D0006941

Fingernail
MOON

Fingernail
MOON

The True Story of a Mother's Flight
to Protect her Daughter

JANIE WEBSTER

DOUBLEDAY
NEW YORK LONDON TORONTO SYDNEY AUCKLAND

PUBLISHED BY DOUBLEDAY
a division of Random House, Inc.
1540 Broadway, New York, New York 10036

DOUBLEDAY and the portrayal of an anchor with a dolphin are trademarks
of Doubleday, a division of Random House, Inc.

Book design by Bonni Leon-Berman
Star map illustration by Jackie Aher

Published by arrangement with Hodder and Stoughton, a division of
Hodder Headline PLC

ISBN 0-385-49529-3

CONTENTS

Foreword ix
Prologue xi

To
Ellen Mari Michelle
and my parents

FOREWORD

WHEN MY DAUGHTER AND I FLED AMERICA, STAYING WASN'T AN option. Dropping everything to board a train and then a plane for an unknown destination, I did what usually only happens in the serendipity of dreams and fantasies. No return tickets were purchased. As sojourners, home was wherever we plopped our bags and rested our heads, sometimes for a week, other times for months.

The financial restrictions of our journey radically altered the comfortable lifestyle we had left behind. Becoming stranded without money was a constant concern. We survived to tell the story because of the unwavering support of my parents, Jess and Kathleen Webster. Even with sustaining financial support from them, our lifestyle was sometimes dispiriting and always exhausting. Their assistance kept us going and their prayers, united with those of friends in America and around the world, lifted us above whatever treacherous ground we traveled.

Writing this book dredged up painful memories that had begun to settle in the riverbed of my soul. As a chronicle of our fugitive years, this intimately personal book omits many particulars concerning the legal case, as well as descriptions regarding my daughter's abuse. Since the abuse had been perpetrated by her father, my husband, someone she and I had loved, the pain embeds deeper in the strata of past experiences, cutting a wider swath for both of us. At more than one point during the writing, I bargained with God: "I'll go around the world again if You will take away the pain of reliving this story." The encouragement of my editor and of my family and friends restrained mental flight, returning me to grapple with whatever I didn't want to write about. They patiently read the manuscript, offering helpful suggestions and heaps of "You can do it." The book also passed the litmus test of my daughter's scrutiny and benefited from her ideas.

Receiving little instruction on how to survive as a fugitive, I learned as I went. The intent of this book is not to be a manual on how to successfully flee with a child. Many events critical to our survival have been omitted. These omissions do not diminish the debt of gratitude I feel to people whose support helped us along our way. The outcome of our flight would have been quite different had it not been for the faithfulness of friends in the countries we visited. In hindsight, some of the precautions may have been unnecessary, but at the time, they had seemed vital to our security. I don't judge anyone who decides not to run from an abusive situation, nor do I advocate becoming a fugitive to protect a child. My vision is to work for the safe shelter of children so that fleeing wouldn't be necessary.

Within the physical journey was hidden a spiritual one. Purposes nested within each other like boxes, all enclosed in the primary objective of protecting my daughter. Writing about the journey has been like uncovering box lids to reveal purposes, some understood better than others. When incidents such as arriving in a new country with no place to stay soured the journey, they were mitigated by the sweetness of observing God's power to engineer circumstances for our good. I saw firsthand (and continue to see) God's unique ability of transforming difficult circumstances into intriguing results. Although my daughter and I would not have chosen such a journey at the outset, neither of us would trade our experiences for anything. Now that the physical journey has ended, the spiritual one continues, affirming that God can be trusted.

PROLOGUE

AS MICHELA AND I WAIT IN THE SNAKING LINE AT THE AMERI-
can Express office in Brussels, I refuse her request to sit near the
travel brochures. She must be within arm's reach in case a quick
departure is necessary. Panic paralyzes swallowing when I imagine the consequences if the Moneygram transaction fails. I possess only enough cash to fund a frugal return to Italy. My anxiety
isn't lessened by the hysterics of an American woman who has
lost her Travelers Cheques. Leaving the American Express office,
she beats her head with her hands and wails at her husband, who
quietly looks at the floor, either from embarrassment or remorse.

By the time I step up to the agent, my throat is collared by
fear, making speech difficult. Handing over my passport, I explain
that a Moneygram from the States has been sent in my name, the
designation being "international." The train of thought derails
abruptly when the tracks end. No plan exists for safeguarding
these Travelers Cheques from being traced; cashing them could
leave a crumb in the forest trail to our whereabouts. Acting as if I
have changed my mind about the Moneygram, I ask to speak to
the office manager—privately.

Michela and I are directed to an office where he listens as if I'm
the fifth fugitive to cross his path this day. Without emotion for
our circumstances, he advises how to avoid having the numbers
of the Travelers Cheques traced. If larger denomination checks
are requested when receiving the Moneygram, they can be exchanged for lower denomination checks with no cross-referencing. The transaction, which is free of charge, makes tracking the

original check numbers impossible, particularly when the checks are exchanged at another American Express office in a different country.

Although the manager's apparent lack of interest in our plight is reassuring in one way, his purpose may be to keep me calm and settled until the police arrive. At the counter, I watch the actions of the agent like a hawk, intent on noticing whether her fingers type numbers from my passport into the computer. Retrieving my passport would require lunging over the counter to snatch it before grabbing Michela's hand and running into the street.

After a reasonable number of questions and giving a bogus address in Kentucky, the Moneygram comes through without a hitch. Desperate to flee the location where our global position is momentarily nailed down, I must remain on the spot to sign the checks. I request as many $500 Travelers Cheques as available to avoid signing $10,000 worth of $20 checks. This large sum of money from my parents doesn't come to us from their surplus, but from their limited retirement savings. The fingernail moon is indelibly stamped on every check, reflecting their pledge to be there for us, whatever the sacrifice.

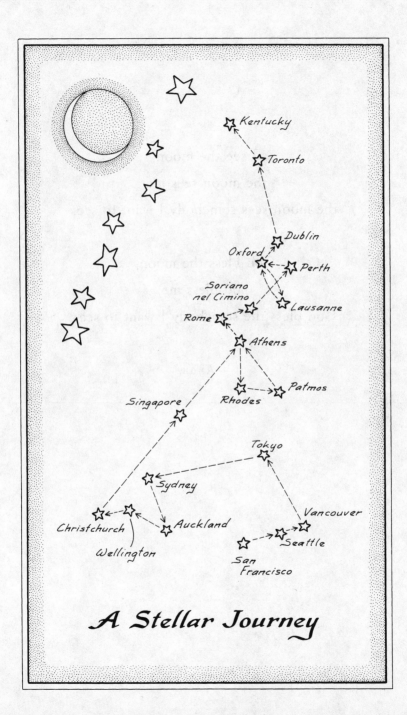

A Stellar Journey

I see the moon,

the moon sees me,

the moon sees somebody I want to see.

God bless the moon,

God bless me,

God bless the somebody I want to see.

—*Anon.*

1

How Long, O Lord?

A cold coming we had of it,
Just the worst time of the year
For a journey, and such a long journey . . .
—T. S. ELIOT, *JOURNEY OF THE MAGI*

ONCE IN THE TRUCK, I TELL MY DAUGHTER, ELLEN, THAT WE
are going for a ride. As a six-year-old, Ellen lives in the present
and going for a truck ride is the only explanation she needs. She
has no inkling that she is embarking on a long journey. Neither
of us knows that we will never return to our home and life in San
Francisco.

Earlier in the evening as I prepare for this moment, excitement
surges so strongly through my body that I doubt whether I could
carry on a conversation without revealing my intentions. Don't
let the telephone ring, God. Alone in the house, I pace between
the kitchen and my bedroom as I pack last-minute items. The
cast-iron skillet on the kitchen stove alludes to the possibility that
I may be going from the frying pan into the fire. Should I take my
daughter and risk the unknown, or should I stay and risk what I
know?

As I secure the house to depart, fly-on-the-wall observers
might discern that I am going out for the evening, but they would

be wrong. After placing the supper dishes in the dishwasher, I say goodbye to my kitchen by pondering for an inordinate amount of time on what to do with the leftover chicken. If I put it in the garbage can, it could be weeks before the garbage is put out for collection. Eventually, I store the chicken casserole in the refrigerator, thinking perhaps Ellen and I could eat it tomorrow evening. Laughing nervously in the quietness, I wonder if I will "chicken out" at the eleventh hour. Thus far, the most irreversible action has been pouring milk down the drain. No train tickets have been purchased, and the $100 bills, which are becoming moist next to my body, could be redeposited. Few friends would be the wiser if I decide not to go through with the plans for this evening.

The doorbell shatters the silence like the breaking of glass. The arrival of this encounter with Jim, Ellen's father, brings both relief and apprehension. Every inch of my body is as taut as a stretched rubber band. At the time arranged, he brings her home following a two-day visit. I do not encourage him farther than the hall, fearing that his suspicions may be aroused by the emptiness of the refrigerator. Ellen wriggles on the carpet as her father discusses plans for picking her up after school on Monday, forty-five hours from now, the lead time before Jim becomes aware of our departure. My voice sounds high-pitched and unsteady, altered by the pounding pulse in my throat. I want to blurt out that this might be the last time he sees his daughter, but the urge dissipates in fear. After the door shuts, I anguish whether my intentions to flee with Ellen have been transparent. If Jim suspects anything, he could phone the police, or even wait on the street and track us himself.

Timing is critical. When the doorbell rings later, I fear that Jim could be returning something Ellen left behind in his car. What a relief to hear the voice of my coworker Stephen, who is helping us escape. Turning off lights as we go through the house, Ellen and I meet him downstairs after he backs his truck into the garage. While Stephen distracts Ellen, I transfer our luggage into the back of the truck. Ellen eagerly slips into the front seat, expecting a truck ride before bedtime. As I stand in the dark garage after the truck has pulled into the driveway, all that remains to be done is activate the garage door-closer and hasten under the cascade of descending metal. Now that the truck is in full view of neighbors and passersby, I charge from the house as if an explosion is imminent, intent on leaving the premises as quickly as possible. If Jim is watching, hopefully he will think I am running to escape the rain. Before the garage door makes contact with the asphalt, the three of us are on our way toward the Bay Bridge. I look back over my shoulder at our rain-soaked stucco home without becoming a pillar of salt.

The beads of rainwater on the windows distort the view inside and out, hiding from the outside world the three occupants of the truck. For the first time in my life, I attempt to disguise my appearance, but I draw the line at changing hair color. When everything else is changing in my life, I need to recognize myself in the mirror. Amid the rain spots on the rearview mirror, my appearance has been significantly altered just by stuffing hair into a cap and wearing glasses, but I shiver at the thought of being identified while stopped at a traffic light. So I sit on my left hip, facing the interior of the truck and my daughter's side.

As we cross the Bay Bridge, I wonder if another big earthquake will strike at this moment, our journey beginning and ending in the water below. No perceptible earth movements occur to impede our advance; the only upheaval seems to be along the fault lines of my emotions. The downpour creates the illusion of traveling within an insular bubble that bursts upon arrival at the Amtrak station. Since the ticket office is closed, the waiting passengers remain in vehicles to keep warm and dry. I dread contact with the outside world, fearing that someone will recognize me.

The onward rush of recent days comes to a standstill as the scheduled arrival time of the train comes and goes. Waiting is insufferable when freedom depends on leaving city, county, state, and country quickly. Conversation between the three of us takes place in fits and starts because there is little to talk about; the past is slipping away, and the future is a slippery unknown. The absence of conversation releases my mind to speculate on what could happen to us as fugitives. If money runs out, will strangers believe our story and extend mercy? One friend advises hiding in a convent, as in *The Sound of Music.* "How long, O Lord?" is the pivotal question, thinking about returning before committing to departure. The knowledge that sleeping in our beds is only thirty minutes away is comforting. Our vulnerability overwhelms me.

Waiting generates questions from Ellen: "Mommy, are we going on a train? Where are we going?" With meager enthusiasm, I tell her, "Sweetheart, we are going on an adventure. I'm not exactly sure where this adventure will take us, but it will be exciting." As a six-year-old who reads fairy tales, Ellen views know-as-you-go travel differently from me. Serendipity is a matter of course in adventure stories like *Alice in Wonderland,* which have prepared her for boarding an "adventure" train. Telling her about spending a night in Seattle would inform Stephen of our plans. If friends and family aren't aware of our whereabouts, they can answer investigative questions truthfully, "I don't know." Ellen's response to our "adventure" concerns me more than the uncertainty of times and places. The greatest unknown is how she will respond to being cut off from family, friends, home, school—and father. Will she resent me for turning her life upside down, or thank me? A friend, an adult survivor of child sexual abuse, believes with all her heart that Ellen will be grateful. Whatever the outcome, Ellen's trust in me will be put to the test.

As a gift for our journey, Stephen presents me with a roll of coins for making phone calls. The expediency of this thoughtful gift takes me a step further toward resolve. When the train is an hour late, the roll is opened on the spot to call a distant Amtrak office. The estimated arrival time is one hour from now. I worry about what effect this delay will have on the rendezvous in Seattle with Tiffany, the daughter of a San Francisco friend. The store of change diminishes further when I call Seattle to confirm our arrival tomorrow evening. Reluctantly, I entrust my precious message to an answering machine.

The onward rush begins once more when the train pulls up to the platform. During the "pause," a change has occurred within me. The emotional cord with life in San Francisco has been cut. All thoughts of sleeping in our beds have vanished. I accept the mandate to protect Ellen from being sexually abused by her father again, and I am ready to run with my decision.

Action is an antidote for fear. Holding Ellen's hand, I spring toward the train like a cat toward its prey. Stephen sets our suitcases on the platform and leaves without saying anything; his words and deeds have already wished us well. Besides, customary farewells don't fit the context of this goodbye. Lifting the bags into the dark passageway between the cars, I place Ellen beside them. For an instant, I hang suspended with one foot on the train step and the other dangling. The unknown pulls at my ankles like weights, holding me back until I shift my gaze upward toward my daughter's expectant face. The point of no return overtakes the eleventh hour as the train moves toward Seattle.

I MET MY FUTURE HUSBAND, JIM, ON A BLIND DATE IN KENtucky before our senior year in high school. During that romantic summer, we saw each other every day until Jim returned to boarding school in Virginia. After leaving high school, we both attended universities in different states, anticipating the prospect of four melancholy years of dating others as well as each other. During our sophomore year, when Jim was a student at Yale University in Connecticut and I was a student at the University of Kentucky, it dawned on us that telephone, travel, and dorm fees would go a long way when applied toward joint living expenses. Wanting to be with Jim as well as wanting a university degree, I believed that the two desires were not mutually exclusive. I accepted Jim's marriage proposal and transferred to Southern Connecticut State College (now University) and became his wife. Not having clearly defined goals, I merged into the multilane expressway with others on their way to becoming teachers. In contrast to my vague career aspirations, the future course of Jim's medical career was well charted.

During the second half of our senior year, our money ran out. Since the education degree did not have a strong hold on me, I willingly pulled out of student teaching to take a temporary job in New Haven and graduated with a liberal arts degree in history and political science, minus the teaching credentials. Clueless as to how I would use this degree, I was content to focus on Jim's career, which both of us understood would take precedence over mine.

After our university graduations in 1970, Jim's medical career necessitated hopscotching the country to attend medical school and graduate school in Nashville; residency training and being chief resident in medicine in San Francisco; and a postdoctoral fellowship at the National Institutes of Health in Bethesda, Maryland. During Jim's medical training, my income from working at the medical centers where he trained helped support us. When he began earning a salary, I worked part-time and earned an associate degree in architecture and building construction. Our life together yielded both pleasant and challenging memories.

Then, in 1982, a few months following our fourteenth wedding anniversary, I discovered that Jim's professional success had masked a personal torment that he had never shared with me. Following his return home to Bethesda from a medical meeting in San Francisco, I found an admission ticket to a sex shop in his shirt pocket at the dry cleaner's. I stared at the ticket in disbelief, knowing the reputation of this establishment, which even the city of San Francisco closes down periodically for lewdness. Wanting to explain away this loathsome ticket, I told myself that Jim may have gone to a sex show as a lark with friends from the meeting. Patronizing such a place went against the kind of person Jim was, his reputation. I resisted overreacting emotionally until hearing his explanation, but I felt as limp as the cotton shirts on the counter.

That evening Jim confessed to frequenting sex shops as a prelude to involvement with prostitutes. Unbeknownst to me, his episodic involvement with prostitutes had begun during the second year of our marriage. For hours, I listened as he poured out the dark pain of his duplicity. Jim had been a master of deceit, even to himself. He coped with deception by building a wall in his mind that divided his life into two segments—faithful versus unfaithful husband—each blocking awareness of the other side. Regardless of which side of the wall he found himself, he was convinced that he was a loyal husband, believing each appointment with a prostitute to be his last. Years later, this mechanism of deception would terrorize me concerning his relationship with his daughter. The power of denial erected another wall, separating the abusing from the loving father.

What a release he experienced as the burden of deception lifted! I would have rejoiced to witness such liberation of a soul if my emotional load had not become heavier as his lightened. I had had no inkling that there was a dark side to my intelligent and controlled husband, who expressed affection and emotions, although rarely insecurities or fears. What he told me went against everything I had believed to be true about him, and that made me angry. Jim's confessions directly opposed the years of my trusting his faithfulness. I was angry at two people: Jim for betraying me but more angry at myself for trusting him all those years. I didn't feel like breaking china, ranting or raving, or getting even. Jim's revelations pierced deep, as emotional acupuncture might cause numbness to feelings. A veneer of repose settled on me, but when I was alone, a spontaneous fusillade of the word "duped" would shoot from my mouth.

Neither of us were certain if our marriage would survive this crisis of trust. Jim told his parents what had happened, but I refrained from telling mine. He pleaded for my forgiveness and a second chance at being a faithful husband, confessing his hope in God to help him. During our marriage, Jim had attended church regularly, even Bible studies and prayer groups, the latter mostly at my instigation. When his outward interest in God waxed and waned, I had attributed it to the demands of work. Now I understood that the guilt from failing to control his sexual desires had driven a wedge into his relationship with God, as it had with our sexual intimacy. Early on in our marriage, I had suggested marriage counseling, but Jim had refused. Now, when our pastor recommended a counselor to bridge the crevasses in our relationship, Jim agreed. Initially, we participated in joint and then separate sessions. As our home life settled and moved on to other concerns, Jim relaxed, seeing that I did not intend to leave him or expose his actions. Choosing to attend fewer counseling sessions himself, he encouraged me to continue, intimating that it might help me become a more satisfying sexual partner. According to his thinking, the responsibility for fidelity in our marriage was shifted on to my shoulders.

Forgiving Jim was possible, but taking the responsibility for his unfaithfulness carried a relational cost. Forgiveness liberates and multiplies love, but accepting misplaced responsibility strikes at the root of love. When the roots go deep, one strike may not fell the tree, but vitality is sapped from its life. I had dreamed of walking hand in hand through life with my childhood sweetheart, becoming old together, very old. Blissful happiness had never been part of the dream, but faithfulness and togetherness had been essential. Was this dream salvageable without the faithfulness? I didn't know how to modify it to make it work. Resolving to work through anger and resentment as best I could with God's help, I prayed that Jim's faith in God would strengthen his self-control.

During this time of relational upheaval, Jim faced a career

change: deciding on a medical school faculty position to follow the current postdoctoral fellowship. It was the most inopportune time to make a major life decision. In hindsight, taking off a year from the medicine circuit could have been lifesaving, but the concept probably never entered Jim's mind. Returning to San Francisco had been our first choice, but now I perceived the city differently, as a place with painful associations, not a place for a new beginning. Since both of us desired a fresh start in new surroundings, Jim applied to other medical centers and was offered a faculty position in Arizona. When he was offered an assistant professorship in San Francisco, I pleaded that he refuse it, having no peace about returning there, but at decision time Jim could not resist the pull of his first choice, a plum of a position.

NEW BEGINNINGS AREN'T ONLY GEOGRAPHICAL. AT THIRTY-FIVE years of age, only a smattering of sand remained in my reproductive hourglass. Being a mother had not interested me until the panic of a childless future gripped me. What if I desired to open the door of motherhood next month, or next year, I asked myself, and it was too late? Whether my panic stemmed more from an attempt to restore dismantled dreams than biological considerations was impossible to gauge. Jim had never pressed me about having children, although he was supportive about becoming a father. Six months before moving from East Coast to West Coast, I happily became pregnant.

Morning sickness and moving three thousand miles during the last trimester of pregnancy diverted my attention from misgivings about living in San Francisco. Jim drove our car and beagles across country while I traveled by air. Alone on the plane, I reflected on Jim's comments about the newly identified disease, AIDS, which is sexually transmitted and had appeared on the San Francisco infectious disease scene in 1983. Most cases had been reported in the homosexual population, but anyone would be at risk if a sexual partner were infected with the HIV virus. During our first week of living in San Francisco, the *San Francisco Examiner* printed a story about prostitutes and the risk of AIDS, but settling into a new home and anticipating a new role as a mother pushed concerns about the disease to a cerebral back burner.

The birth of Ellen, our new daughter, diverted attention from the marriage, bringing delight to our life. Jim became a "rising star" at the medical center, advancing from assistant professor to associate professor and taking on directorship of a clinical research laboratory. For the first time in our lives, financial pressures were not needling us. To the outside world, our marriage of twenty years, our healthy daughter, and our lovely home may have appeared enviable.

In 1985, when Ellen was a year old, I entered graduate school at San Francisco State University as a part-time student in geography. Training as an architectural draftsman had kindled my interest in using cartography as a tool for studying disease distributions. Later, as I sat in a restaurant in Switzerland with Jim and some of his medical colleagues, a thesis topic developed from their conversation: mapping the distribution of favism, a blood disease, on the island of Rhodes in the Mediterranean.

My rise in academia had not been as meteoric as Jim's, but graduate student awards had opened opportunities to present papers. On one such occasion in October 1988, when Ellen was almost five years old, I presented a paper at a cartography meeting, which required me to be away from home for several nights. Returning from the meeting, I found that Ellen wasn't happy to see me, as I had expected she would be. As the evening progressed, her conversations and physical interactions with her father bewildered me. At bedtime, I felt uneasy about Jim's effusive compliance to Ellen's whims and her control over him. In my absence, she had slept in the bed with her father and seemed to resent my presence.

During the following days, I noticed changes in Ellen's personality and behavior. She clung to me when we passed men on the street, manifesting for the first time an unnatural fear of men.

When I asked her about the nights she spent with her father while I had been away, she commented, "Mommy, in my mind, I wish you had been there."

One day when the three of us were eating lunch at home, Ellen initiated a conversation about keeping secrets. All of us agreed that secrets were not a good idea, except when buying birthday gifts. Ellen pushed the conversation further by mentioning that her father had asked her to keep a secret about something he had done. Without responding, he left the table to retrieve something from the kitchen, as if he had not heard Ellen's comments.

Ellen persisted: "Daddy told me not to tell you, Mommy, because it was our secret."

When I asked what the secret was about, Jim mumbled that there hadn't been any secret.

"But, Jim, Ellen said that you did have a secret and told her not to tell me something." Again, Jim ignored my comment.

Troubled by Ellen's comments about secrets, I recalled some recent publicity about "red flags" and the sexual abuse of children.

Until now, Jim's relationship with Ellen had appeared healthy, except for his disregard of my strong objection to his showering with her. Unexpectedly, an issue that had never before confronted me was causing an avalanche of confusion and questions having no answers. Unable to ignore the changes in Ellen's behavior and what I had heard her say, I was at a loss to know what action to take. Expressing my concerns to Jim would jeopardize our marriage, which was worth preserving for Ellen's sake. She deserved a childhood living with both parents. Besides, I wasn't convinced that Jim had sexually abused her. With this in mind, I proceeded cautiously, taking my own counsel.

At the San Francisco Child Advocacy Center, the counselor who heard my concerns confirmed the existence of "red flags" and suggested that I make an appointment with Ellen's pediatrician for a physical examination. Thankfully, this exam disclosed no physical evidence of sexual abuse, but Ellen's responses to questions prompted her pediatrician to recommend that she be evaluated by a psychiatrist specializing in child sexual abuse. Hesitant to subject Ellen to such an evaluation, I sought a second professional opinion without involving her participation. When I presented the family history and changes in Ellen's behavior to a clinical psychologist, he concluded that more investigation was justifiable and reported her case to Child Protective Services.

When the report reached the district attorney's office, I was contacted by a detective and a representative from Child Protective Services, both men. They asked to interview Ellen alone at a neutral place, not her home. Because of Ellen's fear of men, I pleaded that women investigators be assigned to her case, but learned that this request could only be met if Ellen were evaluated at the child abuse clinic located in the same hospital where her father worked. This bureaucratic inflexibility was incomprehensible, but my petition fell on deaf ears. What if Ellen and I came face-to-face with Jim at the hospital? What if Ellen were evaluated at the hospital clinic and the sexual abuse was not substantiated? Rumors could sully Jim's reputation if the visit were not kept confidential. Having worked in medical centers, I was aware how gossip and speculation spread through departments like wildfire. Not convinced that Jim had sexually abused Ellen, I only wanted to leave no investigative stone unturned.

Reluctantly, I agreed to Ellen being interviewed at nursery school. After notifying the director, I told Ellen that two men would be asking her some questions at school. Before her class Halloween party, Ellen was interviewed for fifteen minutes by two men she had never seen before. When I asked her about the interview, she said that they had asked her questions about a doll; they had been nice, and she hadn't been afraid. When I pressed her about the questions, she didn't want to talk about the interview. By phone, the inspector from the district attorney's office informed me that the interview with Ellen had revealed no evidence of her having been sexually abused by her father. When I expressed doubts that a four-year-old would have trusted two male strangers with intimate details about what had made her feel uncomfortable with her father, the inspector said that they had not been wearing uniforms during the interview. When I expressed doubts that a reliable conclusion could be reached during such a brief interview, my request for further investigation was denied. When I mentioned Jim's past involvement with prostitutes and my concern about his current involvement, the tone of the inspector's voice signaled that the penny had dropped concerning the case. The inspector intimated that marital distrust of my husband may have influenced my thinking about his relationship with our daughter. Whatever I said as a mother concerned for the welfare of her child was received through the filter of a vindictive wife. For now, the case was closed but could be reopened if new evidence appeared.

I rejected the validity of the report filed by the district attorney's office. The conclusion could be correct, but the interview had been too brief and threatening to Ellen to prove anything. Lack of substantiation on these terms did not necessarily mean that abuse had not occurred, particularly with a young child who is hesitant to talk with strangers. Screaming silently about my inability to expose the truth, the weight of the solitary burden was crushing.

When the plague of doubts and uneasiness did not go away, I heeded the advice of Ellen's pediatrician and made an appointment with the child psychiatrist she had recommended. I worried about the effect of more questions on my four-year-old daughter, who had already been questioned by her pediatrician and two strangers at school. The child psychiatrist evaluated Ellen during three weekly one-hour sessions. During these weeks, I stayed close to Ellen but refrained from instructing her not to tell her father about the "talking" sessions with the doctor, not wanting to validate secretive tactics. Although Ellen had opportunities to mention the office visits to her father, to my knowledge she didn't. At the completion of Ellen's evaluation, the psychiatrist concluded, "It is my opinion that Ellen was sexually abused by her father by contacts that were physically painful and emotionally devastating."

Believing my daughter and pursuing the investigation of her father were choices with consequences. On the evening I confronted Jim with my fears, I asked Ellen's adult babysitter to spend the night in our home as a safeguard. In the past, Jim had never acted violently toward me, but our relationship had not come up against anything as formidable as this accusation. After Ellen had gone to bed, I informed Jim of our appointment the next morning with a child psychiatrist who, after evaluating Ellen, had concluded that he had sexually abused his daughter. An explosion of anger did not occur, but his actions were chilling. As he stood leaning against the kitchen cabinet, Jim's hand hovered above a cooking knife on the counter, never touching it. Except for this incident, his demeanor was stunned, incredulously offering denials but never erupting into rage as I had feared. His emotions were controlled until the next morning at the psychiatrist's office, when, after being presented with Ellen's verbal and physical responses to play therapy, Jim exploded with angry denials. Ellen's psychiatrist encouraged him to seek another professional opinion. For a second time, Ellen's case was reported to Child Protective Services.

At my request, Jim moved out to his own apartment. For a while, the three of us dined together at restaurants, hoping to ease Ellen's adjustment to the new living arrangement. Although we reassured her that the separation had been our decision, Ellen assumed the responsibility for her father's departure, confiding that she blamed herself "for what Daddy did to me." The threesome outings became less frequent as tensions between Jim and me crescendoed. Although Jim resented my insistence that he arrange for a chaperone when Ellen visited his apartment, he complied, on one occasion expressing fear of going to jail.

———

DURING THE NEXT YEAR, JIM AND I RETAINED LAWYERS TO initiate the dissolution of our marriage and to resolve the custody of Ellen. In a preliminary family court hearing, Ellen's psychiatrist stated that she had treated Ellen on a regular basis, for one-hour-weekly sessions during the previous six months. Concerning this therapy, she testified, "I believe that Ellen has improved and has successfully begun a healing process. She feels much safer and more secure than she did when therapy first began six months ago, when she was angry and clinging toward her mother. Ellen is now opening up to me verbally, regarding what ensued between her and her father. She has told me several times in words that her father sexually molested her."

Six months after Ellen's initial evaluation, Jim requested a second psychiatric evaluation. The judge ordered a family evaluation by a different psychiatrist, one who had a clinical appointment at the medical center where Jim worked. The psychiatric evaluation, eight months after the beginning of Ellen's therapy, revealed no evidence that she had been sexually abused by her father. It was recommended that I receive counseling, which would be "salutary" to align my "misguided" thinking. The dictionary definition of "salutary" is "producing a beneficial or wholesome effect." "Beneficial" for whom? What's "misguided" about listening to the words of your child and taking action to protect her welfare? Not to have taken action would have been "misguided."

Soon after this second evaluation, Jim requested that Ellen attend a dinner party at his apartment. When he telephoned, asking to pick her up earlier than we had planned and before dinner guests would be arriving, I refused, not wanting Ellen to be alone with him at his apartment. In a low raspy voice, which I had never heard before, Jim threatened to kill me and "lay me out flat." He warned that Ellen's psychiatrist would regret meeting him in a dark alley where he would cut her into pieces, sending each part to different locations. The macabre nature of Jim's threats and his strange voice was terrifying. He was only five minutes away from me by car. Believing that my life was in danger, I attempted to defuse his threats by calmly speaking them back to him. Eventually, he regained his normal voice and apologized for threatening me. I listened for a retraction of his desire to carry out the threats, but I heard only a disavowal of intention. Verbal exposure to the depth of Jim's anger convinced me that my well-being was also at risk.

2

Money in My Shoes

The owl and the pussycat went to sea
In a beautiful pea-green boat,
They took some honey and plenty of money,
Wrapped up in a five-pound note.
—EDWARD LEAR, *THE OWL AND THE PUSSYCAT*

DURING THE AUTUMN OF 1989, A YEAR AFTER CONFRONTING Jim with the psychiatrist's conclusions about Ellen's sexual abuse, I was preoccupied with the forthcoming court hearing where the allegations of sexual abuse would be examined by a judge with relation to Ellen's custody and visiting rights. On October 17, I was shaken out of my single-track thinking when the earth moved under my feet, as it did for everyone in San Francisco. When the building I was standing in did not "pancake" after fifteen seconds of jolting, I ran outside with the other students to the shrill sound of car alarms activated by the shaking. I panicked, realizing that Ellen was sitting at Candlestick Park with her father, waiting for the first baseball game of the World Series to begin. On the car radio, I heard that concrete had fallen at the ballpark, expressways had collapsed, and the Marina District was burning. All I could do was wait at home as the city darkened without electricity, but glowed orange on the horizon from the fires. After several hours of watching the street from the front window, headlights pulled into the driveway. Ellen and Jim were safe, despite their top-tier seats at Candlestick Park.

The earthquake seemed a minor blip in the seismology of my life when compared to appearing at the family court hearing in early November. The San Francisco Court Building was still festooned with yellow police tape, alerting pedestrians to structural damage. Aftershocks were on the mind of the judge, who instructed us to duck under the sturdy oak tables if the building began shaking. For five days in a closed hearing, the judge listened to testimonies and read depositions on whether Jim had sexually abused Ellen. On the fifth and final day, Jim, appearing to be ill, testified in a barely audible voice, denying all allegations of sexually abusing Ellen.

After the hearing, my lawyer speculated that legal protection for Ellen, in the form of supervised visits with her father, was unlikely, since her sexual abuse had not been substantiated by legal evidence, such as photographs, physical evidence, or an admission of guilt by the perpetrator. In the legal sense, the words of an almost five-year-old and the psychiatrist's findings were considered secondary evidence—circumstantial. Jim's reputation and his position as an associate professor of medicine could work to his advantage by giving credibility to his denial.

Two days after the hearing, Jim phoned me from the hospital, where he was a patient after collapsing at his apartment and struggling for hours to reach the telephone to call for help. His diagnosis was pneumocystic pneumonia, a complication of AIDS. Hearing that Jim had full-blown AIDS, I fell to my knees by the phone and wailed, crying for my childhood sweetheart and the husband I had adored when ignorance was bliss. Within minutes, my mind leaped to the present and the possibility that Ellen and I could be HIV-positive.

The next day Ellen and I were tested at the San Francisco Blood Bank. For more than twenty-four hours, our future hung in the balance, abducted by the present. Shock deadens the sensation of consequences. The diagnosis of HIV-positive for either or both of us was beyond what my imagination could conjure. Before the anesthesia of surprise had worn off, I learned that our tests were negative. For the moment, I rejoiced, although I knew that subsequent testing would be necessary to confirm these results. The uncertainty of Ellen's sexual contacts with her father made the outcome of her future tests less secure. For me, God had worked the pain and frustration of our marriage for my physical salvation.

Jim's immediate medical condition was life-threatening, and his prognosis was uncertain. Although the diagnosis had struck me like a thunderbolt, the possibility of Jim being HIV-positive did not come totally out of the blue. During the past year, he had had frequent and persistent respiratory illnesses, often searching for decongestants in the medicine cabinet when he had come to pick up Ellen.

At Jim's request, I visited him in the hospital at a time when the woman he was seeing would not be visiting. It was as if the hospital room had been declared an allegation-free zone. Jim's vulnerability and his close proximity to death opened the way for us to comfort each other. His happiness about our HIV-negative tests comforted me, and my sadness comforted him. The unfortunate timing of his reinvolvement with prostitutes had occurred when the prevalence of AIDS was increasing at an alarming rate in San Francisco. When I asked him why he, an expert in infectious disease, had not protected himself, he simply said, "I just didn't."

I left the hospital terrified that Jim would infect Ellen with the HIV virus if he abused her again. After the court reconvened in January 1990 for the judge's ruling, Ellen could spend every other weekend and alternating holidays at her father's house, unsupervised. Her protection would depend on whether the judge decided the sexual abuse by her father was substantiated. Putting Ellen at risk of sexual abuse again could now be life-threatening.

The idea of running with her had been like a winged seed blowing about in my mind, which now began to germinate in a fertile recess.

A MYRIAD OF CONSIDERATIONS SURFACED AS I CONSIDERED shutting down our lives in San Francisco. Whatever the future, selling the house was a given, a function of the divorce proceedings, rather than the custody issue. Although our house had suffered no major structural damage during the earthquake, potential buyers were looking cautiously at houses in an earthquake zone, and selling the house quickly, or even to our financial advantage, was unlikely. The greatest challenge to preparing the house for sale was relocating Arcturus, our beagle named after a star. Several weeks before Christmas, Ellen and I reluctantly sent him to my parents' home in Kentucky as cargo, requiring a change of planes in Cincinnati on a winter's night. When my parents picked him up at the airport, Arc was in good condition but suffering from a raspy, overused bark. Arc's departure before putting the house on the market solved two problems: eliminating the doggy smell and arranging for his passage to Kentucky without arousing suspicion.

If Ellen and I were to flee America, passports would be necessary. Although my passport was valid for years, Ellen didn't have one, nor even an appropriate photo to submit with an application. Taking a passport photo of Ellen would be too risky in case she mentioned it to her father. I had to take a chance with a slightly out-of-focus, nonregulation-sized vacation photo of Ellen.

On a mid-December afternoon, an official at the San Francisco passport office measured the photo of Ellen and rejected it, advising me to resubmit the application with a suitable photo. Walking away, I prayed that God would intervene and returned to the same person, stressing the importance of his accepting this application without delay. Without looking up, he directed me to another official in the same room, presumably with higher bureaucratic authority. She grimaced when the photo measurement turned up short, and I held my breath until she asked me where I wanted the passport mailed. Without my asking, she offered to process it as a "rush order." By the power of Amazing Grace, Ellen's passport arrived at my parents' home in Kentucky before our Christmas visit.

The problem of what to do with the car was solved when it was stolen from the front of our home two weeks before Christmas. Why anyone would want to steal a fourteen-year-old Toyota wagon for a joyride was beyond comprehension. After a few days, the car was found parked on a street in South San Francisco, having suffered no damage; it was as if the thief had used a key to unlock it. Stupidly, the thief had left in the car a video charge slip with his name on it, but submitting this information to the police would have involved me in an investigation I did not want to pursue. My mind was preoccupied with a higher goal than tracking who was responsible for the car theft. I would have benefited more if the car had not been found, but the theft seemed more for my annoyance than for anyone's profit. Bartering with a teenage neighbor, I agreed to give him a car I no longer wanted to drive in exchange for his painting the dog's room.

ELLEN SPENT CHRISTMAS DAY WITH HER FATHER, AND I SPENT the day with the flu at the home of a friend who did her best to make me comfortable. As a spiritual Christmas gift, my friend Linda wrote a Bible reference, Ezekiel 34:11–31, on notepaper in the shape of a sheep. Verse 12 became regular reading: "The LORD God said, I will look for lost sheep and take care of them myself, just as a shepherd looks for lost sheep. My sheep have been lost since that dark and miserable day when they were scattered throughout the nations. But I will rescue them and bring them back from the foreign nations where they now live. I will be their shepherd." As a sheep in the fold, I had lost trust in the

Shepherd, Jesus. The bottom line was that I didn't trust men, Jesus, as man, included. Although I had attended church regularly during the last few years, I had rarely opened my Bible, dangerous reading for anyone attempting to avoid God. I read these verses in Ezekiel again and again, asking myself if the Shepherd could be speaking to me.

The day after Christmas Ellen and I flew to Kentucky to celebrate the holiday with my family. My grandparents presented me with money for legal fees to appeal against the court's decision if necessary, but my lawyers had offered little hope that an appeal would reverse the ruling they anticipated. If I could not protect Ellen legally, then putting distance between Jim and Ellen was a contingency plan. Moving with Ellen away from the Bay Area was much preferred over becoming a fugitive with her. During Christmas week, I applied to the doctorate program at the University of Kentucky and was offered a position and a scholarship contingent on completion of my master's thesis. With this offer came a glimmer of hope that we could move to Kentucky, separating Ellen from her father without living on the run.

While Ellen and I were still in Kentucky, Jim applied for a court order requiring Ellen to return to San Francisco by his birthday, a few days away. The order seemed unnecessary, since he knew that our return flight reservations were scheduled for the morning of his birthday; his action suggested that he believed we might flee and was trying to put the law on his side. Possessing passports and money, I had considered leaving the country with Ellen during Christmas week, but departure from Kentucky would have linked my family too closely to our fleeing. Besides, legal loose ends remained in San Francisco—the judge's ruling on the issue of Ellen's sexual abuse and on my petition to move to Kentucky. Perhaps the lawyers would be wrong. Running away was still the last resort.

Speculation ended in January 1990 when the judge ruled that sexual abuse of Ellen by her father had not been substantiated. The judge ordered that Ellen be monitored by a psychologist who would detect any evidence of future abuse. This "wind in the sails" approach of protecting Ellen was not acceptable to me. Physical custody of Ellen was awarded to me, but in March she would begin staying with her father unsupervised. The judge ruled that I was free to move to Kentucky to pursue my doctorate, but Ellen's residence must remain within a fifty-mile radius of San Francisco. If I were to take Ellen for any reason farther than the nine counties of the Bay Area without Jim's consent, I would risk being charged with a felony. The same applied to Jim.

Asking lawyers for advice about becoming a fugitive was pointless, as they are obliged to direct clients toward law-abiding behavior. Psychiatrists advised against fleeing with Ellen for various reasons, including her possible frustration and anger at living on the run. The consequences of being captured (through media exposure, the work of private detectives, or the efforts of the FBI) would put me in prison and Ellen in full-time custody with her father—a worse situation than if we hadn't fled in the first place. Hiding in foreign countries was also less secure, due to international reciprocal agreements regarding child custody disputes. The consensus among the lawyers, counselors, and psychiatrists was "Don't do it." But this advice had been delivered professionally—not without compassion, but not as Ellen's parent.

Desperately needing to talk with someone who spoke from my perspective, I attempted to contact Elizabeth Morgan, a doctor who served a prison sentence for concealing the whereabouts of her daughter, who had been sexually abused by her daughter's physician father. At the time, she could not speak to me directly, but she sent a message: "Go to jail to protect your daughter." In my case, going to jail would create more problems for Ellen than it would solve, as I was the only family member who could take her into hiding. Contacting several mothers who had attempted living as fugitives with their children, all had either surrendered or been apprehended—although none of these women discouraged me from going on the run to protect my daughter. In every case, their children now lived with the fathers. Counsel on what I should do was divided into two camps: professionals who said no and the mothers of the abused children who said go.

As Jim's physical condition had improved, he defiantly claimed that he would beat AIDS. During his medical training, I had witnessed Jim's triumph over hepatitis B, continuing to work at the hospital until the yellowness of his skin, not the severity of the symptoms, forced him to stop working for a few days. Certainly, AIDS was more life-threatening than hepatitis B, but Jim's physical stamina had seemed invincible, above reproach from God and man. If anyone were cured of AIDS, I believed Jim would be the one.

Man's counsel left me turning in circles. I needed to speak with someone other than a friend, family member, or involved professional, someone who understood the God connection in decision-making. Although God and I had not been too close recently, I consulted a priest, who did not know me, asking him, "What should I do?"

He wisely did not answer the question directly, but he counseled, "Listen to what you cannot accept and let that guide you." Along the lines of determining what you can and cannot accept, he mentioned counting the cost of decisions, as in Luke 14:28. "For which of you, when he wants to build a tower, does not sit down and calculate the cost, to see if he has enough to complete it?"

Walking home, I established what I could not accept: Ellen being sexually abused again and becoming HIV-positive. The cost of protecting her could be a prison sentence, if I—we—survived the journey.

That night I opened my Bible, letting the pages fall where they would. God directed my attention to Joshua 1:7–9. "Only be strong and very courageous . . . Have I not commanded you? Be strong and courageous. Do not tremble or be dismayed, for the Lord your God is with you wherever you go." These Scriptures sealed my decision. Unlike Joshua, I had not trusted God to guide me through the wilderness. Disappointment about my marriage and now Ellen's abuse had compelled me to keep God at arm's length, but He was wooing my heart. Despite fearful second-guessing and not trusting God's protection, I knew what I had to do. The first step was to alert my parents to make flight reservations for San Francisco.

NAILING DOWN A SAFE AND RELIABLE MONEY PLAN BECAME A priority during the next two weeks. As expected, home buyers were moving at a snail's pace, so money from the sale of the house was out of my reach for now, and probably forever if I became a criminal. The legal appeal money from family would now become the fleeing money. At the onset of the journey, I planned to carry cash, lots of it, leaving credit cards at home. Only a few weeks remained to transform the family money (which had been deposited) into portable cash. Withdrawing thousands in cash did not raise eyebrows at my bank, which served wealthy Asian clients; the limiting factor for the bank was the amount of available cash, which necessitated making arrangements ahead to target "cash-on-hand" days. I had hoped to carry $500 bills, but I was told by the bank official to be grateful for the $100 bill, since the U.S. Treasury had contemplated discontinuing it to make drug transactions more cumbersome. Bit by bit, I accumulated $28,000 in crisp, thick $100 bills, squirreling them away in my wardrobe closet, which had never been so well appointed.

Living on the run offered two options: organizing our own way, or linking up with an underground network. Hiding within a network with frequent location changes did not appeal to me. In a vacant city office, I met with a legal adviser to discuss how to live as fugitives and how to connect with the underground network. Listening to stories about mothers who had fled with their children, I learned that most either surrendered, were caught, or died on the run in America. One mother in hiding with a child was stopped for a traffic violation and apprehended "in bad shape, scarcely able to care for her own needs." Some parents who were caught went to prison; others did not. Either way, custody of the children almost always was awarded to the parent who had not committed the crime of child abduction. Such dreadful outcomes sent shivers through my body, as I speculated on what it would take to put me "in bad shape." The legal adviser confirmed that Jim's position and resources could jeopardize our safe hiding in America. I was warned not to trust assurances from Ellen's father if he offered to make legal deals for our return; many women were now sitting behind bars as part of such deals. The FBI, not private detectives, posed the greatest threat to our capture. As a result of this clandestine meeting, I devised a mental list of "never" and "always" actions: never open a bank account; always fly non-American air carriers; always use our legal passports; never mail anything directly to my parents; always call from public pay phones; and never call my parents' home. For this prudent counsel, I offered the legal adviser one of the crisp $100 bills, but she encouraged me to save it for the trip.

The privilege of planning an open-ended global itinerary thrilled me, even under these circumstances. Poring over atlases and maps, the sparkling jewels in geography's crown, delighted me. When I asked the geography faculty at San Francisco State University hypothetical questions about living abroad, New Zealand came up most often. Its geographic isolation, English-speaking culture, and reputation for being behind global times in crime made it an attractive destination for a mother and child on the run.

Fearing that my home phone might be bugged, I called airlines for fares and flight times from the pay phone at the supermarket. Both air reservations and advance purchase savings for any international flights were off-limits, since I would need to use my passport name. Amtrak accepted phone reservations for two under the name Chris Kramer, on February 3, 1990. I had chosen Chris for its nongender status and Kramer from a movie about a wife who left her husband, albeit under different circumstances. To my ears, Chris Kramer sounded legitimate.

A WEEK BEFORE OUR DEPARTURE MY PARENTS ARRIVED IN SAN Francisco. My mother did not doubt that I was taking the right action, believing that my well-being was in danger as much as Ellen's. My father reluctantly gave his blessing on our becoming fugitives, fearing that living on the run would be too risky for his only daughter and granddaughter. As a jury member, he had seen what happened to offenders who violated court orders. Although my mother abhorred the possibility of my imprisonment, she believed staying in America was a greater risk.

The stack of $100 bills totaling $28,000 was almost two inches high. Shopping with my parents, I tested numerous money carriers, targeting various anatomical locations, eventually buying a sternum necklace, a leather belt with a zippered hideaway, and a midriff pouch. Although I creased the bills with an iron, the money in the leather belt bulged as if it were a seed pod ready to burst its contents to the wind. To prevent my leaving a trail of $100 bills through some airport, my father sewed the zipper closed with dental floss to ease the stress. The cash was divided among the hiding places, with $2,000 in the sole of each shoe, $8,000 in the sternum necklace, $4,000 hiding behind the dental floss, and $12,000 at the midriff level, giving me the appearance of early pregnancy. I worried that clothing would be insufficient cover for such a quantity of cash. Would the scent of money track me?

For when the cash ran out, my parents and I discussed sending American Express Moneygrams, which could be designated for an international "money pot," thereby absolving my parents from the responsibility of targeting the pickup point. Although this computer transaction offered flexibility in retrieving U.S. dollars in the form of Travelers Cheques, Moneygrams would pinpoint our global location at American Express offices through passport identification.

Limiting our luggage to two carry-on suitcases, I can't risk an airline losing all our belongings. Packing clothes for a journey of unknown duration to an unknown destination, likely to span all seasons, called for my mother's pragmatism. She advised taking more of my clothes than Ellen's, since her clothes would be replaced along the way. Consulting Ellen about what toys and treasures to pack was not possible, but my mother's intuitive relationship with her granddaughter was a close second. A few favorite books and Little Ponies, a doll from New Orleans (a gift from her father), a stuffed dog, a colored pencil set, as well as her comfort cloth—a diaper never used for its original purpose— were stuffed into a diminutive school backpack.

Packing my clothes required more strategy, since I would not be shedding clothes periodically unless my weight ballooned. Heavy and bulky items, such as my favorite boots, were painfully excluded from the to-go pile on the bed. One coat, one jacket, one sweater was the general rule; going two by two was reserved for underwear, T-shirts, shoes, and socks. Most items, except for corduroy slacks and a winter coat, met an all-season standard. My three-inch-thick Bible was the only book in the pile. Pictures of family and friends, checkbook, credit cards, and driver's license were left behind, as either adding to the pain of separation or threatening to expose our cover in hiding. My mother added safety pins, a sewing kit, and vitamins to the heaping pile. In a waist pack, I carried a pen, small notebook, Swiss Army knife, a house key (just in case I changed my mind on the way to the station), and a wallet with smaller denomination bills. When the two suitcases were full, I said goodbye to "friends" of the cloth, hanging in the closet, who didn't make the cut. In a few short hours, I would be saying goodbye to everything my eyes rested upon. The suitcases could not even carry the rudiments of my life, much less the comfort items, such as a jewelry box.

Contacting my parents on the journey would require stealth

and organization, knowing that their phone line would be tapped by the FBI. My mother composed a list of U.S.A. contacts, identified by initials, with telephone numbers minus the area codes. This enigmatic phone list would travel with the cash for future reference, not pointing toward anyone in America if the list were lost, or found on me.

The possibility existed that Jim might send bogus messages to alarm or confuse my parents. Through the use of a code word, my parents could trust the authenticity of the message, as being from me. All evening the three of us wracked our brains for a phrase, meaningful only to us. In the wee hours of the morning, my mother remembered a special night in our backyard when I was about eight years old. My parents had looked up at the crescent moon, thinking of the trail of nail slivers I left behind from biting my nails, which turned out to be a lifelong habit. They reminded me of what had been said many years ago in Kentucky as we had gazed at the moon. Mother had said, "Janie, when you are grown and away from us, look at the fingernail moon and know that we are thinking of you. We'll always be there for you, wherever you go." Our journey could not take Ellen and me beyond my parents' love and encouragement, nor farther than the "fingernail moon," which became our code words.

When the day of our departure dawned, stormy and rainy, I remembered the verses from Ezekiel, given to me a month earlier on Christmas Day. The airport goodbyes to my parents, who were returning to Kentucky, tore at my heart. Their farewells to Ellen had been in the driveway the night before, when Jim had picked her up for an overnight visit, and could not include all the things they had wanted to say to her. That goodbye could express only the emotion of a twenty-four-hour separation, since both Jim and Ellen believed she would be reunited with her grandparents the following day. Letting go of their only daughter and granddaughter would be the most difficult path they would ever walk. The pain of what the future might hold could break, or even kill them. My parents and I agreed that if anyone, even one of them, died while we were on our journey, Ellen and I would not return. Looking at their tearful faces, I wondered if I would ever see them again. I knew that they were thinking the same thing.

In less than ten hours, all preparations for the journey had to be completed on my own without the companionship of my parents or my daughter. When Jim brought Ellen home in the evening from the overnight visit, departing swiftly to catch the night train to Seattle was crucial.

3

Crossing the Rubicon

*A pause—in which I began to steady the
palsy of my nerves, and to feel that the
Rubicon was passed.*
—CHARLOTTE BRONTË, *JANE EYRE*

IN THE DIMLY LIT TRAIN CAR, PASSENGERS ARE SETTLING FOR
the night. I am disgruntled that so many people have decided to
travel on this particular Saturday night in the dead of winter.
Ellen manages a chunky school bag and a collapsible luggage cart
as I balance the load of two suitcases and a shoulder bag. On the
bumpy way to our seats, I look furtively from face to face, fearing
that I will recognize one. Looking at the clumps of luggage surrounding our seats, I wonder how the two of us will manage
carrying our home on our backs when even a train aisle challenges our capabilities.

When the conductor appears to collect our tickets, I explain
about the ticket office being closed, thinking nothing of pulling
out three nicely ironed $100 bills. Familiarity in handling 280 of
them the night before has bred in me something akin to con-
tempt. He makes a big fuss about his inability to provide change
and the other passengers look my way, the last thing I want to
happen.

Ellen settles easily into sleep, but every cell in my body is on alert. The speed of the train's forward motion makes me giddy. Pinpricks of light blur in the windows like surreal moving pictures punctuating the darkness. The push-pull of the past gives way as each mile of track puts more distance between us and San Francisco. The alarm will sound when Jim goes to Ellen's school on Monday afternoon, less than two days from now. I wonder where in the world we will be by then, when the lead time ends and the chase begins. Will I wake up in San Francisco tomorrow morning, comforted that I have been traveling in my dreams? Anything seems possible tonight.

As I had embraced the dark cover of night, so I welcome the dazzling sunlight of the morning, finding myself not in San Francisco but whizzing along the edge of the snow-covered Cascade Mountains. Watching Ellen awaken, I think only of finding coffee. In the dining car, chrome table accessories glisten to compensate for not being silver, and we breakfast on delicious pancakes. It's easy to believe that we are embarking on an adventure until the waiter comments on the out-of-the-ordinary method of payment from the night before. I cringe that the conductor told the waiter about a woman who flashes around $100 bills. Keeping a low profile is my intention, but within the first hours of becoming a fugitive, my indiscretion causes a crisis of confidence. Perhaps, as my father had been concerned, I won't be able to pull it off.

During the afternoon, I concentrate on entertaining Ellen and avoiding conversations with fellow passengers, which goes against the grain of my personality. Ellen and I play tick-tack-toe, challenge each other to a brown versus white cow-counting contest, and read to one another. For years after, Ellen talks about two memories from the first day of our journey: eating pancakes in the sunny dining car while looking at the snow-covered mountains and passing through the city in Washington State where her kindergarten boyfriend had moved. Why speeding through his city on a train should bring her so much pleasure is a mystery.

What a contrast between how a six-year-old and a forty-two-year-old emotionally perceive the fleeting proximity of a former boyfriend! Ready acceptance of what the present holds will stand Ellen in good stead for the future.

When the train arrives in Seattle after dark, I phone Tiffany immediately. What a relief to hear her unrecorded voice! While we wait at the station, I tell Ellen our immediate plans: spending the night at Tiffany's home and then taking a long flight the next day. Questions from Ellen are few, either due to tiredness or because she senses that I do not know where we are headed on this "adventure."

After dinner, when Ellen is tucked in bed, Tiffany and I focus on destinations and airline timetables. Crossing the Canadian border to reach Vancouver International Airport is the first leg of tomorrow's journey, but where to go from Vancouver is up for grabs. I am encouraged that Tiffany, only an acquaintance, has invited us to her home and has even taken a day off from work to help us on our way. As a ground rule, or rather air rule, a non-American air carrier will be chosen, on the assumption that any legalities for accessing passenger lists would take longer. Tiffany suggests booking with a lesser-known Canadian airline, which flies to the Orient. A flight to Tokyo, with seats available, leaves tomorrow afternoon. Risking seat availability, I make no reservations until the last minute, in case anyone attempts to trace our escape path. Discerning the optimal level of cloak-and-dagger maneuvers for each situation is frustrating. As a novice fugitive, I take the admonition "to err on the side of caution" as a *modus operandi*.

The next day starts early to accommodate the two-hour drive to Vancouver International Airport before the afternoon flight to Tokyo. When the Canadian official waves us through the border checkpoint without inspecting passports, I sigh with relief to be traveling on Canadian soil. The cocktail of emotions also includes sadness at leaving my country. Looking over my shoulder once again, I view the welcoming sign for cars entering the

U.S.A. and wonder how much time will elapse before a sign welcomes our return.

At the airport, reality exceeds fantasy. In the past, I may have imagined spontaneously boarding a plane for Europe, but my imagination had not stretched to flying off to an unknown destination. As we say goodbye to Tiffany in front of the terminal, I realize that Ellen and I may not see a familiar face for a long time. Walking away from Tiffany's car, I feel the magnetism of the past and the resistance to its pull as we enter the terminal. Ellen and I tread on the boundary of a new identity, laying aside past history, even our names. At this juncture, pausing to adjust to this unfamiliar turf before charging toward the airline reservation desk would have been wise.

I ask the representative about afternoon flight departures, and she confirms that the 1:30 P.M. flight to Tokyo has seats available. Fearing a stopover in Hawaii, I blunder by asking if this flight stops on U.S. soil; if I had asked whether the flight was nonstop, no flashing "red lights" would have been activated in her mind. Then, as if ordering ice cream, I say, "I'll take two one-way tickets to Tokyo." Noticing the top of Ellen's head below the counter, she inquires where we will travel after Tokyo. It is within my power to restore her confidence by saying X, Y, or Z destination, but I only shrug, saying, "I don't know," not wanting to reveal our plans to visit Australia.

Her eyebrows rise again when there is no luggage to check, confirming her suspicions. Now she has no inhibitions about informing me of the necessity of purchasing round-trip tickets, something about Japanese immigration officials requiring incoming passengers to have ongoing tickets, covering the airline for the responsibility of getting us out of Tokyo. The policy doesn't make sense, but what can I do? Ellen and I need to be on that flight, even if it means purchasing round-trip tickets. When she asks for a credit card number, I lamely tell her that I didn't bring it with me. Pulling out thirty-five $100 bills from the money pouch inside my slacks, I count each one out loud for fear of making a mistake. My mind flashes back to a comment made by a bank employee in San Francisco: "You should be grateful for $100 bills because they might be scrapped by the government to make drug transactions more difficult." Indignant that this woman should suspect my money is drug-related, I want to blurt out, "Although I'm fleeing, I am not a criminal." Scraping her hand across the counter to gather the bills, she delivers a parting shot: "People don't generally travel this way."

Fuming about the purchase of useless tickets, I ask a different reservationist at another counter about the round-trip ticket policy to Japan. His puzzled look answers my question, but nothing can be redeemed at this late hour before boarding. All I can do is take care of it in Tokyo. I buy Ellen a coloring book on horses with the leftover Canadian currency, and color with her until I am no longer angry.

The flight is fully booked, Ellen and I being among the few non-Asian passengers. I cringe when our seatmates photograph my blue-eyed, fair-haired daughter, unable to explain my concern that the photo could be sent to a Japanese relative who lives in San Francisco and might see Ellen's picture on a milk carton. Freakier things than that have happened. While Ellen plays with the plastic fishes that held the soy sauce, I think about our midnight arrival in Tokyo with no place to stay and ask the kindest flight attendant for a hotel recommendation.

Leaving the airplane in Tokyo, we walk along corridors that could be in any country until Japanese characters dominate, making the surroundings appear like an exaggerated version of San Francisco. With no luggage to claim, we soon board a courtesy bus, having reserved a room at the hotel recommended by the flight attendant. Heading toward the center of Narita in the darkness, I strain to see the lay of the land. At the hotel desk, I dread showing my passport for registration, but there is no alternative. While we sleep upstairs in our room, my name will be registered on paper downstairs for everyone to see. Judging from the expense of the hotel, our stay in Japan will be brief.

The hotel room could have been a Holiday Inn in the States, except for the Japanese characters on the phone and on the complimentary shampoo. Ellen amazes me by unpacking her toys and arranging her treasures on the nightstand. Although I don't sense that I'm thousands of miles from home, my body is confused—should it gear up for a new day or welcome the bed? I relax, knowing that our departure, if discovered, has not yet been confirmed. Once Jim knows, I can no longer rest in complete assurance that I won't be captured, but tonight I can sleep peacefully.

BRIGHT SUNSHINE FILLS THE HOTEL COFFEE SHOP THE NEXT morning. By now, the lead time is over. Monday in San Francisco has come and gone. Jim has been to Ellen's school, not finding her there. He has listened to my recorded voice on the answering machine. He has knocked at the door of the dark house, whose key I have in my pocket. More disturbing than all of these, he has telephoned my parents, who would have acted surprised and worried by our disappearance. Beyond this, I don't want to know what's happening on the other side of the Pacific. All my energy is riveted to surviving on this side, but before we move on, I want to take advantage of seeing Japan. Eating at Japanese restaurants in San Francisco has prepared us for a breakfast buffet of fish and miso alongside bacon and eggs. Ueno Park in downtown Tokyo is the unanimous sight-seeing suggestion by the coffee shop employees, who take a warm interest in an American woman and child traveling alone.

Neither the zoo monorail nor the vibrant plumage of the Austral-Asian birds nor the pandas at Ueno Park grab Ellen's attention as much as a dinky playground with automatic rides. Entering the teahouse for lunch, we are expected to remove our shoes and place them by the entrance. I am uncomfortably aware of the value of my shoes, and choose a table as close to the door as possible so that I can cast an anxious eye in their direction.

Sitting on mats at low tables, we order green dumplings. Chicken and dumplings are my father's favorite food, but he wouldn't like these.

The following day I decide to stay closer to the hotel and airport, since the flight to Sydney leaves in the evening. The shops along the narrow, crowded streets of Narita intrigue Ellen, but her face brightens at seeing the Golden Arches. McDonald's is wonderfully predictabe and familiar to our palates. Leaving its spacious interior, we merge with the ever-present crowds in the street. Inquiring at a travel agency about receiving credit for the round-trip tickets, I panic on learning that the crediting operation must be accomplished at the airline offices in Tokyo, not at the airport, as I had planned. It is already early afternoon; taking a train into downtown Tokyo could jeopardize catching our evening flight to Sydney. Yesterday the round trip to the city took four hours, but if I don't make the effort, $1,000 will be lost. Staying another day in Japan doesn't enter my mind. The frantic compulsion to keep moving hasn't taken me far enough from San Francisco.

At the Narita railway station, the departure board is a challenging puzzle. As I struggle to understand the location of transfer points for a direct train, a Japanese woman who speaks English offers to help, even waiting with us on the platform until we board the correct train for downtown Tokyo. Other passengers kindly give Ellen lots of attention, which makes me nervous. At the Qantas office, I learn that a refund from the Canadian airline must be obtained to apply as credit toward our tickets to Australia. This credit can only be transacted by a Qantas official at the airport when we purchase the tickets. Returning to the street, I briskly walk to the Canadian airline office, spurring Ellen on with the admonition, "If we don't hurry, we will lose $1,000, which could buy a lot of Happy Meals." Fortunately, airline offices congregate in Tokyo, since Ellen's walking tolerance has been reached. On receiving the refund from the Canadian airline, we break into a run toward the train station. If the hotel van departs for the airport without us, we miss the flight to Australia and our efforts will be all for nothing.

In choosing trains for the return trip to Narita, I am on my own—no one steps forward to direct me. It doesn't take long to realize that we have boarded the wrong train traveling in the right direction. This local train stops at every hamlet and will arrive in Narita long after the hotel van has departed for the airport. Across from us, a Japanese businessman obviously understands my hand-wringing comments to Ellen and spontaneously suggests that we disembark at the next station to catch the express train that is following this train. Hoping this man knows what he is talking about, we risk it and abandon the certainty of the slow train. The express train comes, as he said it would, arriving at the Narita station seven minutes before the van departs from the hotel. I look for a taxi but don't see one. A walk that took fifteen minutes earlier in the day must take seven minutes in the dark. Running through the streets as fast as Ellen's legs permit, we are still several blocks from the hotel. Turning a corner, I see the van parked at the entrance. Before I can gasp with relief, the headlights flash on, signaling that the driver is preparing to depart. Clutching Ellen's hand tightly, I gesture wildly with my free arm to attract the driver's attention, my eyes fixed on the headlights. At the entrance to the hotel parking lot, I communicate again with my arms the need to retrieve luggage from the lobby. Breathlessly, we collapse in our van seats and the wheels begin to move. Ellen beams at winning the race against time, and I am forever committed to buying her Happy Meals.

Finding the Qantas official at the airport is analogous to catching mercury. People at each airline desk have seen him, but no one can pinpoint his whereabouts. While we are waiting at the Qantas desk, eager to check in and sit down with our carry-on luggage, he appears and approves the credit voucher toward the tickets to Sydney. The frantic pace ends abruptly as we settle to wait for boarding.

Ellen, who has received little attention during the day, except for being pulled in this or that direction, needs to be prepared for the long flight ahead. I mention our destination, Australia, but it doesn't mean much to her until I talk about kangaroos.

"Mommy, will we see kangaroos?"

"Probably not, because we will be staying in a city—Sydney."

"Will we go back to America after visiting Australia?"

"Not for a while. We are on an adventure and there are several places I want to visit before returning to America." There is much more to say but introducing the future in small doses seems best, particularly when both of us are exhausted.

ON OUR DESCENT INTO SYDNEY, I SCAN THE HORIZON FOR the Opera House, whose majestic aerial view turns out to be the extent of our sight-seeing in Australia. When the airline representative checks our passports, he finds no embassy-approved visas to pave the way for our entering Australia. Pretending to pay attention on how to obtain them, I am kicking myself inwardly for not researching this detail more carefully. I had planned to stay in Australia for a while before moving on to New Zealand. In this quadrant of the hemisphere, where land masses are few, we have Hobson's choice and must travel on to New Zealand.

Ellen and I are restricted to nine hours in Australia, which in effect means nine hours in the airport. The prospect of boarding another plane makes me irritable. When Ellen asks about our plans, I am too preoccupied about dealing with another airline to answer. Will Air New Zealand be suspicious of an American woman traveling with a young child and no luggage to check? I ask myself. At the Air New Zealand reservation desk, I receive quizzical looks when I ask whether Americans need a visa to visit New Zealand. For an instant, I fear another round-trip ticket situation, but this time I possess more savoir faire than I had in Vancouver. The airline agent does most of the talking and one-way tickets to Auckland are issued with few questions.

Weariness from hopscotching latitudes and longitudes, as well as crisscrossing datelines and time zones, settles on both of us as we anticipate the four-hour wait before the flight to Auckland. Exhaustion dulls the disappointment of bypassing Australia, a country I had wanted to see. Even in the air-conditioned terminal, the heat of summer from outside makes us drowsy. The midmorning bustle of the terminal does not keep us from slumping in the vinyl seats, encircling our cases with arms and legs, and snoozing for a short while. Ellen is refreshed by the nap; her curiosity about this "adventure" awakens again and questions tumble out.

"Do Bebe and Granddaddy know where we are?"

"No. It's safer for them if they don't know where we are."

"Does Daddy know where we are?"

"No, he doesn't know where we are. No one does."

"I hope that Daddy isn't sick in the hospital. I love Daddy, but I want to live with you, Mommy."

"Ellen, he wasn't in the hospital when we left San Francisco. He was feeling much better. Do you remember how well he looked?"

Remembering her father in good health, Ellen relaxes. Although she doesn't ask any more questions, I tell her again why I took her away. "Sweetpea, I left America because I want you to be safe. You said that Daddy made you feel uncomfortable. I was afraid that he might touch you again, so I left San Francisco to protect you. Your father is very angry with me for taking you away. He's not mad at you; I'm the one who decided to leave with you." Ellen wants to talk about something else.

After lounging and snacking, we walk the corridors to stretch our legs from the last flight and loosen up for the four-hour flight to Auckland. While we are sitting at the gate, waiting to board our flight, I introduce another issue. "Ellen, you need to choose a new name."

"Can I pick a name?"

"Yes. I'm keeping the name Chris. Would you like to be called

Katie, Elizabeth, Emily, Zoe, or Catherine?" I ask, suggesting the names of friends she has left behind.

"I don't know what name I want to have. Will our last name be the same?"

"No. I'll choose a new one when we get to New Zealand."

Later, Ellen perks up on hearing a name paged through the airport loudspeaker system. Without hesitation, she announces, "I want my name to be Michelle."

On the Air New Zealand flight, I sit next to a young man from New Zealand who has been traveling in Canada. Somewhere over the Tasman Sea, as Michelle practices writing her new name, I ask my seatmate about the availability of temporary jobs and the cost-of-living expenses in New Zealand, irrelevant issues for most tourists. He suggests fruit-picking as employment, but moving from pillar to post with the fruit harvest sounds awful, particularly for a child needing to attend school. Feigning mild indifference, I ask him what last names are common in New Zealand. From the list he recites, I choose Williams, since William is my father's middle name.

On the flight, Michelle becomes curious about our new country of residence.

"Michelle, the biggest surprise about New Zealand will be the temperatures. The southern hemisphere is experiencing summer, so it will be warm."

"Mommy, can we go swimming if it's hot? Do they have beaches?"

"Probably. It's the same ocean, the Pacific, that we walked along in San Francisco."

Her excitement encourages me. By the end of the flight, my seatmate is clued in to our circumstances and offers the name and telephone number of his parents if I ever need help, a foretaste of New Zealand's extraordinary hospitality.

We land in Auckland, where nothing bridges the coolness of the airplane cabin and the sweltering outside temperature. At the top of the plane steps, Michelle and I are smacked with an invisible wall of 90°F heat, which intensifies as we descend to the runway. I yell to Michelle, "It's warm enough to go swimming!"

Inching along in the serpentine line of passport control, I kick our suitcases along the floor in front of us. If passport control suspects something and refuses us entry, could we face another air flight? And to where? Back the way we have come? Their questions are perfunctory. "Visiting New Zealand on vacation? . . . For how long? . . . Where will you be staying in Auckland?" Before we have learned to pronounce Auckland without it sounding like "Oakland," our passports are stamped with three-month tourist visas.

Judging from the numbers of travelers in the airport terminal, February is a popular tourist time in this hemisphere, particularly among young trekkers from Europe. Using a courtesy phone, I call motel after motel, hearing the same thing: "No vacancy." I surrender the phone to another traveler when Michelle persists about going to the rest room. When we return to wait for a phone, Michelle collapses from the heat in a limp heap on the floor, despite the air-conditioning. Back on the phone again, I try a backpackers' hostel with the same name as a church camp I once had longed to attend in America as a teenager. They have a room. After receiving assurances that the hostel is located in a safe neighborhood, I take it.

A van shuttles passengers from the airport, which is located in the country, into the city, where the hostel is located, giving us door-to-door service. An old but respectable building along a tree-lined boulevard turns out to be the backpackers' hostel.

The owner apologetically explains that a mixup has occurred; the occupant of the room that was to have been ours will be staying longer. Since no other rooms are vacant, our only option for the night is to share a room with a young working woman.

With grave hesitation, I ask, "Won't she mind strangers moving into her room?"

"No, she's used to it when the season is busy. It will be fine with her. With you in the room, her rate will decrease. Anyway, you probably won't see her because she returns late at night and leaves early in the morning for work."

We are shown a small room with no air-conditioning, no fan, no breeze from the single window, and no working girl, but Michelle and I are too tired to look for a room elsewhere.

In a twin-sized bed, the heat from our bodies creates a tropical environment under the sheet. I want to fling the sheet (and caution) to the wind, but I am afraid our roommate will notice the money belts on my body and the shoes by my side. Putting two and two together, she might hit me on the head, take the shoes, and rent a cooler place to live.

When she arrives during the night, I check out her silhouette through slitted eyes, appreciating that she doesn't turn on the light. From her moves, she is accustomed to getting ready for bed in the dark with strangers in the room. When I open my eyes in the morning, her bed is empty and all our cash is accounted for.

Sharing a room with a stranger robbed me of more sleep than the heat had. The first priority of the new day is to find a private room that can be locked. Walking to a nearby neighborhood with large homes, one of them has been converted to a youth hostel. Supposedly, the house was once the residence of a Maori queen, but no hint of past splendor remains. In the cool of the morning, the cubicle of a room seems pleasant enough without air-conditioning. Although it does not have a window, louvers in the door ventilate it with air from the screened porch. Above all else, it is private, lockable, and cheap.

Now Michelle and I are free to explore the city of Auckland, whose sunshine, tropical warmth, and spatial sprawl remind me of Southern California. It's understandable that the air feels the same because their latitudes have hemispheric symmetry: Auckland is 36° South, and Los Angeles is 34° North. The museum at the Domain introduces us to the cultural heritage of the Maoris (the indigenous people group in New Zealand), who fashioned massive blocks of wood into seagoing boats, decorating the carved wood relief with paua shell. During the demonstration of dance and music, one Maori-style song is reminiscent of how "Amazing Grace" is sung in the mountains of Kentucky (minus the drums and grass skirts). Are my homesick ears bending sound waves? Once the music and dance ends, Michelle's tolerance for touring the museum plummets. Under a canopy of shade trees on the museum grounds, I brief her more about our new life in New Zealand.

"Michelle, people in New Zealand will ask us where we are from in America. You need to tell them we lived in Cincinnati, Ohio. Don't mention that you lived in San Francisco, or that you were born there."

"Where is Cincinnati, Ohio?"

"Do you remember the airport we would fly into when we visited Bebe and Granddaddy in Kentucky?" She nods. "Well, Cincinnati is the big city across the river from the airport. I don't like telling a lie, Michelle, but it wouldn't be safe for us to mention San Francisco."

"Can we call Bebe and Granddaddy on the phone?"

"No, not for a while yet. When we do talk to them, we can't tell them where we are."

As the afternoon heats up, the shade trees offer less comfort. Wilting in summer heat, Michelle pleads to cool off in a swimming pool, but going to a public pool is problematic, since wire baskets are out of the question for storing the amount of cash I'm wearing. In blue jeans and athletic shoes, I don't blend in with the others around the pool. Since I can't enter the water, Michelle's swimming space is restricted to the edge of the pool at the shallow end. Squatting and walking alongside her, I avoid the puddles of pool water to keep the money in my shoes from getting soaked. Feeling ridiculous and hot, I long to jump into the refreshing water, but hearing Michelle's shrieks of delight as she bobs up and down is worth my discomfort.

The hostel takes on a different personality when the sun sets. The first-floor communal room becomes a party room with a makeshift bar. Throughout the day, the management has turned no one away. Sleeping bags are strewn on the floor, particularly on the screened porch outside our door, and cigarette smoke hangs above them in the still air. The plywood walls of our room block ventilation and some of the ubiquitous mosquitoes, which enter through the louvered door, but do not keep out the audible sighs of lovemaking from the adjacent cubicle. Sleep eludes me as I worry about a cigarette igniting a sleeping bag, turning the upstairs central core into an inferno. Thankfully, Michelle sleeps easily and deeply.

The next morning, Sunday, we awaken earlier than the sleeping bodies we step around outside our door but too late to attend church. Arriving at the Auckland Cathedral as services are ending, I initiate a conversation with the organist about recommendations for another hostel. The afternoon is spent walking in the heat to check lodgings that are all either too expensive or without vacancies. By late afternoon, Michelle and I give up searching and resign ourselves to spending another night with mosquitoes, smoke, and passion one room removed.

The coolness of the park revives Michelle. As she climbs on the base of a large monument, I talk with a mother who turns out to be the wife of the organist I had spoken with earlier at the cathedral. Amazed that our paths should cross on the same day, she invites us home for refreshments. As a place to live, she advises me to consider Wellington, which is cooler than Auckland and would be more comfortable for heat-sensitive Michelle. Besides, Auckland, like Los Angeles, requires a car, whereas Wellington is more compact for traveling on public transportation. Circumstances and counsel point toward Wellington, but before packing up again, I need to catch up on sleep—several nights' worth.

Walking back to the cathedral, Michelle and I attend Evensong for spiritual refueling and to pray for protection at the potential crematorium. Years later, I learn from a New Zealander that this hostel was damaged by fire a few years after our stay. Listening to the hymn "Loving Shepherd" in the coolness of the cathedral

soothes both of us. After the service, we kill time by walking in
the neighborhood, intending to return to the hot hostel just before bedtime. On the way to get something to eat, I recognize a
couple from the hostel who also recognize us. When they turn
out to be Americans, I edge away from conversation until I learn
that the woman is a nurse-therapist for abused children. A flood-
gate of feelings is released as I seek a sounding board as well as
validation. Michelle asks her how other abused children feel.
Speaking as a therapist, our new friend confirms that our situation
is not unique. As the four of us eat Indian takeout on park
benches, I thank God for the encouragement received through
this compassionate couple. Staying the extra night seems to have
had a positive purpose. Back at the hostel, we talk about America
and exchange mementos. Giving us their address and telephone
number in America, they offer their cottage in Vermont as a
hiding place.

The heat and the day's activities once again cause Michelle to
sleep soundly. It being a Sunday night, the hostel guests do not
party with the same intensity as they had the previous night. The
next morning a young woman who is sweeping the porch recommends a hostel in Wellington, assuring us, "It's much nicer than
this one."

Not ready to make the daylong train journey to Wellington, I
find out the names of several motels and hostels at the cathedral
office. Most turn out to be either too expensive or lacking vacancies—the same story as the previous afternoon's search—but one
refers us to a budget hotel. By midafternoon, we have settled into
a room that is not as cheap and smells of mildew, smoke, and
stale carpet, but it is private, lockable, and air-conditioned. The
amenity list lengthens.

To celebrate our deliverance, Michelle suggests visiting the
zoo to see the kangaroos she missed in Australia. Sadly, the intense heat discourages many of the animals from venturing out
into their enclosures. I make a beeline for the bird enclosures
while singing to Michelle a song about the kookaburra I had sung

as a Brownie Scout around a campfire between bites of s'mores. The mighty, mighty king of the bush isn't laughing merrily on a gum tree this afternoon, but then why should he, perched on a dead tree trunk in a hot cage?

The nocturnal house offers a refreshing respite from the heat and a view of a bushy-tailed opossum, resembling a koala more than its American cousin. In the darkness, our eyes are opened to the plight of flightless birds in New Zealand. These birds, with their exotic Maori names, such as the kakapo, haven't fared well in standing their ground against the domestic cats introduced to New Zealand by immigrating Europeans. Viewing the shy kiwi, I wonder if Michelle and I stand a chance in New Zealand without taking flight. Will New Zealand's scant human population be sufficient cover for us to maneuver safely as fugitives? If only the ratio of sheep to people were reversed: sixty-four million people to four million sheep. My fears are reinforced when the owners of our budget hotel and their son cross our path at the zoo.

BEFORE GOING TO SLEEP, MICHELLE AND I THANK GOD FOR the cool, quiet room, and pray for Jim, that God will change his heart. Michelle prays that her father is not in the hospital. As she sleeps, I try to calculate how many days we have been on the run. Crisscrossing the International Date Line and spending nights on planes has left me confused. New Zealand doesn't appear to be a jumping-off place for Antarctica and the South Pole, but when I imagine myself and Michelle near the bottom of the globe, I feel acute isolation from the people I love. By now, over a week since our departure, the legalities for my arrest will have been set in motion. Deportation back to America and separation from Michelle could occur at any time if I'm caught. The honeymoon period of life on the run is over.

4

The Light Down Under

Where there is a great deal of light,
the shadows are deeper.
—GOETHE

THE *SILVER FERN* LEAVES AUCKLAND FOR WELLINGTON AT 8
A.M., requiring an early morning sprint to the train station. To my
dismay, the money exchange isn't open, and I possess no New
Zealand currency. Although the tickets have been purchased, I
have no way to buy food and drink during the all-day train ride.
Michelle will suffer hunger and thirst, due to bad planning on my
part. On the train, I appeal to the conductor to take American
dollars for food, but he explains that won't be necessary. The
price of the tickets includes lunch and an afternoon Devonshire
cream tea: a pot of tea and a scone served with strawberry jam
and whipped cream. Could our Shepherd be preparing a table
before us? I ask myself.

Outside Auckland, the farming plains give way to hills loaded
with sheep, a visual clue of the skewed ratio of sheep to people in
New Zealand. As we feast, I think of Psalm 23. Michelle and I
need a guide who knows the terrain and how to steer us away
from threatening ravines. Can I trust God to carry us around and

over dangerous pitfalls? Trust is growing, but painful memories jab holes in my trusting heart.

Elevation changes are dramatic along this route; the train traverses breathtaking river gorges on stiltlike viaducts. At one point, the train tracks make a giant cursive E on the landscape to climb the sharp rise onto the Central Volcanic Plateau. As the train hugs the coast traveling south to Wellington, the volcanic peaks and scrub landscape are softened by dazzling views of the Pacific Ocean. At Paraparaumu Beach, the setting sun highlights the stark silhouette of Kapiti Island, looking like a rock-camouflaged offshore submarine rising to the surface. The island was once a sanctuary for a Maori warrior chief, but now it harbors species of birds on the fringe of extinction.

At dusk, Michelle and I get our first view of Wellington. Windy Wellington is much cooler than Auckland; hopefully, it will be energizing for Michelle. On the station platform, Michelle balks, expressing her tiredness: "I'm cold," then a few seconds later, "I'm hungry," then "I'm thirsty," all legitimate complaints but particularly annoying at a time when there is no way to obtain local currency. I have no idea where to find the backpackers' hostel where we have a room reservation and shrink from heaving luggage and a tired child through a city of hills in the dark. Hailing a taxi, I propose a condition to our fare. The driver obliges by exchanging an American $50 bill at a rate that doesn't seem too far out of line. The change from the taxi ride (in New Zealand dollars) will provide for hostel and dinner expenses until the banks open the next morning.

The hills and chilled air of Wellington remind me of San Francisco. As the taxi zigzags up a hillside, I glimpse the hostel's neon sign. Our private room juts from the hillside, taking the full brunt of the wind while offering a magnificent view of the harbor, which is beginning to sparkle with lights. The lofty steeple of a church that caught my eye on the way up the hillside dominates the foreground as a signpost.

Our curiosity about exploring Wellington is nil. Hiking down the hill, we stop at the first restaurant for a late dinner, climbing back up again at a time of night when an exhausted six-year-old child should be tucked in bed. Michelle is asleep before her head hits the pillow, but for adults exhaustion doesn't necessarily pave the way for sleep. Airfares and hotel and restaurant expenses have reduced the $100 bills in the money belt at an alarming rate. Now that the security of moving from place to place is over, I dread establishing ourselves in one place, where a routine will place my feet on the same paths, talking to the same people, day after day. Our life could be readily observed by anyone wanting to find us. Besides, finding hostels and restaurants is infinitely easier than arranging an apartment lease, utilities, school, transportation, and so on.

After visiting the bank, Michelle and I walk to the church with the steeple. The minister, Reverend Brown, enthusiastically embraces our situation after hearing our story. Immediately, he phones a parishioner who has a furnished basement apartment for rent. An appointment with Mrs. Hadley, a widow who lives alone, is arranged for as soon as public transportation can get us there. The prospect of our living in a safe neighborhood with a good elementary school overwhelms me with joy.

Before leaving Reverend Brown's office, I mention the need to safely stow the cash I am carrying. Opening a bank account in my passport name could be traced via computer records. Storing so much "mystery" cash in the church safe might prompt questions from the church staff. When Reverend Brown proposes a safety deposit box, the money storage problem is solved. A telephone call to the bank confirms that no identification is necessary. I leave the church office jubilant that two daunting hurdles have been leaped in one day: a safe place to live, and a safe place to store our money.

Several bus changes are necessary to reach Mrs. Hadley's home, which is located on the other side of Wellington. Our excitement grows as we walk through the attractive neighborhood where children Michelle's age are playing. Seeing Mrs.

Hadley's neat brick home with lovely shade trees and a front yard full of flowers, I thank God for His provision. As we enter the walk to the house, we see Mrs. Hadley holding the door open for several people who are leaving. I introduce myself, and she seems surprised by our presence and flustered when I express interest in seeing the apartment. Minutes earlier, she had rented it to the people we greeted on the porch. Apologizing for the misunderstanding, she insists that she would have waited for us, but she assumed that we weren't coming. Perhaps she hadn't anticipated the time required for public transportation. I know that Reverend Brown had made our appointment definite, but it doesn't matter now; the apartment is gone. Seeing that I am on the verge of crying, Mrs. Hadley invites us in for refreshments. Focusing on the cup of tea steadies me, and the tasty homemade cookies delight Michelle. Mrs. Hadley has no idea of the depth of my disappointment, or how much I need to establish a home away from hostels and restaurants. There's no point in telling her; the deposit furnished by the future tenants cancels all hope of our acquiring this apartment. I ask to see it for future comparisons and perhaps because I still haven't let go of the hope of living here. Seeing the cozy, albeit sparsely furnished, apartment (minus a refrigerator and a bed) rubs salt into my wounded soul. Michelle scampers through the rooms as if we are to be the new tenants, and I ridicule myself for rearranging the scant furniture in my mind, an exercise in futility.

Disappointment quickly changes to despair as Michelle and I walk away from the house. I do not like the way God is handling this situation, snatching this apartment away from us at the last minute, literally out from under our noses. At the bus stop, I can no longer control the tears. Michelle becomes quiet, for she has never seen me cry on a street corner. Although she is disappointed (responding more to my feelings than her own), she doesn't view this missed opportunity as the proverbial backbreaking straw. Since leaving San Francisco, I have been telling her that God will lead and protect us, so she volleys God's faithfulness back at me. While I have been hurling angry potshots at God about His cruelty, Michelle has been securely anchored in the present, not focused on what could happen to her in the future. Giving words of comfort from a faithful heart, she says, "Mommy, don't cry. It will be OK. We have a place to live."

What should have been a celebration dinner becomes a functional intake of food. Still preoccupied with inner contentions about the future, I haven't learned the spiritual lesson of taking life minute by minute as my daughter has. Despair fuels the idea of returning to America: Michelle might be harmed more by this undertaking than by the threat of sexual abuse in San Francisco. Perhaps I misunderstood God's instructions about fleeing with her. At least in America, the support of friends and family could help us face the future, however dreadful. I didn't expect this journey to be easy, but it seems impossible.

Back at the hostel, I peer into Michelle's face as she sleeps, imagining life for her in America if we returned. Pulling from a money pouch the yellow legal-sized page with the telephone numbers, I read the list of pros and cons about leaving San Francisco I had noted at the bottom to aid my decision process. Below the columns, I had written: "None of the nine counties [in the Bay Area] offer hope for the future. I must go beyond them to receive hope. If Ellen were to develop AIDS, I could not live with myself." Michelle is right; hope for the future has not been cut off. Healing begins when I acknowledge that finding a refrigerator and a bed for the apartment could have been costly. Hope for this journey is not about whether I rented an apartment today; as Michelle reminded me, our needs are covered tonight. Life is not turned upside down in the southern hemisphere because February is summer. Disappointments happen in New Zealand, even for people who are not on the run. As I glide toward sleep, I remember a Scripture song using verses from Lamentations: "The LORD'S loving kindness indeed never ceases, for His compassions never fail. They are new every morning. Great is Thy faithfulness. The LORD is my portion says my soul. Therefore I have hope in Him" (Lam. 3:22–24). I have enough hope to last until morning.

The list of available apartments at the rental agency offers no encouragement. When the agent advises walking through neighborhoods to look for advertisements posted in the local shops or in the windows of homes, I wonder how many neighborhoods Michelle's six-year-old legs can manage. To begin our search, we need to change elevations. The agent suggests taking the Kelburn cable car to save climbing a steep hillside, in addition to being fun. Near the top of the incline, Wellington's harbor, encircled by tree-covered hillsides with a mountain range in the distance, comes into view. The spectacular views momentarily lift the pressure of finding a place to live until the cable car stops with a jolt at the top. Michelle and I follow the flow of passengers into an area that appears too prosperous for my budget. After walking a few blocks, wishfully thinking about living in the basement of one of these fine homes or over a garage, the residences end and a row of shops begins. Michelle is single-minded about wanting a cold drink to revive her. Heading toward a corner grocery store, I look for a community bulletin board but find none. As I slowed down to look at the map, a man's voice interrupts my concentration. "Can I help you find what you are looking for?" Streams of shoppers are eddying around the three of us as we stand in the middle of the sidewalk. The man, who is wearing jogging shorts and has a newspaper under his arm, is willing to help. I reply with expectant interest. "I'm looking for an apartment to rent in this neighborhood. Do you know where ads might be posted?" Shaking his head, he responds, "I don't know of any bulletin boards, but a friend of mine may know of an available apartment. He works at this grocery store, the one in front of us. Wait over there while I go ask him." He gestures us toward a pewlike bench and returns in a few minutes, announcing that his friend knows of an apartment located on this street, only a few hundred yards beyond the shops.

On this side of the street, garages are at street level and paths descend the hillsides into the glen below. Trees and thick shrubbery obscure the view of the houses from street level. As we check the street numbers above the garage doors, the man explains that his friend doesn't know if the apartment is available now. Due to a keen interest in knowing more about the apartment, as well as the brevity of the walk, I discover little about the man walking beside me. At the garage matching the number we have been given, a woman and a young girl, who appears to be the same age as Michelle, are washing their car. When we inquire about the apartment for rent, Ruth, the owner, is surprised that anyone should ask. "My husband and I have not advertised it because we're uncertain of our plans. In fact, only one person, the young man at the grocery store, knows that it might be available in the future."

Noticing that the man who helped us has continued down the street, I send a wave of gratitude in his direction.

The girls, who have been eyeing each other curiously, start walking toward the house. As Sara, Ruth's six-year-old daughter, and Michelle peel off to jump on the trampoline, Ruth and I continue to the house. The path, whose curves make it longer than I expect, might be an annoyance when carrying groceries, but its seclusion is ideal for hiding out.

The entrance to the basement apartment is tucked around the corner of the house, not visible from the end of the path. Only one side receives daylight, since the back is pressed against the hillside. The smell of must dominates the small sitting room, which has potential for coziness. The galley-style kitchen is drab but offers a splendid view of the forested glen. A bathtub and refrigerator share the utility room with a washer-dryer. Retracing our steps to the end of the sitting room, a minuscule hallway leads to the bedroom. My nose tells me that we are getting closer to the source of the musty smell. Reluctantly, Ruth opens the bathroom door on the outside corner of the bedroom. On the walls, intricate tendrillike circles of mildew look as if they have been applied with the consistency of design. If mildew patterns can accomplish such uniformity, why can't the freckles on my arm coalesce to form an even tan? I ask myself. Ruth apologetically explains that the walls need to be cleaned before painting can be done. Eager to secure a hold on this apartment, I offer to clean the mildewed walls, a small price to pay for living in a lovely neighborhood near shopping and a school.

Ruth and I retreat from the musty odor to talk upstairs in her kitchen. She asks, "How did you find out about this apartment?" After I explain our encounter with the man on the sidewalk, she reflects, "I didn't recognize him, which surprises me, since I have lived in this village for fifteen years. Does he live here?"

"I don't know. I didn't find out much about him."

Ruth is respectfully curious about our situation: an American woman and child living in a youth hostel and wanting to set up a new life in a foreign country. Although I like her, sharing our circumstances with someone I have known for only thirty minutes makes me cautious. However, trust works both ways. Coming off the street as a stranger, I can offer no references, only the truth, an incredible story that Ruth believes. After she has talked with her husband, Peter, the apartment is offered to us and accepted. Since Ruth and Peter had no idea of renting the apartment yet, scheduling renovations—namely new carpeting—catches them off guard. A week of work in the apartment will be necessary before we can occupy it. They graciously offer their guest room for us to stay in until the work is completed, but I don't feel comfortable barging into their household, no matter how eager I am to swap the transient crowd at the hostel for family life. To accommodate both our needs, the three of us devise a plan. Michelle and I will spend the following night in their guest room before leaving for a week's excursion to the South Island while the carpet is being laid.

On the way back to the hostel, I marvel at the extraordinary sequence of events of the past few hours, bringing us to an apartment (including a bed and a refrigerator) tucked away on a lovely hillside. Michelle and I are not eager to pack our travel bags again, but coming home to our own place and the prospect of attending school will make this trip more like a vacation. Michelle likes having Sara and Frances, her older sister, upstairs as companions. Already, she has been invited to go swimming with them the next afternoon.

TWO DAYS LATER AT THE HARBOR, MICHELLE AND I BOARD THE InterIslander Ferry for the three-hour crossing from Wellington to the South Island, watching the porpoises play in the Cook Strait. Through the Tory Channel, land and water meet abruptly with bush-clad mountains dropping steeply into the fjord. On the South Island, the *Coastal Pacific* train to Christchurch squeezes between rocks engulfed in sea foam and the Kaikaua Mountains.

Christchurch lives up to its reputation as "a distinctive touch of England." The willow-lined River Avon flows gently through the city, carrying boating students. The English breakfast including a grilled tomato, a piece of fried bread, and a piece of bacon is identical to one I remember in Oxford. The spacious sky to the west reminds me of Wyoming, hinting at the Canterbury Plains, which are several hundred cricket fields away, the frontier being closer than England.

After Christchurch, the train crosses the Canterbury Plains and traverses a river gorge on a viaduct higher than Christchurch Cathedral. At Arthur's Pass, surrounded by high mountain lakes and trout rivers, the train reaches its highest point in the Southern Alps. Then, as if by tectonic magic, the plains vanish as the train descends to the sea through lush rainforests—nothing short of a continental makeover.

At Greymouth, we transfer to a bus. Arriving at Fox Glacier, only three of us have no lodging reservations; it is the end-of-summer tourist rush, and all the budget rooms were reserved long ago. The patient bus driver takes responsibility for us, even offering us a room with his family if all else fails. One expensive room at the Fox Glacier Hotel is vacant. Michelle and I and a woman from England decide to share it, splitting the cost.

At dusk, Michelle, our roommate, and I tramp through fern groves and subtropical vegetation, heading for a local tourist attraction, the Glow Worm Grotto. The grotto isn't really a cave but a hollowed-out circular path exposing a cross-section of earth. Sprinkles of light glow with unearthly luminescence amid the subterranean tangles. Shining the flashlight on the spot, we see only roots and clods of earth, taking on faith the presence of small beetles with glowing tails.

The hamlet of Fox Glacier is scenic, but experiencing the grandeur of the mountains requires transportation. The three of us hire a van driver to take us to the glacier where we walk on ancient ice that has been receding since the 1950s. The top crust, dirty from the summer season, needs a dusting of snow to restore its freshness. Our driver warns us not to leave shiny objects, such as jewelry or keys, lying around. Distraught motorists at the glacier have been seen stalking the native kea, a scruffy-looking alpine parrot, who has a reputation for snatching unattended keys.

Michelle and I board a bus to return to the plains, where we view Mount Cook from the other side of the Southern Alps, having been dazzled by its reflection at Lake Matheson on the rainforest side. The Maoris named Mount Cook "Cloud Piercer," but today only a tuft of cloud brushes up against the stone face. In Mackenzie country, the sheep fill the road, eddying to either side of the bus, which stops and waits for the woolly clump to pass. The turquoise hue of Lake Tekapo results from the glacial rock "flour" suspended in its water, complementing the palette of tawny colored grasses. Michelle photographs me hanging on to a bronze monument honoring the sheepdog. Both of us long to stroke Arcturus's velvet ears.

When the InterIslander brings us back to Wellington a week later, Peter is waiting to pick us up. "Chris, have you heard the news about another American girl who has been hiding in New Zealand? Her mother is a doctor who went to prison."

"Dr. Elizabeth Morgan's daughter?"

"That's the one."

"Where did they find her?"

"She was living in Christchurch."

"Oh, good grief. Michelle and I only left Christchurch this morning. It must be buzzing with reporters from America. Has the story been publicized much?"

"It's a big story in today's paper."

"Peter, this isn't good. Why couldn't Elizabeth Morgan's daughter remain in hiding a bit longer, at least until Michelle and I left New Zealand? It flags New Zealand as being a hiding place."

"You're right, Chris. It's not the best timing for you and Michelle."

Becoming even more concerned after reading the newspaper account, I learn that Dr. Morgan's daughter, who is slightly older than Michelle, used the name Ellen in hiding. The choice of New Zealand as a place to hide and the choice of names by Hilary Morgan says to Jim, "Here we are. Come and get us." I feel like a sitting duck, but instead of fleeing I am grounding our position by moving into an apartment and enrolling Michelle in school.

The journey to school consists of hiking up the path, walking past three houses, and crossing a street. Enrolling Michelle as a pupil without documentation is risky. As we wait to speak to the principal, I concentrate on relaxing, not wanting to appear as desperate as I feel. If necessary, I will emphasize the fact that Ruth, a special education teacher known at this school, has trusted us enough to rent us an apartment in the basement of her home. After cordial introductions, the principal asks about

Michelle's age (six), previous schooling (kindergarten) and why we have moved to New Zealand (new start following a divorce). These warmup questions are easy to answer, but soon the conversation turns to passports and immunization records. When she asks to see our passports, I fuss through my bag, apologizing for having forgotten them, along with the immunization record. I hate to lie, knowing that the passports are touching me and that the immunization record is with my parents. She asks me to bring them to the office the following day, but says Michelle can begin classes today if she likes. I check myself from expressing profuse gratitude toward this wonderful woman, who enrolls Michelle in school. The passport dilemma is postponed. Hopefully, the principal, who may suspect the nature of our situation, will never find her mental way back to this administrative detail. I plan to let this sleeping dog lie.

The principal leads us to a classroom, calling the teacher into the hallway for introductions. Within minutes, Michelle and I are standing before a class of twenty-five children whose curious eyes are directed toward the new American girl. Michelle shrinks shyly from this singular attention, but the teacher's warm welcome puts her at ease. She is given a desk next to another new student, Alex, a girl from Christchurch. Stalling for time to see how things go with Michelle, I scan the walls, which are lined with colorful displays of New Zealand lizards and birds, the current topic of study. Having already encountered the wall-climbing gecko outside our apartment, I am relieved to learn that it is harmless. The bird pictures are familiar from the New Zealand paper currency. Each bill denomination features a different native bird, culminating with the $100 bill displaying the takahe, which is making a successful comeback from near extinction. When I leave, Michelle looks self-conscious, but she is talking to Alex, who soon becomes a close friend.

After four weeks of constant togetherness, having a five-hour break from Michelle's company is glorious. On the way to the city center, I walk through a succession of public cut-throughs down the hillside. Lined by wooden fences, these walkways run past people's yards, bringing me nearer the windows of homes beside the path than would be accepted in America. It's tempting to glance in through the windows, at people moving around their cozy-looking kitchens surrounded by familiar things, but I keep my eyes straight ahead toward the views of the bay and the city, looking neither to the right nor the left. I don't want to be reminded of what I'm missing and what I've lost.

The safety deposit vaults are located in the bowels of the Bank of New Zealand. As the talking elevator drones on, I imagine what would happen to the thirty-plus stories above me if an earthquake were to occur; like San Francisco, New Zealand sits on the edge of several tectonic plates. But I feel shaky for another reason: Does today's success of enrolling Michelle in school, coupled with finding a well-situated apartment, preclude the success of this venture? Too much success, like too much failure, can make one feel insecure.

The incandescent friendliness of the vaultkeeper brightens the fluorescent environment. This bank official, dressed in khaki shorts and walking shoes, looks more like a misplaced park ranger, but strolling through the Wellington business district has accustomed me to summer business attire. I complete the safety deposit box application in the name of Chris Williams and hold my breath. Without asking for identification, the official leads me into the vault and pulls out a box, which I take to a tinted glass enclosure offered for the convenience of the bank patrons. For my purposes, the glass could have been tinted even more to conceal these undressing maneuvers from anyone watching from the reception area. Airfares have exhausted the sternum necklace, leaving hiding places only in the leather belt, the midriff pouch, and the shoes. Snipping the dental floss stitches on the zipper with the miniature scissors of my Swiss Army knife, I retrieve the bills, which appear to be permanently creased. Next, I unzip my jeans to pull off the midriff pouch, which displays the same convex curvature of my stomach. Then, removing the inner soles from my shoes, I pull out bills molded, through heat and pressure, into the shape of my instep. To my consternation, several have partially disintegrated. By now, the enclosure smells like a locker room—no laundered money here. I slip the money, totaling $15,000 in American currency, into an envelope, which becomes my bank account. Keeping out the disintegrated bills, I test their currency status immediately. The cashier at the foreign currency exchange accepts them, but her nose twitches.

From the perspective of a fugitive, storing cash in a safety deposit box has a downside. Besides the money accruing no interest, I relinquish immediate access to the money, which can now only be retrieved during banking hours. God only knows what I will do if we need to leave Wellington in a hurry, but the exhilaration of shedding the money dispels all other concerns for the moment. The Maori name for New Zealand means "the land of the long white cloud," and my steps are as light as any of the clouds above me. The brilliance of the sunlight gives the shadows a cleaner edge. Ruth had mentioned the striking radiance of light in New Zealand, advising us to wear sunglasses to protect our eyes. Years later, I learn from teaching geography that a thinning of the ozone layer above the South Pole permits more ultraviolet rays to reach this part of the globe. Will "the land of ultraviolet rays" provide sufficient shadows for hiding? I ask myself.

Walking home through the campus of Victoria University reminds me of the graduate students and faculty I left in San Francisco without saying goodbye. I ache with homesickness, now that some of the survival pressure has been removed. In San Francisco, I was advised not to phone America during the first month or two when everyone would be pumped up to find us. Now my imagination runs rampant, and I fear that one of my three elderly grandparents has died, or that Jim has threatened my parents for information of our whereabouts. The worrying suspense drains me. Will my mother's blood pressure and my father's heart condition be strained by the stress of not knowing where we are? Their survival depends on knowing that Michelle and I are safe. Without hearing from us, my mother may have conjured up the worst possible scenario: our living on the street, our capture, or our deaths. I am not certain which one of these would be the most terrifying to her. I long to call America, but bad news might paralyze tentative efforts at beginning a new life in Wellington.

CREATING AS NORMAL A LIFE AS POSSIBLE FOR MICHELLE AND myself ranks as an objective on the same hierarchical level as staying safe. For Michelle, school and church contacts open opportunities for birthday parties, sleepovers, and dance lessons in a church hall. Sunday dinner invitations fill our schedule and our stomachs with lamb, kumara (the Maori sweet potato), velvety ice cream, and pavlova, a meringue piled with cream and kiwifruit, which elevates "luscious" to new heights.

During the weekends, friends include us on family swim outings at the elaborate public facilities around Wellington, where New Zealanders develop gills when they are not tramping through the rugged outdoors.

School balances Michelle's time, but I suffer from having no weekly routine, except aerobic classes at the university and walking Michelle to and from school. While other children walk to school unaccompanied by an adult, I operate in a different mode, compelled always to be on watch.

To institute more routine in our life, I propose having a Friday night celebration, a weekly event to look forward to. Although the details vary from week to week, the festivities usually include dinner at McDonald's, a trip to the library, and the purchase of an inexpensive gift for Michelle, usually something for school. I am amazed how assigning gift status to a notepad, an ink pen, or a pair of socks magnifies the satisfaction it gives her. When it rains on Friday evenings, we eat pizza or fish and chips at home in front of the rented TV.

On one of our Friday evening excursions, a fingernail moon

shines over Wellington's harbor, reminding us of my parents. The light of the moon triggers a serious talk with Michelle, who releases some pent-up frustrations. When Michelle has had a bad day at school, fiery darts fly in my direction from the short fuse of her temper, because she knows her anger is safe with me.

"Bebe and Granddaddy are thinking of us tonight. Mommy, I want to go back to America and see them in Kentucky. The kids at school talk about their grandparents and ask me questions about Daddy. I don't know what to say. I tell them that I don't want to talk about it."

"Sweetheart, sometimes I don't know what to say when their mothers ask me about your father. I tell them that I'm divorced and starting a new life, but they look at me in a funny way."

"I want to see Sister Elise [Ellen's babysitter in California]. I miss my friends at kindergarten . . . Catherine the most. Does Sister Elise know where we are?"

"No one knows where we are."

"Can we go back to America without seeing Daddy? I love Daddy, but I want to live with you. I want to see Daddy sometime. Is he going to die?"

"It's not possible to go back to America without seeing Daddy. I know that you love him. When we left America, do you remember how well he looked? He still has the illness that gives him trouble breathing."

"What's it called?"

"Your dad was treated for pneumonia, which caused his lungs not to work properly."

After walking a little way in silence, Michelle brings up another concern. "What happened to the toys in my room? The girls here have things that I had in America. When my friends come to my house here after school, there's nothing to play with."

"I know. I wish it were different, but I can't buy you lots of toys because I must be careful about how I spend our money. You remember that Daddy and I were selling the house before we left?

All of our things will be boxed and waiting for us when we return."

Michelle has given up so much. Desperate to make her happy, I entreat, "Don't you like living in New Zealand?"

"Yes, but I'd rather live in America," she says simply. The conversation has come full circle, and the uppermost question in Michelle's mind hasn't been answered.

MICHELLE ISN'T THE ONLY ONE WHO FEELS FRUSTRATED AND lonely for contact with home. In San Francisco, my mother and I had agreed on a U.S.A. telephone contact, Marcella, her close childhood friend. Unbeknownst to my mother, I had arranged for other family friends, Joy and Wayne, to act as the initial contact so that Marcella becomes the intermediary. Planning for the day I call America, using a phone card from a public telephone seems the safest option to avoid calls being traced. Calling from New Zealand during school hours in the early afternoon works out to be bedtime in Kentucky, a mutually convenient time in both countries.

One afternoon about two months after leaving America, when I can wait no longer, I insert my phone card in a public telephone on the campus of Victoria University, but I still worry about the call being traced. My skin tingles from anticipation, not knowing what to expect. The news from home could be good or bad. Feeling as though someone has their fingers around my neck, I press the numbers with slow deliberation. "Hello," says the familiar voice, which does not sound sleepy. "Joy, this is Janie," I whisper self-consciously.

"Janie! I can't believe it's you. Are you both OK? We have been so concerned for you. Let me get Wayne." In seconds, Wayne, her husband, is speaking into the receiver. "Janie, are you and Ellen all right?"

Before he can question me further, I blurt out, "Is everyone at home OK? Have you seen my parents?"

"I talked to my dad, who said that everyone is fine. Your parents aren't saying much, so I don't have much to tell you. I can't push too hard for information because I don't want him to suspect anything—that I'm your contact."

"That's OK. I just need to know that everyone is still alive. My mother will be tight-lipped about all of this. She is not telling anyone, not even my grandparents, when she receives word about us." It is strange to hear familiar voices calling me Janie. I remind myself to say Ellen, instead of Michelle.

"Wayne, I can tell you so little about our life here. Please reassure my parents that God is meeting our needs. Ellen is in school and taking dance lessons. We have an apartment that is safe and in a nice neighborhood, and friends have been wonderfully supportive. Wayne, I don't want to talk too long. I can't imagine how this call could be traced from your phone, but anything seems possible."

"Janie, in your situation, it's better to be safe than sorry."

"I don't know when I'll call again—a month or so from now."

"Call us anytime, any hour. When I call Marcella, this friend of your mother's, I won't give my name."

"That's right. Just say that you are a friend of the family. Don't mention my name, in case the FBI bugs her phone." As the phone card counts down the seconds, I remember another important detail. "Wayne, when you talk with Marcella, mention the words 'fingernail moon.' Then my parents will know the message is from me."

The phone card beeps and then cuts us off. I sigh with relief. For a fleeting moment, apprehension about my family is gone.

ACCORDING TO RUTH, WORKING WIVES AND MOTHERS LIKE herself in our area need housecleaning services. Having arranged with her to do weekly cleaning and ironing to offset the rent, I'm eager to line up additional work. Within a few weeks of advertising on the community bulletin board, I have cleaning jobs arranged from Monday to Friday: too much routine, but the extra cash comes in handy. The mother of Michelle's friend, Alex, accompanies me on several cleaning jobs, picking me up in her 1950s silver Jaguar. We consider starting a housecleaning business together, but Bite the Dust Cleaning turns out to be the right venture at the wrong time. Soon, our passports will identify Michelle and me as overstaying our three-month tourist visas in New Zealand.

Despite all the positive benefits of living in Wellington, the predictability of life here makes me uneasy. Jim could have hired private detectives to track us from Auckland, or the FBI could be making inquiries at fitness centers and churches in Wellington at this very moment. Jim would know where to look for me. Now when I hear footsteps on the wooden boards of our porch, I stiffen and peer cautiously from the windows before opening the door, expecting a confrontation with him. I have no reason to suspect that our hiding place is threatened, but I am losing confidence that we are safe from discovery in New Zealand. Not knowing puts me on edge, the edge of despair.

Restlessness intensifies after our immigration visas expire, but leaving the security of New Zealand troubles me. Michelle could be out of school for an indefinite period of time, and the expense of air travel and living in hotels could exhaust our money supply. Although I have been frugal in New Zealand except for travel excursions, which I look forward to, the stack of bills is dwindling. In the near future, the supply will need replenishing, but few American Express offices exist in New Zealand for receiving Moneygrams. The islands of New Zealand, unlike the countries of Europe, don't provide a compact political-geographical structure for picking up money in various locations.

The pendulum of uncertainty knocks around inner peace. Emotions seesaw between the hope of staying and the despair of going. Life is comfortable here, but it could become unsafe. While I was growing up, my father used to advise me at times of indecision to "Do something, even if it's wrong." I have never understood the wisdom of this admonition until now, when the inability to make a decision is turning me into a jellyfish. Leaving New Zealand might turn out to be the "wrong" action, but then circumstances hint that staying could be "wrong," too. There's no way to know whether my shot-in-the-dark decision will turn out for good or for ill.

After about four months in New Zealand (one month as an overstayer), my body reacts from the tension within. During the wee hours of the morning, as Michelle sleeps next to me in the apartment's solitary bed, I wake up sweating, with a pounding pulse. A swig of antacid gloop gives no relief. If these symptoms are leading to a heart attack, Michelle could awaken to find me dead. On the other hand, this could be an anxiety attack. Her vulnerability makes my heart pound harder. The triage desk at the hospital recommends coming to the emergency room, but that would mean waking Michelle and hiking up to the road at 2 A.M. to meet a taxi, or calling upstairs for help. A few minutes of reflection convince me that receiving medical care at the hospital is impossible anyway, since I can't risk using my passport for registration purposes.

I phone a doctor friend from church, but he is out of town until the next morning. His wife offers to come to our apartment immediately, but nothing can be done. All action in the human realm is blocked. The pounding lets up a bit when I acknowledge helplessness, the inability to control even the beating of my heart, and eases more when I accept death, which is what I fear the most. From the hand of the Great Physician, I receive a dose of peace, just enough to put me to sleep—for a few hours, not eternity.

Early the next morning Michelle and I are awakened by our dear friends, the doctor and his family, knocking frantically at the door. By now I feel fine and the symptoms are gone. Michelle asks, "Why are they here so early?"

———

NOT LONG AFTER THIS INCIDENT, MICHELLE AND I RECEIVE AN invitation that sheds light on the path leading from New Zealand. The leader of a church club Michelle attends invites us for a weekend outing to Paraparaumu, the beach I had noticed on our initial train ride to Wellington. The beach is beautifully littered with jaw breaker-sized pumice, sculptured driftwood, and mottled shells with wedding cake tops. Walking at the water's edge near the foam lines reminds us of our strolls at Ocean Beach in San Francisco, but the sand between our toes in New Zealand has a different feel.

Toward evening, driftwood is collected to make a bonfire for roasting hot dogs and marshmallows. Huddled around the fire to take the chill off the night air, my friend and I discuss our future plans. Her lodger, a young woman from Malaysia, returns to Singapore soon to begin a new job. In Singapore, Michelle could attend an English-speaking school and there may even be employment for me as a tutor in English. Upon arriving in Singapore, she will consult her employer, who is well connected in the city, about helping us establish a life there. Living in Singapore sounds hopeful. In the brilliantly clear autumn sky, the Southern Cross is above the beach and a fingernail moon hangs over Kapiti Island.

MICHELLE'S REACTION TO LEAVING NEW ZEALAND SURPRISES me. Saying goodbye to friends and her school isn't as traumatic as I imagined it would be. Although I tell her that we are still on our "adventure" and Singapore will be a stopover, she believes that leaving New Zealand will bring her one step closer to America. I wonder how long the "adventure" theme will appease her frustration. Would there ever come a time when Michelle might contact America on her own? As always, I can't answer her question about when we will be returning home.

At a final meeting with Reverend Brown, we discuss a departure itinerary as well as the Singapore option. Disappearing in western Australia on a nine-hour visa before flying to Singapore is rejected as being too risky. Stopping over in Singapore, which has a reputation for being safe, is preferable to Hong Kong for a woman traveling alone with a child.

Leaving the country could be risky after overstaying for two months. We don't know how immigration will react to this breach of the rules. Judging from the media concerning the Hilary Morgan case, New Zealand doesn't want to become a haven for fugitives protecting children. Laws pertaining to future custody cases have been proposed to strengthen the power of extradition. Leaving New Zealand from Christchurch may offer less resistance for overstayers than Auckland, an immigration hotspot, and would draw attention away from Wellington if anyone discovers these reservations in the future. Reverend Brown, who has formerly been a pastor in Christchurch, writes a letter to present to immigration (if necessary) verifying that I have not been a burden to the state, or anyone else, during our five-month stay in New Zealand.

Thinking beyond Singapore, Greece offers a good currency exchange rate and relatively inexpensive living costs. Visiting the island of Rhodes, the site of my thesis topic, is an enticement for stopping in Greece. For a woman traveling solo with a child, Athens would be better than Istanbul, which arouses my curiosity as a stopover on our way to Europe. Reverend Brown suggests the Isle of Man, off the western coast of England, for seeking protection in the isolation of an island, as I had in New Zealand, but, looking at the map, the small island looks too confining. I leave my true name and my parents' address with him in the event something drastic happens to us. After our departure from New Zealand, he plans to write my parents a letter of encouragement. Before saying goodbye, Reverend Brown takes a snapshot of me with my back against the generic brick of the church building for enclosure with the letter. In this case, a picture will be worth more than a thousand words, particularly to my mother, whose fears are not allayed by messages without my voice behind them.

OUR GOODBYES COINCIDE WITH THE MIDWINTER FEAST, CELE-brated with dinners and gifts, a pleasant diversion from thinking about leaving a place which feels like home. Bone-tired exhaustion sets in from the emotional fatigue of saying goodbye to friends who have cared for us as loved ones. As I clean the refrigerator and pack our bags on the eve of our departure, I must leave behind many items I would like to take. A box of winter clothes is left behind to be sent to us later whenever and wherever we establish our next residence. The carry-on standard is strained to the limit by our bulging suitcases and an extra tote bag.

Continually, I cross-examine myself to determine whether reason or fear is propelling our departure from New Zealand. The phrase "hit the ground running" pervades my thoughts. Although this is what I need to do in Singapore, little energy remains to hit the ground, running or otherwise. Despite our weariness, Michelle and I are ready when the mother of a classmate drives us to Wellington Airport for the flight to Christchurch and on to Singapore.

5

Under the Juniper Tree

It is enough now, O Lord, take my life.
—Elijah

In the official guide, Singapore advertises itself as being "safe, clean, green, and always hospitable," comforting words for fugitives seeking a haven. Immigration offers us one month of hospitality as fanlike ferns wave welcome in the airport terminal. The hot humid air from outside infiltrates the environmentally controlled air of the terminal. The flight crew has warned me that accommodation options in Singapore are limited to international hotel chains. Opting for predictability and a central location, I make a reservation at one in the city center. Michelle warms to staying in Singapore instantly when she learns that the hotel has a rooftop swimming pool.

The Chinese taxi driver surprises me by being a deacon at a church in Singapore. It is as if God has appeared to chauffeur us in a city where only 3 percent of the population profess Christianity. Handing me a church card, he invites us to attend his church, thus providing a vital contact in a city of strangers in case of an accident or a medical emergency. If my appendix had been removed before leaving America, I would have one less medical emergency to worry about.

Amid rows of stately palms, Singapore is gearing up to celebrate twenty-five years of independence. Banners laud the slogan: ONE PEOPLE, ONE NATION, ONE COUNTRY. Michelle gets a kick from watching the rickshaw bicycles hold their own with cars in bumper-to-bumper traffic. The steel and glass towers are edging out the low, shuttered buildings with street-level colonnades which, in times past, sheltered shopping stalls. Few of these architectural beauties remain; I'm a generation too late to experience the intrigue of old Singapore.

Our hotel room is opulent compared to the New Zealand apartment. Here, we don't flinch when pulling back the shower curtains as we had there, expecting to see gargantuan spiders and rarely being disappointed. Before heading to the pool, I question the hotel receptionist relentlessly about the security of the hotel safe for holding cash. When her voice indicates that she is becoming impatient with my queries, I yearn to say, "You don't understand how vital this money is to my daughter and me. If other hotel guests lose their money, they can get new Travelers Cheques at American Express or call home for money, but I can't." To her, I appear neurotic.

During a break from swooping Michelle up and down in the pool, I write a letter to my parents, intending to mail it on our way out of Singapore to friends in Kentucky, who will then send it on to my parents. Every word is scrutinized for location-giving detail; even the blank stationery is held up to the sunlight to inspect the watermark. Mostly, the letter includes assurances about our well-being and expressions from the lips of Michelle. Important details, such as where we have been, where we are, and where we are going, are omitted. Although the sanitized letter is boring, my parents will hang on every word originating from my hand and dote on Michelle's drawings, signed Ellen.

When the late-afternoon thunderstorms drive Michelle from the pool, I call our Malaysian friend, who has arranged to introduce us to her employer, Mr. Lee, the following afternoon. His administrative connections could be helpful in establishing a life in Singapore. One disadvantage about hiding in Singapore is that Michelle and I do not blend physically with the ethnic Chinese and Malay populations. Presumably, our lives would center in the suburbs, where American tourists tend not to frequent. Trying to predict Jim's hunches on our whereabouts, Singapore doesn't seem to be a contender, although I could be wrong. Several countries down the line, I learn from my mother that the inspector at the district attorney's office in San Francisco had suspected our initial hiding place as being New Zealand, not Europe, as I had guessed.

The sanctuary of the Church of the Good Shepherd is crowded on this Fifteenth Ordinary Sunday, as noted in the church bulletin. If only I could experience some ordinary days, Sundays or otherwise. From the sermon title, *Receiving the Word,* I anticipate words of encouragement from God. The text for the sermon is the parable of the sower and the seeds in Matthew 13, and I try to facilitate God's speaking to me by adapting the parable to our experiences of living on the run. The seed, or gospel, represents my decision to flee with Ellen, falling on various "soils," or circumstances of the journey, symbolized by the growth of the plant. Initially, the seed falls to the ground and is snatched by disbelief immediately, never taking root. Michelle and I are past this stage, where the seminal idea of fleeing sprang up in San Francisco and became rooted in the soil of experience. In the second soil, the words from God are believed for a while, but the temptation to doubt eventually causes the plant to wither and die; in New Zealand, the rocky circumstances of finding a place to live almost cut off the shallow roots of perseverance, but I had endured the temptation to go home. In the third stage, the plant, or journey, is in danger of being "choked" with the thorns of worry, riches, and pleasure; at this point, the last two thorns seem more desirable than suffocating, but the thorn of worry is omnipresent, popping up everywhere to test my spiritual fortitude. In the final stage, the plant survives to bear fruit, symbolizing the journey's end, when protection is accomplished, although God might define fruit-bearing differently from me. Through the sermon, God implies, "Just as a fruit-bearing plant doesn't happen overnight, neither will the purposes of this journey come to fruition without sufficient time." Although I expected this journey to take time, I had estimated it would last six months, or a year at the most; my mother had predicted the journey would last longer. In my impatience, I tend to underestimate time, whether I'm packing to catch a plane or learning to trust God again. I continually pester God with "How long, O Lord?," but more pertinent questions for this journey would be "How long, O Lord, before I trust You? What's the minimum time required?"

Almost forty-two years of living have conditioned me that expectations calibrated at a high threshold in the imagination let me down more times than not. Living by expectations defeats my spirit with the deadliest weapon of all for attacking the Achilles' heel of the heart: disappointment. Life isn't a roulette game operating on the chance of expectations, because God, not I, knows where the chips will fall. God reiterates, "Don't expect, just trust. This journey won't end until trust, as well as protection, comes to fruition. The seed for trust has taken root in Canada, Tokyo, New Zealand, and now Singapore." I leave the church feeling as if the journey is just beginning.

Later in the afternoon at the hotel, Michelle and I are introduced to Mr. Lee and his children. Our meeting is brief, since he leaves on a business trip later in the day, but he suggests that we talk tomorrow when he returns to Singapore late in the evening. He invites Michelle and me to stay at his home, where he often extends hospitality to friends. Although he assures me that our presence at his spacious home would not be an intrusion, I refuse his kind invitation. I don't know him well enough to feel comfortable staying in his home.

The next day is filled with animals, exotic and otherwise:

komodo dragons and penguins at the zoo and parrots riding bicycles on trapeze wires at Jurong Bird Park. Michelle selects colorful hummingbird earrings for her grandmother, ones that will be treasured but never worn. At the Bird Park, what really captures our attention is a sign above the toilet in the ladies' rest room that reads: $250 FINE FOR FAILING TO FLUSH TOILET. Instinctively, I look for cameras but don't see any way to verify a non-flush.

Back at the hotel, Michelle scratches itchy red blotches covering her arms and legs, having provided nourishment for many mosquitoes during the day. A tube of cream from the pharmacy has only a sketch of a mosquito surrounded by Chinese characters to assure me of its soothing purpose. Riding in a rickshaw bicycle during five o'clock traffic diverts Michelle's attention from scratching more than the cream does.

After returning to our room for the evening, I page Mr. Lee as he had requested. Sleep does not come easily for Michelle, who is distracted by the itching. Although ready for sleep, I stay awake for Mr. Lee's call, which comes at midnight from the lobby of our hotel. When he suggests that Michelle and I meet him downstairs, I explain about Michelle's difficulty in getting to sleep. Knowing that Mr. Lee's busy schedule permits few appointment opportunities, I suggest that we talk in our room so that Michelle can continue sleeping.

Desperate to know whether Singapore is to be simply a stopover or a place of more permanence, I ask him about living expenses, English-speaking schools, and opportunities for employment. Mr. Lee, who speaks excellent English, offers encouragement at the prospect of our living in Singapore but no concrete details. The conversation moves toward our personal situations, his of being a widower, and our life of being on the run, which doesn't surprise him, since he has been informed of our circumstances. Moving closer, he puts his arm around my shoulders as a gesture of comfort, but his next move catches me off guard. Confounded by his attempt to kiss me, I jerk backward,

lose my balance, and fall sideways, sputtering that I'm not interested in "that." Both of us are bewildered by the actions of the
other. We avoid eye contact, with conversation continuing awk-
wardly as we contemplate how to escape without appearing to do
so. Struggling to conceal embarrassment and agitation, I do not
want to expose how wounded I feel. Saying goodbye at the door,
Mr. Lee advises me not to stay in Singapore but to look for a man
of similar culture in Canada, or the United States, to marry.
Confusion makes responding to this parting shot difficult. I mum-
ble that marrying is the last thing on my mind, as I'm not certain
of being legally divorced. We wish each other well, and the door
shuts on Mr. Lee and Singapore.

I feel like screaming but don't want to wake up Michelle. In
hushed tones, I express my anger and confusion to the mirror, the
walls, the bed pillows, alternately raging against myself and
against Mr. Lee. How could I have been so stupid not to have
seen it coming? Giving Mr. Lee the benefit of the doubt, a major
cultural misunderstanding has occurred. He anticipated helping
our situation by supplying us with a new name, as well as the
legal documents accompanying it. Addressing the ceiling, I mut-
ter, "God, I interpret this incident as a catalyst to move us on
from Singapore." If possible, I would leave Singapore tonight.
Will the day ever come when I see humor in the humiliation of
this misunderstanding? I ask myself.

The next morning, following the itinerary I planned in New
Zealand, I reserve seats on a flight departing for Athens in the
evening. Since reserving ahead for lodging means staying at an
expensive hotel, I decide to take our chances with tourist information at the Athens airport. Greece will serve as a vacation
stopover on our way to a place of residence somewhere in Europe. Floating in the world without the grounding of roots is
eating away at something inside me. My soul needs to arrive at an
oasis that links me with who I am; it thirsts for the companionship of friends who know me, like Janet in Scotland or Gabriella
in Italy, who both crossed my path in America. Sadly, visiting

these friends known by Jim is risky, but a dry, shriveling soul can be risky as well. If I become too depressed, the journey is over.

Before leaving Singapore, I call Gabriella, who lives near Rome, to alert her that we plan to visit Italy during the next few months. Gabriella and I met while working at the same architectural office, becoming friends before she and her husband, Francesco, returned to Italy. Although Gabriella and Francesco, Jim and I had spent time together socially, Gabriella and I formed the foundation for the friendship. During the turmoil of the past year, letter-writing to friends like Gabriella has halted. She has no idea that Michelle and I are on the run, or any knowledge of the events leading to our fleeing America. Despite the compassion she will feel for Jim and her inclination to give him the benefit of the doubt, I am confident of her loyalty.

Gabriella's familiar voice thrills me. She has been concerned for our welfare when attempts to contact us in San Francisco were unsuccessful. Hearing about our distressful situation is difficult for Gabriella to comprehend during a brief phone call, and many questions must remain unanswered until I see her. Over and over, she repeats, "I can't believe it. I can't believe that Jim would do such a thing. He is a very intelligent man."

ON THE NIGHT FLIGHT TO ATHENS, THE DESERT OIL FIELDS ARE a kaleidoscope of illumination from the plane's window, oceans of blackness perforated by islands of brilliant light. At passport control, no obstacles block our entry, but the stamp of our tourist visa is too smudged to reveal how many months we can stay in Greece. In the harsh fluorescence of the terminal, students sprawl on the floor, using their luggage as headrests to catch up on sleep. The hot, humid air intensifies the odor of vomit, sweat, and plane exhaust. Feeling queasy from the foul air, Michelle and I line up behind others seeking a hotel room at 4:30 A.M.

At tourist information, we reserve a room in the center of Athens and go outside to wait for a taxi in predawn darkness.

When a taxi pulls up to the curb, hands rush forward to grab the back door handle. Holding Michelle's hand and the luggage hinders me in the dash to reach it. I feel empathy with the blind man in the Bible who had strived for years to be first to enter the stirring waters at the pool of Bethesda (John 5:1–14). The man's healing required Divine intervention, which, in my case, slows the responses of those behind me so that my hand touches the next taxi first. When I show the driver the reservation sheet, he looks puzzled. When he doesn't recognize the name of the hotel, my heart beats faster.

Traffic in downtown Athens is sparse at 5:30 A.M. Finding the street is no problem, but the number doesn't seem to exist. Spinning around the block while peering at street numbers, our driver rams into the back end of a taxi in front of us. Without seat belts, Michelle and I jolt forward but are not hurt. Both drivers jump out to inspect the bumpers, shouting and gesturing vigorously at one another. A number of fears have materialized in the thin morning air, a lesser one being that the fare will be inflated to cover the damages. After a few minutes, our driver returns to the wheel in a bad mood, muttering to himself in Greek. On the next trip around the block, he jumps out at an inconspicuous passageway, leaving us alone in the taxi. Is he on a mission to locate the hotel, or to settle a personal vendetta? While I am fiddling to lock the doors, he reappears, unloads our cases onto the pavement, and motions for us to follow him. There, situated in the curve of an arcade, hidden from the street's view, is the Minerva Hotel, where a room is reserved for us.

Stark fluorescent lights reveal a clean, functional lobby. The setup seems OK, but it is hard to judge the character of a hotel at 5:30 A.M. The woman at the front desk is reassuringly nice, but Michelle is put out that there is no swimming pool. The window in our small cheerless room frames a brick wall and holds a window air conditioner that puts out more noise than cool air, but the room is clean and the adjoining bathroom makes it self-contained.

During the dog days of August, Athens is inhabited by tourists and by local residents who have stayed in the city to service the tourists. Their faces wear the expression of wanting to be elsewhere, where the air is cooler and sweeter. While sight-seeing, I carry bottled water for drinking and a bottle of tap water for pouring over Michelle when she overheats. When I suggest climbing the Acropolis, the fortified hub of life in ancient Athens, Michelle is too hot to appreciate the privilege. Anticipating the experience makes me shiver with excitement, even in the heat. The upward path snakes through scrubby trees with dust from an entire summer covering their leaves. At the pinnacle, the sun strikes our heads with blistering heat. Intact monuments have been reconstructed among the heaps of crumbling stones that are strewn around and lying on their sides. Reconstruction of antiquities is unsettling. I prefer to see what Aristotle saw when he proposed the spherical nature of the earth or, if that isn't possible, to see the ancient rubble of what he saw. Michelle is wilting, despite my efforts to cool her with splashes of water. After photographing a flushed Michelle in front of the Parthenon with a camera on indefinite loan from a New Zealand friend, we head down the hillside to buy cold drinks.

As we waited to cross the street at the base of the Acropolis, a large tour bus stops directly in front of us and Tina Turner (known to Michelle as Tina Turnip on *Sesame Street*) steps out. Traffic in Athens stops. She is dressed in a navy suit jacket and slacks, and not an inch of her dynamite legs is showing. As a knee-jerk response, I scan the periphery for paparazzi, fearing that our faces could appear in the background of an American TV show. At the entrance to the Theater of Dionysus on the other side of the street, Tina Turner reverently kisses the ancient stone wall before disappearing inside. I want to call out, "Wait! I have wanted to tell you something for years. Once Ike [her former husband] mentioned on television that you had experienced racial prejudice years ago at a hotel in Kentucky, the site of my wedding reception. I apologize for whatever happened there. I admire your spunk in fleeing from an abusive situation. You did what you had to do to survive, and I want to survive with my daughter." None of these words bounce off the ancient stones, but stay within the walls of my heart. How many times had I left the aerobics class in San Francisco singing "What's Love Got to Do with It"? I am face-to-face with an American woman, a survivor, who I recognize but who doesn't recognize me; not a bad deal for a fugitive. Unbeknownst to Tina Turner, she encourages my survival spirit. Motivated to encourage her in some way, albeit from afar, I determine to pray for her welfare, initiating a celebrity prayer list with Tina Turner's name at the top.

SPENDING TIME IN ATHENS DIRECTS MY THOUGHTS TOWARD MY graduate thesis. Before leaving San Francisco, I had mapped the incidence of favism on the island of Rhodes, using the clinical data of a research pediatrician in Athens. Favism, or Mediterranean anemia, is an acute blood disease occurring in some individuals after they eat fava, or broad beans. Tracking down Dr. Kattamis will be easy if he has remained at the hospital I remember from the credits of the journal article. Hailing a taxi to take us to the hospital, I inquire at the pediatrics department whether Dr. Kattamis is still on staff. He is, but he's not in the hospital today.

When Michelle and I return to the hospital the next day, we wait for Dr. Kattamis to return to his office after his clinic hours. For times like these, the Golden Arches are handy to offer as a carrot for good behavior, but Athens hasn't yet been chained with fast food. As we pass the time in a playground near the hospital, my palms become sweaty, not from the heat but from the likelihood of appearing foolish during an interview with Dr. Kattamis. Anxiously, I sift through clinical symptoms, trying to recall without the aid of notes the ones that apply to favism. The harder I try to remember, the more memory blocks I come up against—not a new phenomenon. In New Zealand, I spent hours trying to recall the names of friends in San Francisco, even my Social Security number, to no avail.

It's possible that this respected physician will have no time to talk with an American graduate student who intentionally presents no academic credentials. Yet, when approached, Dr. Kattamis is willing to answer my questions about favism and is not put off by Michelle's presence. I am the only one uncomfortable until Dr. Kattamis puts me at ease by pulling out tongue depressors for Michelle to play with. The line between family life and professional life isn't as clearly drawn in Greece as it is in America.

After twenty minutes of sorting through facts that have not been at the top of my intellectual pile for months, my brain is weary from the workout. Leaving the hospital, I'm exhilarated by the rush of cerebral juices and the prospect of visiting the island study site of my graduate thesis.

MICHELLE AND I CROSS THE AEGEAN SEA ON OLYMPIC AIR-ways, clapping with the other passengers (mostly Greeks) when the wheels touch the runway on the island of Rhodes. Traveling by bus to the city, we arrive in the late afternoon, after the tourist office has closed. I wish to God that I could make reservations like ordinary travelers, but reserving in advance could risk my arrest at an airport, a train station, or a hotel. If I'm to be arrested, I'd prefer it to happen by chance, rather than ambush resulting from an error in judgment.

Room hawkers swarm around the bus, holding up pictures of houses and yelling fragments of English at us. Retreating back into the bus from the verbal assault, I ask the driver for a hotel suggestion. He offers little hope that a room exists this late in the day during the month of August, but directs us to a hotel three blocks away. Our walk is not in vain. One room remains, a lovely room with a balcony, tiled floors, and a private bath. The rate is too expensive for more than one night, but for this night the room has been reserved for us in heaven.

The swimming dilemma resurfaces when Michelle pleads to go to the beach. The stack of money has diminished to the point of fitting into one receptacle: the midriff pouch, which still contains thousands of dollars in cash. Although I'm only wearing a T-shirt and shorts, the cash becomes drenched next to my body in the intense sun. In the shallow waves, Michelle splashes while I swelter from the ankles up, wearing more cloth on my body than all the other women on the beach put together.

The next day, throwing caution to sea breezes on a Greek beach, I leave the money and our passports in the locked room of the small hotel we had checked into the previous day. More than wanting to swim, I want liberation from carrying so much cash. On the way to the beach, I worry that this relaxation of the rules could be a fatal mistake, leaving us stranded with no money. If the cash were stolen from our room, the loss couldn't be reported to the police. Uneasiness dissipates when I feel the splash of the waves.

SEVERAL MONTHS BEFORE LEAVING SAN FRANCISCO, A FRIEND of mine had shown me gorgeous vacation photos taken in the village of Lindos, located at the south end of Rhodes. Her descriptions had sharpened my interest then, even to the extent of thinking what a wonderful hiding place it would be. Michelle and I board a bus for Lindos, which deposits us at the village center. Here, tourists hire guides to lead them on donkey rides up the steep ascent to the Lindos Acropolis, situated on a towering rocky outcrop overlooking St. Paul's Bay. Supposedly the Apostle Paul came ashore here on one of his missionary journeys. Michelle pleads to ride a donkey, reminding me of her dream to ride a pony in Kentucky. Today is the six-month anniversary of our departure, and I give in.

The donkey guide settles each of us atop a donkey, on a

blanket covering a pillow. When he enters a shop to purchase a bottle of water before the climb, the donkeys, who aren't tethered, become restless. Suddenly Michelle's donkey bolts toward the uphill path. My donkey, stuck with a heavier load, follows at a slower pace. Neither donkey pays attention to my commands. When I realize that the situation is out of control, I scream to Michelle, "Hold on tightly!" Looking happy that her donkey is in the lead, Michelle says something I don't comprehend. In the distance, she bounces up and down, her legs thumping against the donkey's flanks, which may be interpreted as "Giddyap." Soon our donkeys are trotting up the narrow steep path of switchbacks, passing other groups of donkeys on the outside, close enough to the edge to dislodge rocks, which tumble to the switchback below. The blanket underneath me shifts from side to side on the turns, each time tilting my body a little more. As other donkey guides yell to us, we see our guide running on the switchbacks below us. At the top, the runaway donkeys stop on a dime at their watering place, allowing our guide to catch up and rebuke us in Greek, presumably for starting without him. The donkey escapade becomes a journey highlight for Michelle, a rare life occurrence when reality exceeds expectations. For me, it symbolizes the potential for harm's way lurking within every decision.

ON THE PEDIATRICS WARD AT THE HOSPITAL IN RHODES, I interview a pediatrician who has treated patients with favism while Michelle studies a mural of cartoon characters depicting Bugs Bunny in a tunic and Mickey Mouse wearing leather sandals. The pediatrician mentions a mountain village, Embonas, as one place on the island that has a high incidence of the disease. In San Francisco, Embonas had been only a graphic arts bullet on a map.

At Embonas, the bus deposits us at a cluster of tavernas that seem to exist more for the pleasure of the village residents than for tourists. Few people are stirring in the heat of the afternoon. Older gentlemen are sitting and talking wherever shade is available, mostly in doorways. Walking through the narrow streets enclosed by whitewashed walls, Michelle and I smell the scrumptious aroma of food grilling on a charcoal fire. I peer over a parapet to locate the source, and a Greek woman looks up from turning vegetables on the grill. When I convey with my hands the heavenly scent of her cooking, she motions us to join her on the terrace below. In pulverized English, she invites us to have dinner with her family. Her husband, who works in Athens, speaks a few words of broken English. Feasting on peppers, zucchini, eggplant, potatoes, bread still holding the oven's heat, and clusters of red-purple grapes, we communicate using the universal language of gestures. After dinner, Michelle plays with a neighbor's daughter, and our hostess gives me a few dried fava beans for good luck.

SUMMER IS WINDING DOWN, AND THE LANDSCAPE LOOKS TIRED. Intent on making our way toward Athens and on to Italy before school commences in September, I ask anyone who can communicate with me for suggestions about an island stopover on the way to Athens. The consensus is Patmos, the Holy Island, familiar to me as the place where the Apostle John wrote the Book of Revelation in the Bible.

At the tourist office in Rhodes, I purchase tickets for the next available ferry for Patmos. The agent explains that the Monastery of St. John the Theologian has been successful at keeping discos and nightclubs off the island; even the noisy engines of planes are banned. After the ferry tickets have been issued, another agent remarks that she has received a notice requesting that no additional tourists be routed to Patmos, since accommodations are full. When I try to unpurchase the ferry tickets, the agent shrugs: the tickets belong to us, but we don't have to use them.

The ferry for Patmos leaves Rhodes at noon, stopping at a number of islands beginning with the letter K. Other passengers traveling to Patmos confirm that we are arriving during a major holiday celebrating the Assumption of the Holy Virgin. Michelle and I are warned that, without hotel reservations, we may be sleeping on the beach unless we find a room through a hawker on the pier.

On the deck, I stare for a long time at the sea. If the ferry were to lurch and catapult us overboard, no one in America would know where to search for our bodies. When I look at the water, the plunge is appealing, but when I look at Michelle beside me, I recoil from the idea. The waves move whimsically on the surface, concealing the deep below, just as the surface motions of my life, moving from island to island, country to country, conceal a deep sadness. In this abyss, such treasures as my name, my hopes and dreams, and my freedom have sunk to the bottom beyond my reach. Words from the Bible—"Deep calls to deep"—match my spirit. God seems as fluid as the waves buffeting the ferry, nearer at some times than others but mostly beyond reach. I'm grasping for a temporal anchor, a guarantee that everything will be OK, that all of this will be ending soon. But no assurances exist: ". . . all Thy breakers and Thy waves have rolled over me" (Ps. 42:7).

When the ferry docks at 10 P.M. in Skala, the principal city on the island of Patmos, a sea of people fills the pier and spills into the street beyond, the crowd appearing larger than the ferry can accommodate. In the swell of bodies, I see no room hawkers, only passengers pushing to reach the gangplank leading to the ferry. The crowd towers above Michelle's six-year-old stature. I can devote only one hand to the luggage, and the cart bumps through the crushing crowd, eventually tipping over. Unable to right it, I drag it on its side. At the first telephone, I call a number that was given to me on the ferry as a possible place to stay, but the person who answers speaks no English. Looking for a hotel on foot, Michelle and I pass the police station; we will camp on its floor before spending the night on the beach.

After about ten minutes of walking along the harbor with boats on one side and outdoor tavernas on the other, Michelle and I come to a hotel. The owner insists that no rooms are available, but I persist, emphasizing that I am traveling alone with a child. With hesitation in her voice, she admits that one room remains vacant. About ten minutes earlier, a man had asked her to hold it, but he has not returned. Observing Michelle's tired face, she offers us the room. Later, I discover that our steps had been directed to one of the few vacancies in Skala, as well as one of the best deals.

Crowing roosters awaken us the next morning. Judging from the overheard conversation at breakfast, this hotel is popular with French tourists. After a satisfying breakfast of rolls, fruit, and yogurt, I am still hungry, but not for food. My spirit needs nourishment that feeds endurance and perseverance, reserves which have been running low since leaving New Zealand. Although Michelle and I sustain each other by praying together, more intensive spiritual refueling is required—the high-octane spiritual mixture of God's presence in the assembly of worshipping believers.

Michelle and I enter a Greek Orthodox church, blinded by the dark interior until our eyes adjust. The pungent odor of incense catches in my throat. I strain to comprehend the priest, but my Greek vocabulary is limited to courteous expressions like "Good morning" and "Thank you," useless phrases for grasping the meaning of a sermon. The mystery of the service is perplexing. If the onion-shaped dome of the church were lifted, I would see the hillside where the Apostle John received the Book of Revelation, a spiritual conundrum for past, present, and future. Longing for revelation, not mystery, I escape with Michelle outside into the white glare, thinking ahead to the nitty-gritty reality of the beach.

Throughout the day, boats depart from Skala's harbor for beaches around the island. While buying water, Michelle and I miss the boat we had intended to take and board the next one. At the beach, when we can stand the penetrating sun no longer, we withdraw to the shade of the trees clustered around the taverna a few paces behind the beach. Tepid drinks refresh us enough to repeat the relaxing cycle of water, sun, and shade. A shade segment of the cycle is extended when I meet a minister and his daughter from Louisiana. Without spilling all the beans about our situation, the three of us discuss God's guidance through the morass of life's circumstances. Their spiritual fellowship primes the pump for another encounter later in the day.

Returning to Skala, Michelle and I cool off our insides with ice cream, but we long for ice, both rare and suspect in Greece. While we linger at the pier with our cones, an English-speaking non-Greek woman asks if I will take their family photo. Within seconds, people I have never seen before are smiling into the camera as if they know me. As our conversation drifts in a personal direction, I discover that Meridel and Jay are originally from Toronto and now serve God in Israel. While Michelle and their young son, Daniel, inspect a titanic yacht belonging to the Sultanate of Oman, I tell Meridel and Jay our circumstances without reservation, not understanding why I trust these strangers immediately. Our story comes as no surprise to them. Both are authors of books on family life. One book, written by Meridel, chronicles the story of a young child who has been sexually abused by her father.

After establishing spiritual common ground, they suggest praying with me. At first, I feel uncomfortable about huddling together on this public pier, but the desire for God's intervention in our circumstances overcomes self-consciousness. When Jay encourages me to listen to his wife's prayer because her words have spoken meaning into many lives, God rivets my attention. Hearing a husband say, "God speaks through my wife. Her prayers carry authority," attunes my ears for listening. As they pray on my behalf with their hands resting lightly on my shoulders, I am no longer concerned about what other people on the pier are thinking. Their words aren't extraordinary, only powerful. Meridel prays, "God will use your situation, your life, in a mighty way. Follow your heart. Trust that God will guide you by your heart."

Opening my eyes after hearing these words, more from consternation than elation, my first thought is that I won't be alive to see
"mighty" things, knowing that godly purposes are sometimes accomplished through death as well as life. Words such as "resolution" and "soon" would have been more comforting, but I'm left
with "trust" and "follow."

Meridel suggests that I contact Youth with a Mission (YWAM),
a Christian organization with a vision for bringing the gospel of
Christ to the world. They are acquainted with a staff member,
Barbara, who serves at a YWAM base in Switzerland. Meridel is
uncertain whether she lives in Lucerne or Lausanne, this information being in Israel. The initiative for pursuing the address rests
with me after Michelle and I reach Italy and Meridel and Jay
return to Israel.

Leaving the pier, I hold Michelle's hand as I always do for
security, as well as for the pleasure of clasping her small hand. At
this moment, her arm prevents me from floating upward, as an
untethered hot-air balloon might do. The awe from praying has
created a lightness in my step, as if my legs will take me wherever
I want to go without effort. Neither of the day's spiritual en-
counters has come about through my initiation: not the meeting
at the pier, nor the earlier conversations at the beach. In time, I
will contact Youth with a Mission in Switzerland. Whatever the
outcome of "mighty," God had answered my morning prayer
mightily.

Feeling as if in the presence of family, I confer with Jay and
Meridel about the viability of traveling to Italy next while the
children sculpt a sand castle. In the light of the sun, they pray
with me again, now for the release of destructive emotions from
the past. I visualize releasing the bindings on my skis (wherever
they are). Hearing in my mind the snap that permits the boots to
be lifted from their constraints, I remember that delicious feeling
when leg muscles, weakened from hours of tension, are relaxed.
As terrain changes for a skier on the slopes, so the relational
terrain of my life has gone from singleness to marriage to separa-

tion and probably divorce by this time. Emotional bindings from the past aren't easy to shed and can make living in the present feel like skiing through wet sand. An accusation from Jim calls to me from across thousands of miles: "What gives you the right to take my only child from me when I am dying?" and a familiar refrain: "If only you hadn't . . . I wouldn't have." The power that I laid aside to accommodate responsibility for Jim's actions must now be reclaimed. Empowerment is a process requiring time, unlike the immediate snap of a ski binding. Faith, like empowerment, is a process, "the assurance of things hoped for, the conviction of things not seen" (Heb. 11:1).

On the boat ride back to Skala, Daniel's cap blows overboard in the strong wind. I promise to send him one from Kentucky, adding parenthetically, ". . . if and when I return."

STANDING IN LINE AT THE FERRY OFFICE, I FEEL DIZZY AND nauseated. Earlier, at the beach, Jay and Meridel had encouraged me to make a ferry reservation for Athens as soon as possible, since tourists leave Patmos in droves during the latter half of August. By the time we reach the agent, the cold sweat of impending sickness grips me. Abruptly, I run out of the office, calling to the agent that I will return. Michelle giggles nervously as I vomit into a flowerpot outside. Knowing that I don't have much time before the next episode, I purchase tickets for a ferry leaving Patmos in one week's time and quickly return to the hotel.

Throughout the evening, I become weaker from frequent vomiting in our room's sink; the toilet down the hall is too far away. Michelle becomes very quiet, continually asking me if I feel better and bringing me more glasses of water than I can possibly drink. Attempting to allay her fears, I assure her that my sickness is temporary, probably caused by something I ate or drank. Once when I had food poisoning in San Francisco, Jim had started an intravenous solution during the night to combat dehydration, hanging the IV bag on our hall tree by the bedside. Having a resident physician in attendance had been reassuring, but tonight I must deal with dehydration alone.

Fortunately, Greeks do not retire early. At 2 A.M., between vomiting episodes, Michelle and I descend two flights of stairs to search for food: not for me, but for Michelle, who missed dinner. Although the hotel bar is still open, there is nothing to eat, not even crackers. Breakfast is the only meal served at this hotel, and the kitchen is locked. We purchase an armload of soft drinks from the bar. Toward dawn, the vomiting stops, and the corner of the illness is turned.

At breakfast, Michelle eats all the bread rolls in the basket. The hotel manager matter-of-factly states that many people get sick at this time of year, because the quality of the drinking water deteriorates when the water table is low. Our vulnerability to something as common as food poisoning or water contamination has threatened both of us. If I were to contract a serious illness, how would Michelle manage? No one had been there during the night to meet her needs. When I don't function properly, Michelle suffers; her well-being correlates directly to mine.

In the evening, I feel like walking to buy food until I see octopuses drying on lines. Passing one of the tavernas, Michelle and I recognize a museum curator from Amsterdam whom we met at the beach. Motioning us over to his table, he introduces us to his American friend and invites us to join them. I decline, discreetly mentioning my recent illness. When the friendly American woman asks where we are from, I say, "Cincinnati." Asking her the same question, I stiffen when she answers, "San Francisco." Yearning to talk about home, I mention that I have visited San Francisco and we swap earthquake stories. My stomach churns when she tells me that her daughter lives on Taraval Street, a street in the neighborhood where I shopped, dined, and banked. I panic when, pulling out a camera, she offers to take our photo and send it to us in Cincinnati. Implying physical urgency, Michelle and I make a speedy getaway.

A weakened body is fertile soil for anxious thoughts. Seeing the mother of someone who lives in our area of San Francisco leaves me shaking inside and out. Michelle handled herself brilliantly by not mentioning anything about San Francisco, particularly since her favorite Mexican restaurant is on Taraval Street. Possibly this woman has recognized Michelle's face from a milk carton photo or from media publicity. I have no idea how much our disappearance has been publicized in San Francisco. For all I know, Michelle's face could be well known in the Bay Area by now. My skin bristles at how interconnected the world is. When Michelle remarks that I should not have talked about San Francisco and the October 1989 earthquake, I feel defeated. Michelle's right; her astuteness amazes and encourages me. Thanks to my indiscretion, we could be sitting ducks on this island for the next seven days until our ferry departs. Like the would-be King David on the run for his life from King Saul, I need a sanctuary, a cave to hide in.

THE MONASTERY OF ST. JOHN THE THEOLOGIAN SITS ABOVE the Holy Cave of the Apocalypse where the Apostle John received inspiration for writing the Book of Revelation. Removing the icons and religious symbols would restore the cave's interior to look much as it did when the Apostle John stayed there. No reconstruction here. Whether the massive Y-crack in the ceiling was caused by the voice of God calling to John from an opening to heaven is open for speculation. Certainly, the voice of God is powerful enough to crack rocks, but He can also speak in the gentle blowing of the wind.

No ropes or barricades keep me from touching the recesses in the rocks where the beloved friend of Jesus laid his head or supported his hands while praying. A level rock ledge was used as a desk by John's secretary and scribe, Prochoros, who recorded the heavenly vision. In this cave, where the Apostle John was imprisoned in exile, he must have longed for home, just as I do.

The first sentence of the brochure given to visitors reads: "Your

coming to this holy place is not a chance event in your life."
Based on Revelation 3:20, "Behold, I stand at the door and knock:
if any man hears my voice and opens the door, I will come in to
him, and will eat with him and he with me," the visitor is asked,
"Will you open your soul to Christ, or will you keep it closed,
condemning yourself to fatal isolation?"

These words transport my mind through the cave walls beyond time and place. When I was a youngster, the familiar picture of Jesus standing at a door and knocking had been on the
wall of my Sunday school class. At that time, I didn't question the
physical image of Jesus, who, being Jewish, must have resembled
the Greek monks at this monastery more than the fair, clean-
shaven Jesus I grew up recognizing.

The depiction of this verse brings back memories of sitting in
church before air-conditioning. Cardboard fans with Jesus on one
side and a funeral home advertisement on the other fluttered in
every pew during the summer. Holding the wooden handles,
some members of our congregation used quick wrist action, while
others made broad sweeps through the air. The air generated by
the fans also kept at bay the ever-present wasps that dangled
above the organdy flowers on the ladies' hats. Taking off the
white cotton gloves would have cooled me more than anything.
How I wish that I could experience the sanctuary of the church
where I had waved a cardboard fan, where I had been baptized
before a mural of the Jordan River, and where I had knelt at the
altar of marriage.

THE FIRST CLOUDS OF THE COMING SEASON ARE APPEARING ON
the horizon until someday, after we have left Patmos, their increase will drench rain on the dusty leaves and fill the cisterns
with good drinking water. As a final excursion, Michelle and I
board a sight-seeing yacht for a day trip to the island of Lipsos, a
couple of boat hours from Patmos. The dazzling white church in
the village is locked; we are about to leave when the Greek

Orthodox priest arrives with friends. He ushers them and us into the sanctuary to see the beginning of a remarkable phenomenon that occurs every year at this time. On August 23, the dried vinelike branches surrounding an icon in a glass case burst into flower. Today, August 21, the tight blooms are just beginning to open, and already there is a faint scent of sweetness through the glass. The miracle lives on, and the priest is overjoyed that God has not disappointed him. I wonder if some years have been more difficult for him to trust God's faithfulness than others.

On the evening of our departure from Patmos, Michelle and I wait on the pier for the arrival of the ferry that will take us to the Greek mainland. Michelle is driven to a frenzy by the ubiquitous bees, which are the price to pay for the sweet-smelling air, which is scented by orange blossoms and jasmine. I am restless and ready to be on our way, troubled by ongoing intestinal cramping. Now we are part of the sea of people on the pier, but, it being the end of the tourist season, the swells have diminished. Studying the faces of the tourists, I speculate that they are thinking about returning to homes, jobs, a life waiting for their reappearance. Recalling the end of pleasant vacations in the past, I felt the same reluctance of resuming the daily routine; now I long for it.

Throughout the night, the ferry hopscotches from island to island, picking up and letting off passengers. The gliding motion of the ferry doesn't exacerbate the queasiness in my stomach as the bouncy tourist boats did. Michelle and I share a sleeping cabin with a woman from Athens who has spent the month of August at her house on Patmos. After I express to our cabinmate my wariness of taxi drivers with whom I can't communicate, she engages a taxi for us when the ferry docks at the port of Piraeus, instructing the driver to take us to downtown Athens. This driver knows about the Minerva Hotel, where Michelle and I are welcomed as returning friends.

At an English-speaking church near the hotel, the minister, an American from Illinois, preaches from the gospel of John about healing. My heart leaps for joy when Michelle writes on the service bulletin: "I love myself. I love You, God." These words validate the healing that is occurring in her spirit. Survival presses too heavily to detect whether my spirit is healing.

After the service, I pray with the minister while his wife entertains Michelle. As an encouragement, the minister recalls the story of Elijah running into the desert to escape Jezebel, who seeks to kill him (I Kings 19). Sitting under a juniper tree, Elijah, who is too tired to travel, says to God, "It is enough now, O Lord, take my life." Through the ministry of angels, God strengthens Elijah with a forty-day supply of bread and water, enabling him to reach his destination, Mount Horeb, the mountain of God.

Like Elijah, the specifics of my God-ordained destination are hidden. I too do not know how much farther, nor how much longer I must travel. My grandfather used to tell me how, as a young truck driver in Kentucky, he would order a 500-mile cup of coffee to help him make it through the long-haul nights. I need strong coffee, as well as Elijah's supernatural nutrition, to sustain me during this journey, which passes through the 3-D wilderness of despondency, despair, and discouragement. Michelle and I have wandered long enough in the desert.

6

Don't Leave Home Without It

*Tickets and traveling documents: these should
be kept in a handy place where you can
check them several hundred times.*
—Miss Piggy

LIKE SO MANY OF OUR JOURNEYS, THE ALITALIA FLIGHT FROM
Athens to Rome arrives in late evening after the tourist information office has closed. Passengers walk purposefully through the
exits of the airport, confident of where they will be sleeping.
Michelle and I linger at the baggage claim area, asking the rental
car agents for a hotel suggestion. One of them approaches me
about a friend who owns a small new hotel in downtown Rome,
only a phone call and a limousine ride away. Michelle's eyes
widen with anticipation at the mention of "limousine." Explaining
that we do not require a limousine, I ask if lire could be deducted
from the room price if we were to take a taxi. No, I'm told, the
limousine comes with the hotel package. Since the hour is late
and the room rate doesn't seem exorbitant for Rome, I accept the
offer, expecting to ride in a Cadillac instead of a limousine. But,
to Michelle's delight, a long black limousine awaits us at the curb.
Concerned that this "new" hotel has no brochure, I am too preoccupied to enjoy this superfluous luxury.

Although I recognize landmarks from previous trips to Rome, the hotel address is meaningless. The silence of the driver, who speaks no English, gives me the heebie-jeebies. We could be calmly riding to our demise. Michelle, oblivious to the tension I'm feeling, rolls around in the spacious backseat, holding an imaginary cigarette holder and prefacing every comment with "*Darrrr-ling.*"

The limousine stops at an inconspicuous street entrance where a neon sign in a third-floor window advertises the Europa Hotel. The luggage bumps against the walls as we climb the flights of stairs. Living in Italy will teach me that a plain, even poorly maintained exterior can conceal an exquisite interior. Despite the inelegant access, the lobby of the hotel is attractively decorated with high-tech furnishings. After settling in a room that matches the modernity of the lobby, I phone Gabriella.

After seven months without seeing a familiar face, the next morning I am in the presence of a close friend who validates the Janie in me. With Gabriella, it isn't necessary to conceal the truth about my identity; I only need to explain why we have become fugitives. Having seen toddler pictures of Michelle, Gabriella greets her as Ellen. Gabriella's familiarity with our past in America forms a bond with Michelle. On the drive to her home north of Rome, Michelle enthusiastically agrees to being called Michela. Now I must remember to say Michela, not Michelle, not Ellen. My name reverts from Chris back to Janie, since family members, who won't be told our circumstances, have heard about Janie, Gabriella's American friend.

The security layout where Gabriella and Francesco live with their two children is a fugitive's dream. At the entrance to the residential development, a guard monitors the coming and going of residents and visitors. At their private gate, a friendly, albeit on-guard German shepherd dog stands alert to movements surrounding the house. Although the security arrangement eases my mind, Michela and I are staying at the home of friends who are known to Jim.

Seven years earlier, Jim and I visited Gabriella and Francesco when they lived in Rome. Although their residence has changed, finding their new address through Francesco, a research physician in Rome, would be easy for Jim, one doctor to another. In Singapore, the need to be with friends who know me had been irresistible, but now I question the wisdom of staying where the chances of being caught are greater. Emotional security could become a threat to our physical security. Any ring of the telephone could be Jim or a private detective.

Despite the risk, Michela and I are eager to catch our breath and savor the taste of family life after several months of living in hotels and eating in restaurants. Adapting to the household's rhythm of work and school, Michela delights at having residential playmates. Gabriella and Francesco present her with a new outfit for her first day accompanying their five-year-old son to an Italian-speaking school. The gracious hospitality of this family is glorious but must be temporary.

ON A NEW ZEALAND CALENDAR, THE FOLLOWING WORDS HAD been written in the block for September 15: "Home, please God, grant me this gift for my forty-second birthday." Expecting to celebrate my birthday in Kentucky, I calculate when we must leave Italy in order to arrive home by September 15. From the pantry of my imagination, the dinner menu would include fried banana peppers and a birthday cake with gooey icing. It's tragic to admit that this party is dependent on Jim's death, but praying for his death won't get us home any sooner. God's displeasure with such hateful motives would only add to my discomfort. Besides, I don't want Jim to die; I only want us to be free and safe. I am convinced that God cares as much for Jim as He cares for me, so this spiritual catch-22 will be with me for as long as Jim lives.

As an encouragement, Gabriella and Francesco introduce me to a priest who learned English at a seminary in Toronto. Father

Josef suggests that I contact an Italian priest in Toronto who will be returning to Italy soon for a vacation. Discussing Toronto as a hiding place frightens as much as it thrills. Living on the other side of the Atlantic would put me in closer proximity to my parents, as well as Jim and the FBI.

Father Josef has confident assurance in God's guidance of those who put their trust in Him. Through God's faithfulness, Israel found safety in the wilderness, as Michela and I have found protection and provision during these last seven months since leaving America. As drinking water issued from the desert rock for the Israelites, air tickets were issued to us at the last minute on crowded planes. As manna had appeared daily in the wilderness for the Israelites, hotel rooms had been available for us during peak tourist seasons. When Gabriella hears Father Josef's comments, she acquaints me with an opera by Verdi, *Nabucco*, which echoes the longings of the Israelites living in exile by the banks of the Euphrates.

> *Go, my thought on golden wings*
> *Go alight upon the slopes, the hills where soft and warm the sweet*
>   *breezes of our native land are fragrant!*
> *Oh, my country so lovely and lost on remembrance so dear and*
>   *ill-fated.*
> *Golden harp of the prophetic bards, why do you hang mute on*
>   *the willow?*
> *Rekindle the memories in our breasts, speak to us of the times of*
>   *yore!*
> *Just as for the cruel fate of Jerusalem, intone a strain of bitter*
>   *lamentation.*
> *Otherwise let the Lord inspire you with a melody to give us*
>   *strength to suffer.*

Writing these passionate words on the flyleaf of my Bible, I remember Indian-summer breezes swishing through the willows by the frog pond at my parents' home, as well as walking through the mist at Ocean Beach in San Francisco to the tune of foghorns. Perhaps the Israelites appreciated the beauty of the Euphrates as I cherish the loveliness of living in Italy, but it doesn't prevent my longings in exile from traveling to America on golden wings.

I'm happy that Michela is seeing the sights of Rome; this could be her last opportunity. On the way to the telephone office to call America, we pause on the Spanish Steps, which flow like lava into the piazza below. The amber walls of grainy stucco are capped with terra cotta, earth tones which envelop me. Fountains at the base of the steps shoot water to arrest their advance. I throw a coin into one, and make a wish.

With Michela standing beside me at the telephone office in Rome, I make the birthday call to Kentucky. Joy and Wayne, the Kentucky contacts, have talked with my parents face-to-face, gleaning as much information as possible without asking direct questions. Consulting their notes, Joy delivers my birthday message: Mother and Daddy are there for us and spend their time wondering where we are; Arcturus, our beagle, is their joy and comfort; Ellen would have liked eating on the patio this past summer—no bees; all three ninety-year-old grandparents are doing well; but there's no news about Jim. The dream bubble of traveling to Kentucky bursts in my face. Remembering the prayer of the Israelites from the opera, I modify it to express my own heart, "God, I don't want to be inspired with a melody of suffering; just give me strength to suffer disappointment."

Our journey will be extending past my birthday, which necessitates making a decision about future plans. When I call Meridel in Israel to request YWAM's telephone number in Switzerland, she doesn't have it. However, Lausanne is the location. Before saying goodbye, she reminds me to let God lead through my heart. At the moment, my heart is too crushed to be led beyond the American Express office in Rome, where I exchange Greek drachmas for Italian lire.

Looking at the calendar later in the day, I cross out September 15, writing the same plea on my mother's birthday in October, my father's birthday in November, and Jesus' birthday in December, knowing that I could be setting myself up for disappointment but doing it anyway.

MICHELA AND I ARE INVITED TO LUNCH WITH FATHER GIANNI, the Italian priest who works in Toronto, at his family's home in Viterbo. He advises that Italy is better suited for our situation than Toronto, where a car is required and the cost of living is higher. When Father Gianni offers to funnel letters to my parents via his office in Toronto, I take him up on it. Although hiding out in Toronto seems unlikely, the city is bound to figure in the journey at some point. During the last month, four people of faith with Toronto connections (two in Patmos and two in Italy) have crossed our path. If I have the choice, Toronto will be our portal for reentering the U.S.A.

A decision about remaining in Italy must be made soon. We have been staying with Gabriella and Francesco for two weeks, and their privacy needs to be restored. The uncertainty of moving forward and the inability of staying where we are puts our future plans in limbo. According to medieval Christian theology, limbo is an abode of the soul not admitted to heaven but not condemned to punishment either. On the paradise-punishment continuum, living in limbo seems closer to punishment than paradise, while living in Italy is on the approach to paradise.

No direction regarding our future exists until Gabriella's family offers us an apartment in their palazzo, a multistoried building in the hill town of Soriano nel Cimino, where they gather during the summer months. The apartment remains vacant for the rest of the year, primarily because it lacks a heating system. It is offered to us rent-free for the autumn, winter, and spring months if I agree to arrange for heating and pay the utilities. Trusting Gabriella's judgment, I enthusiastically embrace the housing offer, sight unseen.

Situated in the Cimino Hills, Soriano is surrounded by dense woods and chestnut groves. The village of eight-thousand residents swells in the summer when Romans escape to their vacation homes. The precedent was set in the thirteenth century when Pope Nicholas III built a castle on the pinnacle of the hill as a summer residence. The present town descends the hillsides as if stucco buildings have flowed from an eruption at the medieval castle, which is now idle after serving as a penitentiary.

Two of the apartments at the palazzo are occupied. The one above ours is occupied during the summer by Gennario, Gabriella's father, who returns to his home in Viterbo when the weather becomes cooler. The apartment next door to ours is occupied year round by Augusta, a widow and friend of the family. Our apartment has two furnished bedrooms, a bathroom, a kitchen with a gas stove, a refrigerator, and a wood-burning stove, and cavernous ceilings throughout. The bedroom windows have functional shutters opening over the garden; in one bedroom, French doors open on to a balcony with a view of the castle. Princess Michela chooses the bedroom with the balcony.

To become better acquainted with our neighbors (particularly when Gabriella is present to translate), Augusta serves refreshments on the terrace, enlisting Michela's help. With sunshine filtering through the grape arbor, Gennario, Gabriella, Augusta, Michela, and I celebrate our new home by eating grapes and ripe figs and drinking coffee (milk for Michela). When Gabriella offers to loan us bed linen, moving in is only a matter of returning to her home for our suitcases.

In celebration of my birthday and our new home, Gabriella suggests an excursion to Viterbo, the town of her childhood, about half an hour's drive from Soriano. At a wholesale warehouse of Italian leather goods owned by Gabriella's brother and sister-in-law, Michela and I are invited to select gifts of Italian leather shoes. For years, my mother has chided me about assembling a lopsided wardrobe, heavy on shoes, although rarely Italian. How I wish she could see me walking up and down the rows of elegant shoes, opening the box lids to breathe in the robust, sinewy bouquet—*paradisio!*

Now that the door to Kentucky has been closed for the time being, there's no point in crying over spilled milk, or, specific to Italy, Four Roses Kentucky bourbon, which is ubiquitous among the rows of liquor bottles at the cappucino bars. My birthday dinner celebrates our first day of residence in Soriano. Augusta's extraordinary culinary skills are manifested in a meal of home-made pasta, grilled beef, roast potatoes, a salad of tomatoes, basil, and *mozzarella fresca*, the delectable duo of prosciutto and melons, fresh figs, pastries filled with cream, and coffee, served in the dining room of Gennario's apartment. In Gabriella's absence, goodwill translates when languages fail us.

SHOPKEEPERS AND RESIDENTS IN SORIANO ASSUME THAT I AM German from my appearance, judging me to be English when I speak. Few suspect that I'm an American until I tell them. Suppos-edly, Michela and I are the only Americans living in Soriano. Only a handful of residents speak English, mostly young adults who have traveled abroad or teenagers who are studying it in school. The Sorianese have a strong *dialetto*, or dialect, as do English-speaking Kentuckians. On one occasion, an Italian from Rome enters a shop in Soriano to ask directions. Not understand-ing the *dialetto* of the shopkeeper, the Roman looks at me to clarify. Although I can't translate, I'm pleased to have been mis-taken for an Italian, not an American.

The sounds of Soriano are as predictable as the fragrance of crushed grapes in the autumn air. Below our windows on the hillside is a hazelnut factory where thousands of nuts can be heard tumbling in large drums. Perhaps they will find their way into jars of the delicious Italian breakfast spread made of choco-late and hazelnuts. Dispensing with a knife and bread, I eat it with a spoon, sitting in the kitchen after Michela has gone to bed. Eating the chocolate under a dangling lightbulb makes the gorging seem more unhealthy. To counteract the consequences of the chocolate, I religiously attend the *palestra*, or gym, in Soriano.

From farther down the hillside, the toots of a 1930s train can be heard when it enters or exits the tunnel bearing the weight of the town above. The only sound that doesn't soothe is the siren blast from the piazza at 8 A.M., noon, and 5 P.M., reminiscent of air raid sirens in war movies. To counterbalance the jarring resonance of the sirens, which the residents no longer notice, the bells of Trinita Chiesa soften the air several times an hour with their gentle tones.

Although Michela is absorbing Italian like a sponge, she can't enroll in Soriano's elementary school until she is fluent. Learning Italian and school subjects at home doesn't work; we already spend too much time together. Holding Michela's interest in studying when the garden and Augusta's attention beckon her consumes more energy than I possess. The daily tasks of communicating in Italian, walking everywhere and hand-washing our clothes in the bathtub deplete the energy reserves necessary for home schooling.

In the afternoons, while the clothes soak, I rest on the bed, since the apartment doesn't have a sofa or armchair. If the church bells lull me to sleep, I always dream. One recurrent dream is set during my last year of high school. In other dreams, I converse with my parents and grandparents, stroking my dog, Arcturus, whose wordless comfort reaches places within my soul where words don't fit. In some dreams, Jim and I are intimate, as if nothing adverse has happened, until I jump with a start about exposure to the HIV virus. In other dreams, Jim pursues me with harmful intent. On awakening, dream and reality are confounded for a while, the dreams appearing more real than hanging wet clothes to dry on a balcony below a medieval castle.

To help Michela mix with girls her own age, she dances at a ballet school at Viterbo, where friendships extend beyond the confines of the dance class for lunch and play invitations.

Gabriella's sister, Lydia, an elementary teacher in Viterbo, invites Michela to help her teach the girls English after school. For a Soriano companion, Lydia brings her a stray kitten named Pisalina. When I ask a shopkeeper in Soriano for a large cardboard box to use as a house for Pisalina, he looks at me quizzically. Until this moment, I have never made the connection between Pisalina's name and her incontinence. With innocent glee, I have been telling people in the town about Michela's kitten, whose name translates as "Little Piss Piss."

AIRFARES FROM NEW ZEALAND TO SINGAPORE, AS WELL AS THE two months of hotel and restaurant expenses in Greece, have exacted a sizable chunk of the cash reserve I carried from Wellington. Soon it will need replenishing, but the American Express office in Rome doesn't transact Moneygrams. Referring to an American Express directory of services, I trace with my finger possible train routes on a map of Europe. I devise a money pickup plan, hoping to divert attention from Italy if the Moneygram location is detected. Picking up the Moneygram in Brussels could imply that I live in the United Kingdom and have crossed the Channel for an American Express office on the Continent. Traveling past Brussels to stay in Ostend, a ferry port for the United Kingdom, would reinforce this impression as well as avoid the cosmopolitan prices of hotels in Brussels. I remember being told in San Francisco that retrieving money is the most vulnerable time for arrest, assuming my passport number has been red-flagged by the FBI and perhaps Interpol. At the very least, receiving a Moneygram in an American Express office pinpoints our absolute location.

Diverting attention from Italy wouldn't be the only purpose of traveling through Europe. As we have made our way to this side of the Atlantic through the eastern back door, Michela has only seen the Mediterranean side of Europe. I want her to see more of the European landscapes that impressed me in the past. Never

knowing when the journey could be cut short suddenly by discovery and deportation, goals become short-term and urgent
while living on the run.

During the past four months since leaving New Zealand, tension has been building. As anyone standing near me would notice, sighs heave in and out from deep within me. Sighs serve the
same purpose for releasing tension in the body as the jiggling cap
on a pressure cooker does for releasing steam, keeping it from
exploding. Traveling by train in New Zealand had relieved stress.
Once more the anticipation of traveling rekindles the spirit of
adventure that had been doused by the weariness of staying put.

As Michela and I wait in the snaking line at the American Express office in Brussels, I refuse her request to sit near the
travel brochures. She must be within arm's reach in case a quick
departure is necessary. Panic paralyzes swallowing when I imagine the consequences if this Moneygram transaction fails. I possess only enough cash to fund a frugal return to Italy. My anxiety
is not lessened by the hysterics of an American woman who has
lost her Travelers Cheques. Leaving the American Express office,
she beats her head with her hands and wails at her husband, who
quietly looks at the floor, either from embarrassment or remorse.

By the time I step up to an agent, my throat is collared by fear,
making speech difficult. Handing over my passport, I explain that
a Moneygram from the States has been sent in my name, the
designation being "international." The train of thought derails
abruptly when the tracks end. No plan exists for safeguarding
these Travelers Cheques from being traced; cashing them could
leave a crumb in the forest trail to our whereabouts. Acting as if I
have changed my mind about the Moneygram, I ask to speak to
the office manager—privately.

Michela and I are directed to an office where he listens as if I'm
the fifth fugitive to cross his path this day. Without emotion for
our circumstances, he advises me how to avoid having the num-

bers of the Travelers Cheques traced. If larger denomination checks are requested when receiving the Moneygram, they can be exchanged for lower denomination checks with no cross-referencing. The transaction, which is free of charge, makes tracking the original check numbers impossible, particularly when the checks are exchanged at another American Express office in a different country.

Although the manager's apparent lack of interest in our plight is reassuring in one way, his purpose may be to keep me calm and settled until the police arrive. At the counter, I watch the actions of the agent like a hawk, intent on noticing whether her fingers type numbers from my passport into the computer. Retrieving my passport would require lunging over the counter to snatch it before grabbing Michela's hand and running into the street.

After a reasonable number of questions and giving a bogus address in Kentucky, the Moneygram comes through without a hitch. Desperate to flee the location where our global position is momentarily nailed down, I must remain on the spot to sign the checks. I request as many $500 Travelers Cheques as possible to avoid signing $10,000 worth of $20 checks. This large sum of money from my parents doesn't come to us from their surplus, but from their limited retirement savings. The fingernail moon is indelibly stamped on every check, reflecting their pledge to be there for us, whatever the sacrifice.

The geographical compactness of Europe is convenient for exchanging checks. Rotterdam is the nearest non-Belgium American Express office. After a few hours of train riding, we search for the American Express office in Rotterdam. The endorsing of these newly acquired Travelers Cheques takes fifteen minutes. Several hundred smaller checks are issued in the exchange, and all must be signed. The staff moves me from the counter to a desk for signing while Michela sets up an imaginary travel agency in front of the travel brochures. For thirty minutes, I binge on signing my name after writing it only on immigration forms these past eight months. This tedious exercise yields safe, although not secure, money. The thousands of dollars in Travelers Cheques are no more secure than cash. If I lose them, the money is gone. Obtaining replacements via America would be impossible.

To celebrate our success, I suggest seeing more of Holland. Amsterdam is too far away, but the city of Delft, a champion of blue, my favorite color, is a short train ride away.

At one end of the market square in Delft, Michela and I enter Nieuwe Kerk (New Church), whose construction began in the fourteenth century. While I gaze at the stained-glass windows, Michela gets down to spiritual business, using the pencil and paper provided for prayer requests. In large letters, she writes: "God wants everyone to love Him. I love Him best of all. Michela." It's small wonder that Jesus said the kingdom of heaven belongs to people who see God through a childlike heart. Outside the church, a statue honors a local man who symbolized justice with stones spelling out the letters of a Dutch saying: EVERYBODY WALKS IN GOD'S PATHS. I would have added stones saying: WHETHER THEY ACKNOWLEDGE HIM OR NOT.

We walk up and over stone bridges, across canals, and past buildings with cookie-cutter façades and cupolas, where the predominance of bricks reminds me of Kentucky. At the Royal Porceleyne Fles, where the famous porcelain is made, potters with clay-coated fingers create at the wheels. As Michela and I talk about God being the Potter and humans, God's creations, being the clay, the potter, who is Jewish, overhears our conversation and acknowledges the confounding simplicity of this truth. In the Old Testament Book of Isaiah, God knew the kind of spiritual pots Esau and Jacob would inhabit while they were still in the womb. The discretion of the Divine Potter in creating some vessels for honor and others for dishonor is a faith concept I do not understand and probably never will. But I choose not to throw out faith in God with the bathwater of doubt.

After buying pastries to eat on the train, we return to Bruges via Rotterdam, viewing an orange sunset through the iron lattice of a Dutch-style Golden Gate Bridge.

IN BRUGES, MY HEART BEATS FASTER THAN USUAL AS I CALL Mary Ellen, a new contact in Kentucky from the list of telephone numbers my mother had given me in San Francisco. The purpose of this call is to arrange a regular time and day of the week for talking with my parents, ear to ear. At this prearranged time, my parents will come to her home to wait for my call. I learn from Mary Ellen that my parents have talked with Jim face-to-face in Kentucky. Choosing to meet him in a public place, a parking lot, they accommodated his request to see Arcturus. His health had appeared good, except for his hands shaking. My parents had pleaded that he pave the way for our return by dropping the charges against me and by agreeing to supervised visitation when Ellen would stay at his home. Jim had urged my parents to persuade me to return home, via any contacts which they might have with us. He had offered to drop the charges against me if I agreed to give up all custody of Ellen, my having only limited and supervised visiting rights. With a clear conscience, my parents had said to Jim, "We don't have any idea where Janie and Ellen are hiding."

This telephone message hits me like a load of Belgian bricks. The penny finally drops that this journey could last years, much longer than I had anticipated when hopeful grace had launched us out of America. Knowing Jim, he will beat AIDS, as he had said and his good health indicates. That being the case, this journey will last until Michela reaches legal adulthood at the age of eighteen. Enduring another eleven years of living from country to country is inconceivable, and my parents could never subsidize a journey lasting that length of time without selling their home. Before allowing that to happen, Michela and I would return to America. If only I could obtain a work permit to contribute as I go!

Michela and I linger inside the telephone center, ostensibly because it's raining, but actually I'm too stunned to move. Survival depends on shifting cognitive gears for a longer haul. On a defiant impulse, I break free from inertia and call Linda, the friend in San Francisco who gave me the Bible verses from Ezekiel on Christmas Day. Hearing my voice on her work phone, she begins to cry. Neither of us can speak as the seconds count down on the phone card. Michela stands quietly at my side, wanting to talk to Linda, who has loved her as a surrogate auntie, but I shake my head no. The risk is too great that Michela may unintentionally divulge a clue to our whereabouts. Our tearful conversation lasts less than five minutes. From a Bible on her desk, Linda reads the last verse from Psalm 73: "But as for me, the nearness of God is my good; I have made the LORD God my refuge, that I may tell of all Thy works." Once again, I wonder if I will live to tell the story of our journey.

Seeking spiritual grounding, I search for a Christian bookstore in the Bruges directory and find one a short walk away from the telephone office. An English-speaking employee there invites us to attend a church prayer meeting that evening. When I accept, Michela sputters during the afternoon about attending a boring meeting where desserts won't be served. As a goodwill gesture, I offer her a treat now. Riding in a horse-drawn antique carriage through the old city appeases her sense of justice.

At the prayer meeting, about twenty believers sit at a long table, the kind which, at other times, might be laden with dishes for a potluck supper. By design, I sit next to a woman from Toronto who translates the gist of the prayers from Flemish to English. Understanding every word is not critical; it's the praying in concert with other believers that validates my spirit. Although I know very little about these people by the end of the evening (and they know even less about us), spiritually we connect. Despite cultural distinctions, the spiritual union within God's family cuts through my isolation like a knife. God created faith in the context of a family for fugitives like us, or for anyone cut off from loved ones through either death or circumstances.

SITTING ON THE STATION PLATFORM IN BRUGES, I CHASTISE myself for not running faster through the underground passage, thinking of times during the morning when ten seconds could have been saved. Missing the train from Bruges to Brussels by seconds, this delay may cause us to miss the international train connection in Brussels. Anger builds until I notice that our tickets to Lucerne are for two *adult* tickets. In my haste to catch the train, I did not catch the mistake. The satisfaction of converting the ticket to a child's fare changes to panic when I realize that the platform has been changed and we are waiting at the wrong one. Running through the underground passageway, we are once again in danger of missing the train to Brussels. Emerging on the platform as the guard blows the whistle, we dart toward the nearest car steps, making contact with them just before the train moves. It arrives at Brussels on time, giving us only five minutes to reach the track for the train to Switzerland on our return to Italy.

Michela and I arrive on the platform one second after the train begins to move. Walking beside the slow-moving train, I'm indignant that the guard stands on the car steps, blocking the way. I plead for him to let us board, but he's immovable. Shouting rude words in his direction as the train accelerates beyond my capacity to keep up would only generate remorse later. Synchronizing train connections has never been as frustrating or as challenging. A crisis of confidence brings me to an angry halt on the platform.

A Belgian naval officer who has witnessed our attempt to board the train steps up beside me. With appropriate reserve, he says, "There may still be a way to catch the train that you missed, but there's no time to waste."

Offering to carry the suitcase to speed up our mission, he explains on the run that we are taking a local train to play catch-up with the train we have just missed. At the central station, two stops away, the international train makes a longer stop.

Michela and I plant our feet and luggage on the local train as it begins to move, signaling thumbs-up and gratitude to the naval officer from the car doorway. Since the ride is short, we don't bother taking seats but remain poised near the door for springing off at the central station.

As our local train pulls into the station, the international train with window signs for Switzerland is in view, only a few tracks away as the crow flies. But how a crow flies means nothing at a train station. Michela and I run the length of the platform, climb the steps to the bridge spanning the tracks, and descend to the platform. I urge Michela along, even though her breath hasn't recovered from the last run.

If Michela and I had won an Olympic sprint, our spirits could not have been higher than when we step on to the train that eluded us the first time. Congratulating ourselves with high-five signs, we celebrate our victory in the vintage luxury of the dining car. The white tablecloth, polished wood, and brass table lamp imbue our success with intrigue, as if we are traveling under clandestine circumstances on the Orient Express.

AT LUCERNE, MICHELA AND I STROLL ACROSS THE COVERED wooden bridge spanning the river and look out at the Alps in the distance across the lake. Walking through the town, we pass the telephone office, where I impulsively turn in. Searching in the Lausanne directory for the telephone number of the YWAM base, I ring it, asking to speak to Barbara, the YWAM staff member Meridel and Jay had mentioned in Patmos. I get through to her immediately with no time to reflect on my purpose in calling her or why I'm interested in YWAM. After explaining that I'm seeking God's direction, having been given her name by Meridel and Jay on a pier in Greece, I briefly disclose our circumstances. Barbara invites us to visit the YWAM base in Lausanne, although staying at the chalet won't be possible for tonight. Traveling directly to Lausanne hadn't been my intention, but her consideration of immediate hospitality is welcoming. Barbara encourages me to explain our circumstances in a letter. After receiving my letter, she

will check with hospitality about scheduling a date for us to visit.
When she mentions the French-speaking elementary school
sponsored by YWAM, hope fills the telephone booth.

The interdenominational church in Lucerne celebrates World
Communion Sunday by spotlighting the global crisis of fleeing
refugees. The sermon highlights the fugitive Jacob, who fled from
the death threats of his brother Esau (Genesis 27). God had
protected Jacob, a deceiver and supplanter of Esau's birthright,
reassurance that God's protection doesn't depend on a track record of obedience. Scripture confirms that God is not surprised by
our predicament, having dealt with many fugitives on the run:
David hiding from Saul, Elijah hiding from Jezebel, and, as a
heavenly parent, the flight of His own Son.

Through a dream, God had directed Joseph to flee with Mary
and Jesus, whose life was threatened by the plans of King Herod
to kill all boys two years old and under in Bethlehem and the
surrounding villages. The magi from the East had brought gold,
frankincense, and myrrh—international currency for the flight to
Egypt—to this economically poor family, who couldn't have fi-
nanced such a journey without these gifts. God, who had or-
dained the journey, supplied the provisions accordingly.

Few details about Jesus' life as a fugitive are recorded in the
Bible. The departure from Nazareth occurred at night (Matt.
2:14), just as ours had from San Francisco. Joseph may have
avoided the primary roads to escape agents from King Herod
sent out on this search-and-destroy mission, perhaps on the lookout for a Jewish man traveling with a wife and young son. Mary
may have attempted to make Jesus appear older, or even to disguise His sex, but what a difficult age to keep Him quiet. On the
long donkey ride to Egypt, Mary and Joseph must have wondered
how long they would need to live in a foreign country, unable to
contact their family and being cut off from their synagogue, their
land, even from information about King Herod.

As the three of them established a new life in Egypt, Joseph
may have looked longingly at the shops of Egyptian carpenters,

missing his tools, left behind to reduce the weight of what the donkey carried. Mary must have longed for the familiarity of her own hearth where she had prepared the family's meals in Judea, selecting only her favorite cooking pot for the journey.

In Egypt, Joseph received a second dream, informing him that King Herod had died and instructing him to return to Judea. Joseph may have discussed the implications of this dream with Mary after Jesus had gone to sleep. If Joseph were mistaken about God's instructions, returning to their homeland would mean his son's death. At least in Egypt, their son had been safe. Some aspects of living in Egypt may have been pleasant: walks along the Nile at sunset, or the taste of unusual vegetables from the marketplace. On the long journey back to Israel, Mary and Joseph may have had second thoughts about returning home, the remembrance of Egypt becoming more attractive with each passing mile.

Jesus' life as a fugitive sets biblical precedence, offering more than empathy for our situation. Just as Joseph had stayed in Egypt until Herod died, I plan to remain in hiding until Jim dies—unless God speaks clearly through a change in Jim's heart that we should return to America. What was good enough for Jesus is good enough for us.

7

Tunnel Vision

Does the road wind up-hill all the way?
Yes, to the very end.
Will the day's journey take the whole day long?
From morn to night, my friend.

—CHRISTINA ROSSETTI, *UP-HILL*

THE AIR, THE SMELLS, AND EVEN THE FACE OF SORIANO HAVE changed during our two-week absence while traveling on the Continent and beyond. Grape-pickers in the arbor below our windows have crushed enough grapes underfoot to ferment the garden breezes. Mushroom-pickers appear in the village with baskets and boots in search of the edible *Boletus* fungus, whose market value lures hopefuls into the woods surrounding Soriano, where it thrives. A good find can be lucrative, although the hunt is not without risk. Selecting and eating a similar but poisonous species results in a hospital stay for some mushroom-pickers each season.

An autumn chill is in the air, both inside and outside our apartment. A *bombola*, a movable heater with a gas tank, is our source of heat. Although everyone assures us that the *bombola* is safe, they relate unnerving tales about exploding gas tanks. Its heating capacity is adequate for the bathroom, but the bedrooms warm only slightly in its presence. I shiver to think what the apartment will be like during the winter.

Preparations for the *Sagra delle Castagne*, the Chestnut Festival, produce obvious changes throughout Soriano. Boughs from the local chestnut trees decorate the shop entrances, and roasting chestnuts spice the air. Towering medieval-style gates of wood stand at the entrance of each *contrada*, or medieval quarter, of Soriano. The delta symbol, representing the triune nature of God, stands at the entrance of our contrada, Trinita. Below our windows, flag bearers for Trinita have been practicing with a drum corps for weeks. Becoming accustomed to the cadences, Michela and I mark their rhythms—even when the drums are silent.

During the October festival, Sorianese who have moved away return to cram the narrow streets. We watch the pageant from a window overlooking the piazza. One contrada, St. Georgio, stages a drama about a dragon pursuing a young maiden who is saved by the skill of a valiant horseman. The slaying of the dragon releases a bevy of lovely young women held captive in the center of a giant chestnut. For an instant, I imagine the maiden's shock if, when her deliverer had slayed the dragon, he had turned on her as an adversary. Hating the dragon had been straightforward and uncomplicated for the maiden, but the remembrance of past love would prevent her heartstrings from playing a harmonious melody of hatred for her treacherous protector. My "knight in shining armor," as friends had referred to Jim during our courtship years, had now become the pursuer, the adversary. Bit by bit, the stress cracks of sadness are breaking my heart apart, perhaps even undermining its physical function. Dying from a "broken heart" may cause more deaths than it's given credit for. Only God can rescue an exiled heart from lethal sadness.

BEFORE THE WINTER RAINS BEGIN, MICHELA AND I TOUR NEIGHboring hill towns by bus, passing establishments named Pizzeria Ketchup and Café Bar, which confirm the Italian predilection for curious English combinations. In one village, after we have waited a long time for a return bus to Soriano, two *carabinieri*, members of the local police, stop to ask where we are going and assure me that the bus is usually late. When it finally does arrive, Michela and I sit on the backseat at her request.

Looking out of the back window, I notice the *carabinieri* behind the bus, but think nothing of it until the police car follows when the bus turns off the main road. While the bus stops in the piazza, the *carabinieri* wait, pulling out behind the bus when it leaves. At the next village, they do the same. Have they recognized our faces from a crime photo, my American accent giving us away? Blonde hair and blue eyes are conspicuous in Italy. I may have been foolishly stubborn about changing my hair color. Since the *carabinieri* know we are traveling to Soriano, they must be planning to arrest me when we get off the bus.

Arriving in Soriano, I descend the bus steps holding Michela's hand, looking neither to the left nor to the right. In my peripheral vision, I see one of the *carabinieri* approaching the bus. Cutting into my path, he addresses me in Italian, "Excuse me, Signora. Are you staying in Soriano?"

"Yes," I answer, trying to appear calm. I want to run away, but we are hemmed in by two *carabinieri* in front of us and the bus behind.

Pulling out a pad, he asks, "What's the address?"

Playing dumb to the language (which doesn't require extraordinary effort), I gesture up the hill as a statue might, my body stiff with fear.

"Are you here with a husband?" he asks, pointing to his ring finger in case I have not understood the question.

"No," I answer, shooting an involuntary glance in Michela's direction. His question could be leading up to the topic of custody. Desperately, I mentally flip through Italian words to compose a question, and ask apprehensively, "Why? Official business?"

Noticing my tension, he attempts to put me at ease with a

charming smile. "No, Signora," saying something I don't comprehend. "I would like to take you for a ride in the country," turning
an imaginary steering wheel in the air to aid communication.
"Tomorrow?"

Completely taken aback, I attempt to suppress my relief,
which turns to irrepressible joy. Michela, who understands the
intent of his question, starts to smile. Sensing that she is about to
enter this conversation, I send her a mute "Shh" with a glance.
Despite his persuasive efforts to fix a date, I decline the invitation,
unaware that my heartfelt gratitude is being interpreted as encouragement.

As we walk up the hill toward home, Michela asks, between
giggles, "Mommy, does he want to marry you?"

I anticipate this question, having heard it once before in
Greece when a man had been overattentive. Turning to assure her
that marriage is out of the question, I notice the police car inching up the hill behind us. The tone of my voice becomes serious
as I say, "Michela, don't look back. The police car is following us.
Walk past our gate, even if we see Augusta."

Not wanting the *carabinieri* to discover where we live, we hurry
past our kitchen window without glancing in its direction. The
police car continues to creep behind us until we reach the piazza.
Ambling in and out of shops, I keep a lookout until, assuming that
they have given up and returned to their village, we walk home.
Later in the afternoon, when Michela is playing outside, she sees
the police car drive by our gate. I have no way of knowing
whether the *carabinieri* saw Michela in the yard. If the spurned
invitation has caused ill feelings, there could be repercussions for
me. Everyone in the town knows that the American woman and
child live next to Augusta. A knock at the door could turn into an
arrest.

This encounter with the police intensifies the worrisome issue
that aliens living in Italy are required to register at the local
police station. Justifying that the authorities are more concerned
about tracking terrorists than about parents involved in custody

disputes, I had decided not to comply. If Jim suspects that we are hiding in Italy, registering with the police could be tantamount to my calling his lawyer in San Francisco with a change of address.

Unless a schooling opportunity in Italy opens soon, our departure will make police registration here a moot point. Michela has already missed four months of school, and I worry that she is slipping behind in her education, losing ground that can't be reclaimed. The French-speaking YWAM-sponsored school in Switzerland seems the only option. After calling Barbara at YWAM, a mutually convenient date is set for us to visit Lausanne.

ON THE MORNING WE LEAVE FOR SWITZERLAND, I OVERSLEEP. Augusta, mindful of our need to catch an early bus, knocks on our door at 5:30 A.M., thirty minutes before the bus departs. She extends a cup of steaming coffee to jump-start me, and the novelty of her early morning presence sparks Michela into action. Running down the hill with the luggage cart bouncing on two wheels, we board the bus for Orte and the station. Here we catch the northbound train for Florence and Milan. A day's journey puts us at the base of the Italian Alps, where a full moon transforms Lake Maggiore into a sheet of silvery glass. On the Swiss side of the Alps, it's raining.

The Lausanne YWAM base, frequently filled to capacity, is a busy training center for missionaries, having a crossroads relationship with Europe as well as YWAM connections. The main building is an eighty-year-old chalet that was previously a hotel but now houses students enrolled in the training schools. From the upper floors, views open across Lake Geneva to the French Alps. Views in the other direction extend across forested hills and rolling meadows, which have miles of hiking trails. Our room at Canaan House, where guest rooms are located, flows with warm air and hot water. This friendly, supportive environment with its magnificent surroundings could be the promised land of our future.

Michela plays with the children of YWAM staff members while I meet the leaders to discuss opportunities for serving as a short-term volunteer. I don't conceal the fact that my reason for coming to YWAM isn't a missionary call, although I'm prepared to serve God at this beautiful haven that has a school for Michela. Expressing compassion for our situation, the leaders are concerned about whether I could maintain a demanding job on the base while caring for Michela's needs. Concern is also expressed about Michela's adjustment to a French-speaking school without a background in the language. The bottom line is that support for our living on the base isn't extended.

Disappointment is blind to logic. Responding to my dejection, one of the leaders contacts another YWAM base in England, where the work pace would be slower and a local English-speaking school would be available for Michela. After a phone call of introduction, this base in the Midlands of England extends hospitality, but offers no guarantees or even encouragement that an opportunity exists. If I am willing to make the trip across Western Europe and the English Channel, the door of opportunity is ajar. Michela and I prepare to leave for England.

ON THE CONTINENT, THE ROUTE TRACES THE SAME PATH WE traveled several months earlier to pick up money in Brussels: Lausanne, Basel, Brussels, Bruges, and Ostend. A hovercraft lifts us across the English Channel to the white cliffs of Dover, the lock and key of the kingdom. British Rail takes us the last leg of the journey through London and into the Midlands.

The YWAM base is situated in pastoral countryside surrounded by villages with hyphenated names, thatched roofs, and pubs with local stories suggested in their names. The flat terrain is in bold contrast to Switzerland, even Soriano. The base itself is smaller than Lausanne and seems to have fewer people passing through. Michela links up with some girls about her age, who are children of staff and would-be schoolmates.

During the meeting with the base leaders, I once again admit that the missionary call is not my primary impetus for joining forces with YWAM, but I add the fact that I'm prepared to work as a temporary volunteer in hospitality, the kitchen, the administrative office, or wherever I'm needed. Once again, the leadership doesn't support our serving at the base, believing that such a living arrangement would not be the best for Michela and me. As a confirmation, no volunteer opportunities exist that match both my capabilities and the restriction of caring for Michela after school hours.

One of the leaders offers to call some friends of YWAM, Tim and Audrey Couper, about opportunities in Oxford, where the Coupers live with their four children. Audrey teaches at a Christian school, which could have significance for Michela. The Coupers encourage us to stop in Oxford on our way back to Italy.

Nine years ago, living in Oxford had been a desire of my heart. On returning to America from a solo trip to Great Britain, I had encouraged Jim to explore the possibilities of securing a medical position in Oxford, but he never pursued it. Although I remind myself that YWAM's purpose isn't hiding fugitives, their decision feels like a refusal to embrace us. Rejection is a bitter pill to swallow, no matter how acceptable the chaser of understanding. A Bible verse, Proverbs 3:5, is inscribed on a plaque in our room: "Trust in the LORD with all your heart and lean not on your own understanding." According to my understanding, we are shuffling between European countries on a wild-goose chase and spending far too much money and energy, both of which are in short supply. I feel like a pawn piece on a chessboard, wanting to believe that the Hand of God, not man's, is directing the moves to avoid checkmate. As a last-ditch effort, I telephone Janet, a friend in Scotland, but get no answer. After calling her father, I learn that she is on an extended visit to South Africa. The slamming of doors is deafening.

———

EXCEPT FOR THE NEW RAILWAY STATION, OXFORD APPEARS much as I remembered it. Michela and I check into the same bed-and-breakfast I stayed in nine years ago. The proprietor's son has taken over the business, but the establishment remains much the same, despite renovations. The tiny room above the entrance, where the chinking of milk bottles had awakened me at 4 A.M., is now a storage closet.

Michela and I walk along the Thames River (known here as the Isis), watching the punters near the college boathouses. The Thames is joined by another river, the Cherwell, with the broad expanse of Christ Church Meadow filling the Y-shaped conflu-ence of the two rivers. With the Thames at our back, the Cherwell at our side, and the spires of the colleges before us, Michela and I head across the meadow toward the High Street. Cutting through Rose Lane, we play hide-and-seek in a maze of low hedges and rosebushes at the entrance to the Botanic Gar-dens. In medieval times, the gardens had provided the university's school of medicine with healing herbs and plants. Entering the gardens, we sit on the banks of the Cherwell under a birch tree; its peeling bark intrigues Michela. Enamored with this spot near Magdalen Bridge, we designate the birch tree as ours and vow to return to this special place.

The Coupers invite us to their home in the evening. While Michela enjoys the company of their four children, I explain to Audrey and Tim the circumstances of our situation. Both offer support to prepare the way for us to move to Oxford.

The next day at Emmanuel Christian School, where Audrey teaches, Michela and I are introduced to Mrs. Stokes, who would be her teacher. She puts Michela at ease by showing her how to have fun on the computer. Since the school's enrollment is small, Michela already knows a good portion of the students through her introduction to the Couper family. She finds the school setup favorable, but her hopes have been raised too many times re-cently to become enthusiastic.

The rapidity of changing expectations has been unsettling for both of us. A lifetime of decision-making has been squeezed into the nine months since leaving America, and our current meandering leaves us feeling disconnected. Enthusiasm for this adventure is waning faster than the new moon. At the close of the day in Oxford, Michela prays to be back in America by Christmas, a month from now. The desperate search for a place to live has pulled security out from under her. She no longer knows what to expect from our life on the run, but celebrating Christmas in Kentucky is a secure scenario in her imagination. For Michela, leaving Italy to return to America would be joyfully anticipated, but leaving Soriano to move to Oxford wouldn't be worth the painful goodbyes and the difficult adjustments of living in a new country.

Ingredients for a pleasant life come together in Oxford: a beautiful city, the possibility of a good school, and new friends who are willing to help us. But the inclination to establish life in a new country, as I had in New Zealand and Italy, is missing. Living on a YWAM base would have simplified moving: no leases, utility hookups, or start-up expenses for equipping an apartment. All I want to do is return to Italy and rest. Italy is a comfortable niche, but we don't belong anywhere.

THE RETURN TO SORIANO IS NOT TRIUMPHANT, AS I HAD hoped it would be, since the opportunity for living in Switzerland did not materialize. Oxford remains an option, but establishing a home and paying for private education would be costly in terms of both money and energy. Despite the exhausting efforts of our three-week trip, Michela and I are no closer to finding a safe place to live with a school.

The contagion of despair spreads with abandon in my soul, no longer being held in check by hope. Imagined perils clamor for my attention like gongs, but one prevails. What if we are dying of

AIDS? I ask myself. For the first time since leaving San Francisco, the urgency for a second HIV test consumes me. Although the initial tests were negative, the physicians in San Francisco had advised subsequent testing for confirmation. Through Francesco, HIV testing is arranged for us at a hospital in Rome.

Four combinations of test results are possible: both of us being positive, both being negative, and either being positive and the other negative. If my test result were positive and I were to die before her father, Michela would unequivocally return to his custody. It's the oxygen mask principle on an airplane: secure the caregiver's mask first. Whatever it takes, I must remain positive in attitude, as well as HIV-negative, because Michela's well-being depends on it. Life, except for aging, is on hold.

THE VOICES OF MY PARENTS WASH OVER ME LIKE A SOOTHING balm, entering my ears and warmly diffusing through my body. For the first time in nearly a year, I hear their familiar inflections. Precautions have been taken on both sides of the Atlantic to ensure that this maiden telephone call won't be traced. I have made the call from a public phone booth in Viterbo; my parents receive it at the home of their friend Mary Ellen, who is unknown to me as well as to Jim.

Our news is generic: Ellen (not Michela) is taking dance lessons; we live in an apartment (not on the street) and are eating well (not from a soup kitchen). No idle word slips from my mouth. Every one is inspected before freefalling across the telephone cables. When my mother asks about the weather, I answer after excessive hesitation, "It's sunny," not wanting to communicate hemispheric seasons. Knowing that our health is foremost in my parents' minds, I don't mention the HIV testing. A diagnosis of negative would be the perfect Christmas gift.

My parents, on the other hand, are free to provide all of life's details. I demand that my parents be truthful, no matter how dire the news, but I know that my mother will sift whatever she tells me through the sieve of encouragement: Arcturus, who is acting like a puppy, devoured my father's hearing aid; Jim, being in good health, obtained a divorce and married his fiancée last August.

The closure of the marriage, which is welcome, gives me an odd feeling, because it has occurred without my presence and my signature. Hopefully, Jim's preoccupation with a new wife will divert his attention from pursuing us. Her decision to marry, not his, surprises me.

AFTER FOUR MONTHS OF LIVING IN ITALY, UNEXPECTED NEWS arrives several weeks before Christmas. Gabriella's sister, Lydia, has arranged Michela's admission at the school where she teaches in Viterbo. Getting Michela to and from school is the only obstacle. The Soriano–Viterbo trip is about an hour each way, involving walking, a bus ride, and more walking. School, which is six days per week, finishes at 1 P.M. each day to allow the children to eat the main meal of the day at home, but the early dismissal precludes my return to Soriano in the morning. The journey and the four-hour wait in Viterbo dampen some of my enthusiasm, but the opportunity is an answered prayer. Returning to the classroom excites Michela, whose Italian has progressed to the level of translator for me.

Until Francesco telephones with the HIV test results, the Advent season feels more like the anguish season. A week before Christmas the gift of our lives is presented to us and later relayed to my parents. Both of our tests are *negativo*, a word which achieves the opposite effect of its meaning.

At a time when I feel like celebrating, a snowfall blankets the *faggeta*, or forest, in the hills above Soriano. A large number of people from the town, including Augusta, Michela, and me, trek to the forest for an afternoon of sliding down the snowy slopes on plastic bags, which make surprisingly good sleds. Coming in

from the brilliance of sun and snow, Michela and I warm ourselves before a wood fire in the kitchen stove and drink hot
chocolate.

The season is festive, despite being cut off from family and the
familiarity of home. Michela and I decorate a small plastic tree
(on loan from Augusta) and set it atop the *bombola*. Michela is
concerned there won't be any gifts under it, continually asking
me for a number count, as well as whether they are big or small.
On Christmas Eve, Augusta prepares a traditional dinner of fish
before the three of us attend midnight mass. Every seat is taken
and worshippers line the walls, their singing drowning out the
guitars. The unity of believers in Christ, past and present, rever-
berates through the splendor of eighteenth-century architecture
in air heavy with the smell of incense and burning candle wax.
Christmas will never be far from Michela and me wherever we
go, because we belong to a spiritual family with global roots.
Hearing the familiar melodies sung in a tongue not altogether
comprehensible is a preview of eternal harmony.

A week later, toasting the New Year with Gabriella and
Francesco, I reflect that 1991 could be a Jubilee Year, the year of
the Lord's favor when the captives are released. However, our
journey's end doesn't necessarily mean legal freedom for me.
Whatever the future, the blank slate of a new year, void of disappointments and mistakes, inspires hope. Thinking beyond, I wonder where Michela and I will be a year from now.

During the first week of the New Year, Michela celebrates the
new age of seven years. Friends of all ages join us for a birthday
party at the pizzeria where Michela and I often hold our Friday
night celebrations. The generosity of our friends fills the birthday
table with Barbies, school clothes, and toys, but the warm glow
from the birthday celebration quickly fades a week later when
Pisalina disappears, never to return. Our last view of the scrawny
kitten, who has never enjoyed good health, was in the garden,
heading toward the cover of the hillside, possibly to seek a place
to die.

While we are in Viterbo on school days, the winter's cold invades the apartment unopposed until Augusta begins building fires in the wood-burning stove to warm our return. Despite her thoughtfulness, breathing becomes a detectable exercise in the apartment, particularly the bedrooms. Michela develops sequential coldlike illnesses, missing almost as much school as she attends. When the illnesses are passed on to me, she misses even more school.

Energy is ebbing from both of us, as car lights dim when the battery runs low. As a recharging mechanism, I affirm that at least we don't have AIDS, but our illnesses have been too persistent for me not to think about depressed immune systems. Even on healthy mornings, I feel as though weights are strapped to my extremities, preventing me from rising. Relief surges through my body when I manage to pull myself up and away from the soft mattress and place both feet on the concrete floor.

The bed, a place of restoration, can also be a pit of emotional quicksand where I cry after Michela has fallen asleep and where I cry out to God for answers about the future. AIDS isn't the only threat to our well-being. The stress of living as a fugitive is taking a physical toll on my body. During a January telephone call to my parents, I propose returning to America if legal charges against me are dropped and legal protection for Michela, such as chaperoned visits with her father, is guaranteed. This proposal is passed on to the lawyers, but goes nowhere.

When January seems as cold as it can get, the teenagers on the morning bus ride to Viterbo inform us that America is at war with Iraq. With alarm in her voice, Michela asks, "Mommy, are Italy and America going to fight each other?"

Her sigh of relief is audible when I respond, "No, we're on the same side in this war." How different our situation would be if we were living in a country that supports Iraq.

Listening to the Italian television and radio for news about the war is frustrating. After a string of incomprehensible words, I hear "President Bush" and then another sequence ending in "Saddam

Hussein." Purchasing the *Herald Tribune* at a newsstand in Viterbo, I scan the American-published newspaper while walking the narrow streets to Michela's school until one morning a car comes dangerously close to sideswiping me. I have been warned about the danger of walking through the narrow medieval streets; a priest was killed by a car fifteen years ago in Soriano. For my protection during the Gulf War, Michela commandeers the newspaper under her arm each morning, returning it when I promise to read it at the library reading room.

Reading between the lines, I sense that America is closing ranks, gathering into the collective protection of the fold. Wanting to be enveloped, I'm on the outside of the fold in more than geographical terms. If the Gulf War escalates, our protection could be jeopardized by staying in Europe, but Canada, not America, would become our safe haven.

Soriano is well acquainted with the reality of war. Above Michela's birthday table at the pizzeria, a photograph records the aftermath of the World War II bombing of Soriano. Allied forces made up of English and Americans had demolished half of Soriano while capturing the town from the German forces who occupied the school. During the *bombardamento*, hundreds of villagers had been killed in their homes. The young woman who cuts my hair tells of her father, who, as a child, found his father in the bombed rubble; years earlier, his mother had died at his birth.

Tragedy on top of tragedy is not uncommon in Soriano. As a young wife, Augusta had endured the deaths of her infant son and her husband within thirty days of each other. Their only child had lived a few hours after birth while his father lay dying from an illness on a different floor of the hospital. When Michela and I accompany Augusta to the cemetery to decorate their graves with garden flowers, gravestone after gravestone is marked June 5, 1944. Photographs of 1940s vintage have been converted to porcelain and embedded in the gravestones, revealing deaths of all ages. The Gulf War doesn't seem far away while walking in the cemetery at Soriano. In America, cemeteries could begin having more than their share of gravestones dating from January 17, 1991, until who knows when.

THE FIRST ANNIVERSARY OF OUR LIFE ON THE RUN PASSES WITH only a thought of how many more anniversaries must I endure. At the beginning of February, a twelve-inch snowfall blankets Soriano. The frosty weather necessitates feeding the wood-burning kitchen stove around the clock to augment the heat from the *bombola*. The weight of the snow breaks the power lines, rendering the electric heater useless, as well as the electric lights. When the pipes in our apartment freeze, Augusta supplies drinking water, and I wash our clothes in her tub. When the unit supplying the hot water breaks two days later, Augusta's bathtub becomes even busier. At the end of the week, the only reliable comfort in our apartment is the heat from the wood-burning fire in the kitchen stove and the gas *bombola*, which has given no hint of exploding. Eventually, the pipes thaw without bursting, the electricity is restored, and the malfunctioning hot water unit is repaired: each one of these transient difficulties has been mitigated by the warmth of Augusta's care. Experiencing her loving kindness may have been more critical to our well-being than the necessities of electricity and hot water.

The discomforts of our habitation make the prospects of traveling during winter and wartime more agreeable. During every phone call, my mother asks, "How's your money holding out?" Regardless of my response, she always warns, "Don't let it get too low." Putting off an excursion to pick up money could result in the realization of my mother's fear if the Gulf War lasts longer than our money reserves.

The inclination to penetrate Europe as deeply as we had during the autumn money pickup isn't as strong this time around, more from fatigue than strategy. Scanning the American Express directory for an office that transacts Moneygrams and is geographically near Italy, I realize that Monte Carlo satisfies both of these conditions. As a bonus, winter's cold should make the French Riviera way off-season in price.

AT THE STATION IN CIVITAVECCHIA, MICHELA AND I HAVE several hours to wait before boarding the international train that tracks up the west coast of Italy into Monaco via the Italian Riviera. In the waiting room, an Italian grandfather pulls from his pocket a string of pearls, presenting them as a gift to Michela. The spontaneity of this unusual gift catches me off guard. Although he looks and acts kindly, appreciation abruptly turns to suspicion and the fear that we could be unwary participants in a fencing operation. On seeing that the quality of the pearls is suitable for dressing-up play, I blush with penitence. Distrust has been calibrated too high. Determining where to place trust is as erratic as picking one's way through a field of land mines. God help me if I'm wrong in gauging the safety zone. As Michela fingers the pearls in wonderment, these words come to me: "God doesn't make life easy, only possible." As I repeat these words over and over again, they are seared into my spirit by the fire of a Spirit holier than mine. In New Zealand, I had accused God of making life impossible. Trust is growing.

Few people are traveling on the northbound night train. For most of the night, Michela and I have the compartment to ourselves, which is comfortable for sleeping but worrisome for security. Stories circulate among European rail passengers about robbers who spray anesthetizing gas into the train compartments to remove backpacks and handbags. The irreplaceable passports and Travelers Cheques are as close to me as possible, as they always are while traveling. A man from Syria, who speaks little English, shares our compartment for a while. When he gets up to leave at a station stop, I look for him on the platform. The Gulf War has prompted in me an unwelcomed wariness of persons from the Middle East.

With crisp sunlight coming through the train window, I

awaken to views of the Italian Riviera. A quick check of Michela's breathing and my midriff pouch reveals that we have survived the night with our lives and valuables intact. Monte Carlo is sunny and cold, degrees removed from beach weather. The family-run hotel assigned by tourist information is the right price, and the room's temperature makes us feel at home. I am more relaxed about accessing the Moneygram than I had been in Brussels, and our stay in Monte Carlo is like a vacation until our unfortunate choice of movies reinstates trepidation. In *Kindergarten Cop*, Arnold Schwarzenegger saves a mother and son who are on the run from a maniacal husband.

As I try not to think about the movie from the evening before, the Moneygram comes through without a problem. Carrying $10,000 in Travelers Cheques puts me in a good mood, and I wish that I could challenge the fur-swathed women riding in limousines to a cash-carrying contest. Since it's February 14, Michela and I celebrate having each other at the Oceanographic Museum, where a chambered nautilus is as large as a dinner plate and rare specimens of heart-red coral from Sardinia stimulate our imagination about their monetary value. On the outside terrace at the cafeteria, we lunch on fast food and feast on a dazzling view of the Mediterranean Sea. Over our shoulders, the peaks of the Maritime Alps are dusted with snow.

THE GULF WAR HAS PUT EUROPE ON EDGE ABOUT SECURITY, causing passports to be checked and rechecked by border officials. Their questions are routine, but all seem to flip through the pages of my passport, looking at me with mute questions. Their eyes seem to ask why an American woman and child who haven't returned to their homeland for over a year would be traveling alone when their country is at war. The train threads through the Maritime Alps toward the Swiss Alps and on to Lausanne, where I will exchange the newly acquired Travelers Cheques. At the American Express office, I sign such a great quantity of lower denomination checks that the agent offers me the pen, saying, "You've earned it."

Before leaving Italy, I had contacted Barbara, who graciously arranged a few nights' stay at YWAM before returning to Soriano. Four months have elapsed since our last visit, and I'm ripe for another explosion of English. Communication in Italian requires so much energy that speaking English is like being on a verbal vacation.

YWAM's attraction goes deeper than providing opportunities to speak my native tongue and its close proximity to an American Express office. God speaks at Trinita Chiesa in Soriano, but my proficiency in Italian is more suitable for buying bread than comprehending sermons. YWAM is an oasis where our spirits are refreshed with comprehensible words. The organization is programmed without being mechanical, dependable without being predictable, and complete without being perfect.

Believers from a multitude of countries pass through YWAM Lausanne. Some have been persecuted in their home countries for their faith. All, even those from the West, have risked something to obey God's call, the cost of discipleship being higher for some than others. Believers who risk the most trust the most in God's leading along the precipice of faith.

Returning to Italy via the Simplon Express under the Alps, Michela and I must awaken for a 5:30 A.M. change of trains in Verona. As I set the travel alarm, a man from Yugoslavia in the compartment comprehends about our disembarking at Verona, assuring me through gestures that he won't be sleeping.

As the train enters the Verona station, Michela and I are sleeping soundly because the alarm switch has jostled to the off position during the journey. When the train comes to a stop, the man, true to his wakeful word, nudges my arm and points to the platform sign. With a start, I shake Michela, knowing that we have only a couple of minutes to disembark before this train moves in the direction of Yugoslavia. Scrambling to gather our coats and luggage, Michela is still asleep when I put on her shoes and guide her along the corridor. She doesn't awaken until stumbling off the train into the cold night air. Looking about the deserted platform, she begins to cry, but a reassuring cuddle must be postponed until we locate the platform where trains depart for southern Italy.

Winter has lost its grip in Soriano during our week's absence. Warmer temperatures have awakened the harbingers of bloom: daffodils, mimosa, and forsythia. Michela and I welcome spring with greater anticipation. During the previous year, we had lost spring by traveling from winter in America to summer in New Zealand. Two boxes of winter clothes have arrived from New Zealand, bringing whiffs of our basement apartment there. Michela speculates that these boxes, which have traveled on a very slow boat, were delayed by Saddam Hussein in Iraq, but I caution her about blaming him for everything.

Traveling to Monaco and Switzerland, although shorter than other trips, generated more exhaustion. If only I could be released from carrying the mantle of responsibility for Michela's protection for a short time. I fantasize about having a weekend, even a day, without being responsible. Digging deeper into the grab bag of experience to find the silver lining of the dark clouds is wearing me out.

My health is becoming a growing concern. Initially, the suppressed appetite and subsequent weight loss were welcome, but the intensifying stomach pains were not. In the past, losing weight had required effort and discipline. Could an undetected tumor be causing the effortless weight loss? I wonder. The thought of cancer flits through my mind like a little fox in the vineyard, too cunning to be caught or chased away for long. The possibility of AIDS simmers on the mental back burner.

One afternoon in February while walking to pick up Michela at school, abdominal pains make standing upright difficult. The cramping worsens, even after eating bread from a bakery along the way. Hunching over to relieve the stress, I poke at my stomach, fighting pain with pain. My goal is to reach Michela's school. At the entrance, I collapse on the steps.

One of the teachers, a friend of Lydia's, takes me to the hospital while Michela remains with Lydia at her apartment. Laura, a doctor friend whose daughter is a friend of Michela's, meets us in the hospital parking lot with a wheelchair. If internal hemorrhaging is responsible for this intense pain, which prevents me from walking, I could die; Jim used to talk about the danger of patients dying from a bleeding ulcer. What would happen to Michela if I died from a bleeding ulcer? She would eventually be returned to America and end up living with her father, whose legal record is spotless. My parents wouldn't stand a chance of gaining custody of her. Whatever happens, I can't die.

In the emergency room, no questions, paperwork, or registration are required for my hospital admission. Without delay, I am wheeled from room to room for a battery of tests: X rays for abdominal obstructions, a gynecological exam, ultrasound for gallstones, and multiple blood tests. Years of working in medical centers make the hospital environment comfortingly familiar. The surgery ward is a large room with eight barrack-style beds, two to each wall, and two banks of tall shuttered windows. On the hospital chart, I am registered as Jenny, but the ward nurses refer to me as *la Americana*.

Soon after arriving on the ward, I receive an injection for abdominal spasms. Within minutes, all pain is gone. Feeling self-conscious about the dramatic recovery, I walk (without support) down the hall to the bathroom. Finding no soap, paper towels, or toilet paper, I report this to the nurse, who explains that the patient, not the hospital, supplies these amenities. Noticing the empty nightstand, I discover that the patient also provides tissues, water cup, water, and even silverware. As I contemplate my predicament, the teacher who brought me to the hospital appears at my bedside laden with these essential items, plus a robe and slippers from Lydia. Michela, who is concerned but less frightened about my condition, will spend the night at Lydia's apartment.

Test reports reveal no abnormalities, but a final test, an endoscopy, will determine whether the pain has been caused by the eruption of an active stomach ulcer. The periodic bedside visits by Laura and Agostino, her husband, also a doctor at the hospital, have been reassuring, since few of the hospital staff speak English. As I lie in the dark ward, wondering if Michela is sleeping, the day's events are relived. Although I wouldn't have chosen this ordeal, the support Michela and I have received has been overwhelming: medical care without questions and cost, strangers and friends alike ministering to my needs and caring for Michela, hospital visits from Augusta, Gabriella, and Francesco, and being cared for by English-speaking doctors who are friends.

Mornings on the surgery ward begin at 6 A.M. when the lights are turned on, the shutters and windows are opened, and the floors are mopped. Since I am scheduled for an endoscopy, the breakfast rolls pass by me, as does the coffee. In the clinic, neither the doctor performing the procedure nor the assisting staff nurse speak English, so my questions go unanswered. After spraying the back of my throat with an anesthetic, the doctor begins threading the slender tube down my esophagus. Within seconds, I gag, panicking from the buildup of saliva. Unable to speak, I point with staccato jabs at my throat, and the tube is hastily removed. More power to any Italian who can endure an endoscopy prepped only by an anesthetic throat spray. After an injection of atropine to calm the reflexes, the tube is reinserted and the test is completed. The diagnosis is an active stomach ulcer, but not a bleeding one.

On my discharge from the hospital, the staff doctor prescribes an acid reducer and instructs me to abstain from drinking cappuccino (which I adore) and from drinking wine (which will be easier to give up). I laugh wryly when the doctor, who is unaware of our situation, advises me to reduce stress in my life. On leaving the hospital, a severe headache from caffeine withdrawal is my chief physical complaint, compelling me to order a cappuccino at the café opposite. On the way back to Soriano, our friends treat Michela and me to ice cream, which hopefully neutralizes the cappuccino. Michela is relieved to see me walking upright, smiling, and back on the coffee scent.

On Good Friday, Augusta puts an electric candle in her window before the three of us join the venerable *Processione del Christo Morto* through the streets of Soriano. Chained prisoners carrying small wooden crosses lead the procession, followed by two men who alternate carrying a tall wooden cross, which must be propped against the side of a building for the changeovers. A statue of Mary towers above a reclining figure of the dead Christ as musicians with guitars play a dirge. Townspeople, including Augusta, Michela, and myself, follow the procession through the medieval neighborhoods, whose windows are aglow with white lights. Participating in this funeral procession communicates the human suffering of Jesus' death as no Good Friday service (which has its sights on the Resurrection) has ever done for me before.

On the original Good Friday before the Sabbath, this son, brother, friend, teacher, neighbor, and favorite carpenter had died a torturous death, and there seemed to be no hope for the future. One physical death is enough for any man to suffer, but Jesus experienced the spiritual death of every human: past, present, and future. He even suffered the death of those who choose to experience their own deaths rather than accept His death waiver, which remains unclaimed to collect eternal dust. It's no wonder that Jesus sweated blood in the garden while contemplating the exponential magnitude of death He would need to endure.

During the Easter school break, Michela and I learn that she won't be allowed to return to school for the new term. A new administrator requires that she register and submit legal identification and vaccination certificates, which are in America.

Attending school in Soriano now seems unlikely. Michela is disappointed about not seeing her classmates and teacher again, but she bounces back with the resiliency of a seven-year-old. I, on the other hand, feel as if someone has punched me in the stomach, which customarily bears the brunt of anxious circumstances. The closing of school opportunities in Italy means one thing— moving to a new country. Perhaps enough time has elapsed since our departure from America to divert the searchlight from Janet's home in Scotland.

I BECAME ACQUAINTED WITH JANET IN 1981 AT A CHURCH in Washington, D.C., where she worked as a nanny for a British diplomat. Our transatlantic friendship was maintained through letters and phone calls, as well as two visits to Scotland, once on my own and once with Jim.

As with Gabriella, I had not corresponded with Janet during the last year in San Francisco, and she knows nothing about Michela's sexual abuse, or my becoming a fugitive to protect her. When I telephone her, hearing my voice relieves one of her fears, assuring her that I'm alive. With characteristic grace, she forgives the long communication break and welcomes us to her home in Perth at our earliest convenience.

Within the week, Michela and I cross the English Channel on a two-week scouting mission to Scotland. When I call Janet from London about our U.K. location, her health condition stops me in my tracks. Janet is immobilized by debilitating pain in her back, but she won't accept our returning to Italy without visiting her, urging us to come and divert her attention from the pain. Following Janet's encouragement and my heart, Michela and I board a train for Perth, uncertain whether I'm selfishly pursuing the wrong direction or persevering in the right one.

On Janet's living room floor, the three of us eat fish and chips, reclining on pillows. Catching up on the intervening years in Janet's company is a feast for my soul. Like Gabriella, she knows the Janie part of me, which removes the stress of hoping new acquaintances believe and trust me, a stranger off the street with no credentials. Immediately, Janet calls me Chris to safeguard against calling me Janie in public.

Janet meets Michela, whom she knows as Ellen, for the first time, having received pictures of her from San Francisco. Michela readily warms to Janet, quickened by the knowledge that she has known me in America, as well as her father and even Arcturus.

Eight years ago on this side of the Atlantic, Janet, Jim, and I dined together at a Perth restaurant within walking distance of where Janet lives now. At that time, she had lived in a village outside Perth, but her current address would be easy to trace. As the manager of a residential care home for adults with learning disabilities, Janet has no telephone listing in her own name. Her private calls are transferred from the care home next door, a turn of events that figures positively for the security of our visit. Janet and I wonder whether Jim has hired a private detective to monitor her house periodically for our presence. Whenever the doorbell rings during the visit, this thought leaps to our attention.

Before going to bed, Michela asks Janet, "Did you get tired of your mother when she took you around the world?"

Amused by Michela's earnestness, Janet replies, "No. I wasn't as fortunate as you to travel around the world with my mother." Michela perceives this adventure as a rite of passage during childhood, as unexceptional as vaccinations or attending school.

The town house where Janet lives is situated on a hill overlooking the center of Perth. The broad city streets extend across the plain until interrupted by the meandering River Tay, resuming on the other side and extending up a line of hills, dominated by Kinnoul Hill, which hosts the Easter sunrise service. In another direction, the faint outline of the Highlands can be seen through blue haze on the horizon when the sky is clear, the clarity of the natural light reminiscent of New Zealand.

Since leaving the playgrounds of New Zealand, Michela has been on the lookout for a flying fox, a rubber tire suspended from a cable that glides several feet above the ground between two launching platforms. Walking to the playground in Janet's neighborhood, Michela sees from a distance the silhouette of a flying fox, exclaiming, "God has answered my prayer."

Watching Michela gleefully fly through the air, I reflect about coming to Scotland. With Janet's boundless energy constrained, our visit is quite different than I had expected. Doing fun things with Janet could have been the antidote for my persistent weariness, although I wouldn't trade our living room floor talks for anything. Unable to ease her pain, Michela and I may be adding to her discomfort by our presence in her home.

Looking for a baseball diamond at the playground, I don't really expect to find one. My thoughts turn toward baseball, more from its being something American than from interest in the game. If life decisions were organized as a baseball game, I would signal from the mound for a relief pitcher. Walking off the field to sit in the dugout would be fine with me. But I'm not alone on the mound: without someone to pinch hit, field, and run with her, Michela would be vulnerable to whatever pitches came her way. Unaware about what is happening in America, I'm pitching in the dark. It's impossible to discern whether the pitches are even reaching home plate, much less within the strike zone. I don't even know if I am in the right ballpark. All I know is that we are at the right playground.

The Umpire calls me by name: "Janie, take this journey one day at a time, knowing that being in the right playground is as significant as being in the right country."

When Janet's pain doesn't lessen after days of immobility, she enters the hospital for evaluation. Sitting by her hospital bed, we discuss the pros and cons of our moving to Scotland. Ewen, Janet's pastor, has offered us the option of becoming lodgers in the manse with his family, even pointing out where Michela would attend school. Janet offers the extra bedroom in her house for as long as it takes us to become settled in Perth, although staying with her carries risk. A staff member or resident at the home next door could innocently divulge through a telephone inquiry the presence of an American woman and child. Jim knows that Janet lives near Perth.

On the way back to Janet's home, I impulsively visit the walk-in clinic of the hospital whose rooftops I have seen from our bedroom window. Under normal circumstances, I would take decongestants and analgesics for a respiratory ailment that has lingered for several weeks, but normality has no place in our life. Knowing that my vital signs are critical for two bodies, the thought of becoming ill or hospitalized between Scotland and Italy frightens me. When the doctor pronounces my lungs to be clear of pneumonia, I breathe easier. Walking through the emergency room on the way out of the hospital, how could I know that I would be caring for Michela in this waiting room in the future?

AFTER DEPARTING PERTH FOR OUR RETURN TRIP TO ITALY, picking up money is the overriding concern. American Express in America is balking at sending such large Moneygrams, now requiring my mother to specify a country designation rather than "international." The United Kingdom is chosen as the generic Moneygram destination, since money could be wired from the U.K. to any other country in Europe or the world. Picking up money at the American Express office in Edinburgh would be convenient, but if the transaction were detected, any future sojourning in Scotland could be threatened. The American Express service directory notes an office in York, a convenient and beautiful stopover on the way to the ferry for crossing to the Continent.

After checking into a bed-and-breakfast in York—the same one I stayed in nine years ago—Michela and I head to the American Express office for a Moneygram of lesser value than the previous ones. Although the York office is open and equipped to transact a Moneygram, the London office, where authorization is issued, is closed for a Bank Holiday weekend. Remembering what one of my geography professors had said about our living on the run—"Persistence is as valuable as knowledge"—I persist for an hour and thirty minutes. Normally, I would shrink from contacting office personnel on a day off work, but I'm infuriated by the silly rules that have blocked access to my money.

Michela, who has been sitting for several hours without interesting occupation, is bored and unhappy. From her pouty mouth issues a stream of complaints, alternating with pleas for ice cream. Periodically, I hiss idle threats at her: "Unless you shut up, you will never eat ice cream again." Her whining escalates, endearing neither of us to the American Express employees. The climate of our lives always depends on how I respond to pressure, barometric or otherwise. If only Michela could comprehend the difficulties I face and not multiply the pressure, but that's asking too much of a seven-year-old living on the run.

Since no one with authority can be reached on this sunny afternoon (who can blame them?), the transaction must wait until Monday at an American Express office on the Continent. On the way to purchase ice cream, fireworks explode in my stomach from being angry at everyone, even the United Kingdom, for declaring a Bank Holiday weekend.

Boarding the train at York for London marks the beginning of a travel marathon. After taking the ferry from Dover to Calais, we arrive at a station in Paris at 11:30 P.M., discovering that the international train for Basel, Switzerland, departs from a different Métro station. Possessing no French francs, only pounds sterling, and with the currency exchange closed, taking a taxi across Paris or even purchasing Métro tickets for the right station is impossible. Walking through the Paris metro after midnight with a child and luggage puts me on heightened alert. The passageways are mostly deserted, except for a few couples and a smattering of solo men. When we are the only ones along an expanse of corridor, the tread of our footsteps echoes in the eerie quietness. When other footsteps reverberate in the passageway, I look over my shoulder. Turning a corner, we link up with a woman from Ipswich who was on the train and offers to buy Métro tickets for us, accepting reimbursement in pounds sterling. Notwithstanding the tickets, her presence in the underground corridors adds to our safety in numbers until the three of us board the connecting Métro train.

SINCE THE AMERICAN EXPRESS DIRECTORY LISTS AN OFFICE IN Basel, we hang around the train station there, waiting for the tourist office to open for obtaining directions. Once again, efforts at transacting the Moneygram are thwarted: the American Express office has been closed down. If I don't receive a Moneygram soon, we will be without cash in one week's time. After a day and a night of train traveling, Michela and I must reboard a train, the last thing either of us wants to do. Scouting American Express offices down the line, one is a sure bet.

Arriving at Lausanne in midafternoon, I douse the internal fire pit with a carton of milk before taking a taxi to the American Express office, where the Moneygram comes through without a problem. On the shortest possible notice, I call YWAM, inquiring whether a room is available. Locating the person in charge of hospitality requires several phone calls and an hour's wait, during which I look at American Express travel brochures. In the end, we receive the green light to spend the night at the YWAM base.

Before returning to Italy, I discuss attending a YWAM discipleship training school beginning in July. Again, I am encouraged by the director of the school to seek an English-speaking school for Michela. The YWAM door remains closed. Possibly the journey is coming to an end and Italy is the last stop.

AS OUR TRAIN WAITS IN THE BERN STATION BEFORE GOING ON to Lucerne, a changing point for trains to Italy, I jump up with a start. Glancing at my watch, I announce suddenly to Michela, "Let's go. Pack up. We're getting off the train."

Looking up from the colored pencils and paper strewn on the train table, Michela says in bewilderment, "But we don't get off here. You said Lucerne."

Addressing the floor, as I gather our luggage, I say, "I know. I've changed my mind. We don't have much time. I'll explain on the way."

When the whistle signals the train's departure, Michela and I are standing on the platform at Bern, uncertain of which direction to proceed, having only the address of the American Express office. In fifteen minutes, the office closes—if it still exists in this city. I ask directions from anyone who makes eye contact, but no one knows its location.

Looking across umpteen lanes of rush-hour traffic on a street near the station, I see the AMERICAN EXPRESS logo in a second-floor window. The office door doesn't budge in response to my jiggling the handle, but knocking brings several young women to the lobby. Through the glass door, I plead to exchange Travelers Cheques. Although the urgency of the request puzzles the employees, the door is unlocked. The transaction itself takes only a few minutes, but signing the checks extends their workday after hours. In appreciation, the next day's coffee break is my treat.

At the station, waiting for another train to Lucerne, Michela wants to know what's going on.

"Sweetpea, I'm proud of you. You supported me without knowing why, running with me when it didn't make any sense. While sitting on the last train, I realized that we would be arriving in Lucerne after the American Express office there had closed and that we would be leaving for Italy the next morning before it opened. I had forgotten that the Travelers Cheques needed to be exchanged outside Italy." I refrain from mentioning the preoccupation that had caused my absentmindedness: believing our journey would end soon, making the exchange of Travelers Cheques unnecessary.

Opening my Bible on the way to Lucerne, I turn to the Psalms in praise of God's provision in Bern. Throughout these songs from the heart, people who have lost hope in the goodness of God still cry out to Him in their distress. Their monologues of suffering and disappointment about living in exile penetrate the spiritual crevasses in my soul. Lured by the word "hope" in Psalm 130, as the red trumpet flowers signal nourishment to the hummingbirds in my mother's garden, I read: "Out of the depths I have cried to Thee, O LORD . . . I wait for the LORD, my soul does wait, and in His word I hope. My soul waits for the LORD more than the watchmen for the morning; indeed, more than the watchmen for the morning."

When I grabbed Michela's hand in Bern, her trust in me, not her understanding, had been critical. Digging in her heels or dragging her feet would have prevented us from reaching the objective. The same could be said about God's leading and my following when His reasoning is incomprehensible and directional cues are few. I strain to see the light at the end of the tunnel, whether it be the pinprick of an opening or the lights of an approaching train. Janet used this metaphor in her farewell prayer, but this journey has none of the directness of a tunnel; it's more like threading one's way in the dark through a labyrinth of perplexing turns. I want to come out of the tunnel where I have been stumbling around without the light of understanding. Out of the tunnel, the darkness of night is natural and expansive, a fingernail moon shines light on the beauty and delights of the journey's path. But, for now, the horizon remains dark with no hint of morning light.

8

Pipe Dreams

As the rain hides the stars,
as the autumn mist hides the hills,
as the clouds veil the blue of the sky,
so the dark happenings of my lot
hide the shining of Your face from me.
Yet, if I may hold Your hand
in the darkness, it is enough.
Since I know that,
though I may stumble in my going,
You do not fall.
—A CELTIC PRAYER

TIME IS RUNNING OUT ON OUR APARTMENT IN SORIANO. AL-though I know Gabriella's family would never act against our welfare, the apartment will be needed during the summer; that had been our agreement. During the remaining weeks of living in Soriano, every action is gauged for the short-term, even deciding the quantity of coffee to purchase. At the same wholesale leather goods warehouse where the gift of shoes had originated, I purchase three enormous black canvas bags. Although departure from Italy is imminent, our destination is unknown. Only two possibilities exist: Perth and Oxford. Of the two, Janet's friendship gives Perth the edge over Oxford. Uncertainty fuels daydreams about a third destination. Spending an afternoon shopping for Italian gifts to take back to America, I speculate that these gifts could be given soon. Daydreams about rebuilding life in America eventually fall flat after hitting a wall with bars on the windows.

Telephone calls to my parents yield no indication that Italy is the last stop before Kentucky. There has been no news about Jim's health for months. Before any mention of him, every telephone conversation begins with a well-being inventory of family members and Arc, our dog. Mother keeps a list of friends who telephone, asking about us. Their greetings and comments remind me that life in America goes on without me. When my mother's gallbladder is removed, I'm the last person in her life to find out about the surgery.

Michela sidetracks conversations about moving to Scotland with a plaintive plea: "Mommy, when are we going back to America? I feel homely."

Her word "homely" becomes a byword for us, merging "homesick" and "lonely." Michela's remedy to feeling "homely" is to find another place to live in Soriano if returning to America isn't possible. Issues such as school enrollment, police registration, and housing don't trouble her. Except for schooling, all her needs are being met; even speaking Italian no longer frustrates her. She has no complaints about living in Scotland, but she has no inclination to leave Italy. Her sole preoccupation is the forthcoming dance recital, where she will wear a white tutu amid the red-wine velvet curtains, crystal chandeliers, and gold leaf of the theater in Viterbo.

A TRAIN AND FERRY JOURNEY TO THE UNITED KINGDOM WITH three heavy black bags isn't possible. Traveling by air to Scotland is the expedient option, but a standard air ticket from Italy to Edinburgh costs over $1,000. When I reject this fare, the travel agent in Soriano checks charter flights. On a charter flight leaving Rome for Edinburgh on June 22, only two seats remain, each ticket costing half the regular fare. I take them on the spot.

During the weeks in Soriano, all our possessions must either be discarded, returned to their owners, packed for traveling, or boxed for sending. Emotions drain from us with every tearful goodbye. I say farewell to friends at the *palestra* in Soriano, where I have conditioned my muscles to a degree I shall never see again. During our last week, Michela sticks like glue to Augusta, who prepares a goodbye dinner worth returning to Italy for.

At the airport in Rome, Michela is unhappy and tearful about leaving Augusta, her friends, and *bella* Soriano. The farewell would have been more intense if it had included Pisalina, her kitten. The three black bags, which are borderline immovable, are checked and not slapped with a weight surcharge.

When the plane's wheels touch the runway in Edinburgh, Michela and I clap for the crew, which has become an on-the-run family tradition. The flight attendant's welcome is inappropriate for passengers who are moving to Scotland, but refreshing in that it doesn't exhort me to have a nice day. Hoping to pass on my anticipation to Michela, who converts her name to Michelle again, I say with attendant pomp, "On behalf of the flight crew, we welcome you to a new life in Scotland. For those passengers traveling on the run, we hope that your stay will be permitted."

Not wanting to bump other passengers with our excessive carry-on luggage, Michelle and I wait until the plane empties. At passport control, the immigration officer asks the customary questions, which I answer as a customary tourist.

Flipping through my passport without looking up, he asks for the third time, "What do you plan to do in the United Kingdom?"

"My daughter and I plan to visit Scotland and England," I state for the third time.

"Are you married?" he asks, looking me in the eye this time.

"No, I'm divorced."

With an edge of sternness in his voice, he demands, "How do you plan to pay for your stay in the United Kingdom?"

"I have U.S. dollars in the form of Travelers Cheques."

"Are you certain that you have brought enough money?" This question is unanswerable, but I assure him that I could draw upon funds in America if my money were to run out.

"I am concerned that you and your daughter could become stranded in the U.K. with no means of support," and he asks to see Michelle's passport.

I give Michelle a look that communicates, "Let me do the talking" when it dawns on me where his questions are leading; he's concerned that we will end up destitute, living off the government. I watch to see whether any numbers are entered in the computer, but he only flips through the passport pages. After more questions about funding, I surreptitiously retrieve a wad of Travelers Cheques from my jeans and spread them on the counter so he can inspect their validity. I'm too tired to think about returning to Italy, or worse yet, America. Responding to his questions diverts my attention from wondering what will happen to us if we are refused admission to the United Kingdom. I must keep him talking.

"Sir, these checks, totaling about $3,000, will keep me from becoming a leech in your country." Diverting the conversation to less threatening turf, I continue, "In addition to sight-seeing, I'm researching a graduate thesis on . . ." The discourse is interrupted by a slight swirl of his hand in the air, as if he is conducting me to stop the flow of words.

When he resumes another round of questions on marital status, an airline agent interjects from the sidelines, "I believe this woman and her daughter have been delayed long enough. Is there a reason to detain her?" Airport employees on the periphery communicate their impatience to close down this section of the terminal for the night. Coming up with no justification, the immigration officer stamps our passports begrudgingly.

The airline agent escorts us through the deserted terminal wing to the baggage claim area, apologizing for the third-degree questioning I have been subjected to for the past thirty minutes. At this time of night, the currency exchange is closed, and the last buses for the train station in Edinburgh have departed. The airline official phones for a cab, explaining that I have no pounds sterling, only Travelers Cheques in U.S. dollars. The company agrees to change a $50 Travelers Cheque, the last I possess of the lower denomination ones. Using the airline's telephone, I call Janet, but the line is busy. The agent offers to telephone her about our arrival time in Perth.

Arriving at the Edinburgh station four minutes before the last night train departs for Perth, there is no time to change money or even purchase tickets. On the platform, the conductor is about to blow the whistle, but he sees our sluggish approach. At the nearest car entrance, he helps me hoist the three bags onboard to expedite the train's departure.

Groaning in disbelief, he asks, "What do you have in these bags? Bricks?"

"No," I reply. "Gold bullion!"

"So, you're a lady of mystery." Having no ready reply, I respond with a Mona Lisa smile.

When the conductor appears again to collect tickets, I have none. Having witnessed our catching the train on the run, or rather on the crawl, he produces two tickets. However, the leftover change (in pounds sterling) from the cab ride is only enough to buy one ticket, a child's fare at that.

"Well, lady of mystery, since British Rail doesn't accept gold bullion and won't force a wee lass to ride the train alone at this hour of night, you ride free," concludes the conductor.

The distance from the train station at Perth to Janet's home is a comfortable walk in the daylight, but not after midnight with a tired child and three cumbersome bags. Although the remaining pounds sterling weren't sufficient for an adult train ticket, the leftover coins are the precise amount for cabfare to Janet's home, including a tip.

Lights are ablaze on the porch and in the living room, signaling that Janet hasn't gone to bed. The helpful airline agent whose intervention facilitated our admittance into the U.K. had kept his word.

FOR SEVERAL DAYS, THE THREE BLACK BAGS REMAIN IN THE ENtrance hall, waiting to be dragged up the stairs to a second-floor guest room. I move through the house with the nimbleness of a garden slug; fatigue has converted well-toned muscles into rubber.

Janet's back condition has improved, although a good portion of each day is spent resting in a supine position with the hope of averting surgery. My homelessness and Janet's comfortlessness bond us, as mutual affliction does. Both of us regret our limitations for serving the other. Janet needs a chauffeur, but driving is off-limits for me. I need help in finding a place to live, but the constant pain prevents her from searching the byways of Perth with me.

Michelle's frustration about leaving Soriano triggers disagreeable behavior. At mealtimes, she complains if something other than pasta is served. When the only television in the house is not programmed to her wishes, she throws a fit, earning her the nickname Squeak. Michelle holds me personally responsible for the weather, a daunting onus during a wet summer in Scotland. Janet introduces me to a word that has the right onomatopoeia for diffusing anger: "throttle."

To give Janet a peaceful break, Michelle and I spend a few days in Kinloch Rannoch, the Highland village where Janet grew up. I want to introduce Michelle to the rugged terrain that impressed me years before. The city and then the forests in the river valley are left behind as the road across the moor rises in a succession of plateaus, which Janet's father counts as thirteen steps. The shaggy Highland cattle with their crescent horns browse in the heather, which softens the stark edge of the landscape with mauve and purple tints. The River Tummel flows dark with peat, the color of Guinness, as Janet says.

Nothing obscures the silhouettes of the mountains. The symmetry of Schiehallion, "the mountain of the fairies," contrasts with the craggy projections of neighboring mountains. Its conical shape inspired the invention of contour lines for communicating elevation changes on maps, and its magnificent bulk figured in eighteenth-century experiments to determine the weight of the earth. The geomorphology of the Grampians awakens the sleeping giant of geography within me.

As Michelle and I sit before a coal fire in the sitting room of the bed-and-breakfast, I initiate a conversation to clear the air and hopefully ease the tension between us. Trying not to sound high-handed, I begin: "Michelle, you know that we couldn't stay in the Soriano apartment."

"You could have found us another place to live in Soriano."

"I tried, but apartments were few and far between. The one we visited was too expensive. Anyway, finding a place to live wouldn't have solved the problem of registering with the police, or schooling for you in English."

"You could have taught me at home."

"We tried home schooling, but it didn't work. It wasn't your fault. I was too tired to teach you."

"You just wanted to come to Scotland to see Janet."

"Yes, it's nice living near Janet. She's a good friend who cares about—"

Michelle interrupts, "She likes you more than she likes me."

I am tempted to quip, "That doesn't surprise me, given the way you have been acting," but such a remark would have only driven the wedge farther between us. Michelle is waging emotional war on two fronts: grieving the loss of, first, America and now Soriano. In New Zealand, she had expressed frustration about being uprooted from America, but now her hostility has intensified. Scotland is several countries removed from New Zealand, and her weariness from being on the move has increased, as has mine. Although I have made no commitments to her about returning to America, comments in New Zealand, such as "We're heading toward America, in the direction of home, but the journey could take a long time," had quickened hope. Keeping the future vague seemed the only option, but her hopes have been dashed with every new country. Michelle's protection and happiness are becoming mutually exclusive.

Michelle isn't the only one unhappy about being away from America. When I learn that my twenty-fifth high school reunion is occurring during the Fourth of July weekend, I once again lean on a self-defeating coping mechanism. The ludicrous scenario of attending a school reunion doesn't stop me from placing a last-ditch telephone call on July 2 to Mary Ellen in Kentucky. Pumped on 1966 maturity, hope evaporates on learning that Jim has recently taught at a medical symposium. Yet again, I prey upon him, rather than pray for his change of heart.

On the Fourth of July, while Americans barbecue hamburgers and watch fireworks, missing a school reunion has reduced me to tearful misery. Graduates within miles of the festivities won't even bother to attend, and others would gladly trade a reunion weekend in Kentucky for a weekend in Scotland. For me, the reunion celebrates something deeper than being twenty-five years past high school. It is a symbolic link with the past when life was less complicated, under the protection of family. The reunion signifies normality: talking about children, jobs, accomplishments, marital status, and so on. If I showed up, I might win the prize for traveling the farthest, but what would I say about my life? "Well,

I'm divorced, homeless, and living out of three large bags, carless, unemployed, and supported by my parents, and wanted by the FBI on charges that could send me to prison for a very long time. Promise not to tell anyone that I am here, cross-your-heart-and-hope-to-die." Such blathering sounds too much like high school.

After eighteen months in hiding, missing a school reunion becomes an emotional watershed, just as birthdays had been in Italy. Flailing on a sea of dreams, the surge of circumstances threatens to hurl me over the dam of false hopes toward an emotional crash on the other side. Survival depends on draining the pit of pipe dreams, enabling me to embrace life as it is. Only God's detonation is powerful enough to break through the damming false hopes. Will my soul survive the upheaval of blasting? When I am drained of false hopes, will I survive walking in the pit of reality?

ON THE OTHER SIDE OF THE REUNION WEEKEND, THE DRAINING of the pit begins with the determined resolve to establish ourselves in Perth. Scanning the listings for apartment rentals, following up newspaper ads, and checking the bulletin boards in the local shops produce only two apartments meriting a visit. Neither is suitable for our needs. Janet leaves no stone unturned in calling friends about available housing opportunities. Although Ewen and his wife, Sue, reconfirm their gracious offer for us to be lodgers at the manse, I resolutely hold out for a place of our own.

When a month's search yields nothing, I question whether Perth is where we are meant to be. I also question God's purpose in directing us here for only two months. Exhaustion from moving eighteen times in as many months has shortened my temper with Michelle, who is bratty about everything. Although Janet encourages us to stay at her home as long as necessary, I need a place to live where our tension is inflicted on no one but ourselves. Janet and I agree that contacting the Coupers in Oxford could open a new door of opportunity. My telephone call to them comes two days before their departure on a YWAM mission trip to the Czech Republic. After expressing interest in registering Michelle for the new school year at Emmanuel Christian School, Audrey encourages me to call Mr. Wilson, the principal, immediately. Only two days remain in the current school year, and Michelle's application must be submitted before it ends.

After several agonizing rings, Mr. Wilson answers. Prefacing the inquiry with apologies for calling him at home, I express my interest in enrolling Michelle. Saving the details of our situation until meeting him in person, I make an appointment for 11:30 A.M. on Friday, the day after tomorrow. Putting down the receiver, I hastily prepare for a train journey that begins at seven o'clock the next morning. Momentarily, Michelle is stunned by the abruptness of the travel plans; then, as if a light switch is flipped, she remembers that predictability is not part of our routine.

Traveling to Oxford could be another wild-goose chase, although Oxford has the same thing going for it that New Zealand had: disassociation from the past. As a safe haven, all connections would be new in Oxford.

Before falling asleep, I listen to the bleating of the sheep in the field next to Janet's town house, an anomaly in an urban residential neighborhood, even for Scotland. Wherever Michelle and I have sojourned on this journey, sheep have been a part of the landscape: the hillsides of New Zealand and Soriano and now Scotland. Their cries cue my thoughts to an Old Testament leader who had needed reassurance from God on the eve of a momentous decision. Gideon, chosen to lead the Israelites—significant numerical underdogs—into battle, petitioned God to confirm His decision on the threshing room floor. According to Gideon's preconditions, dew was to appear only on the fleece, not the ground. When it happened, Gideon was still not convinced. On the second night, Gideon requested that the fleece be dry and the dew be only on the ground. On both nights, the dew had complied according to Gideon's terms (Judges 6:36–40). The wet and dry fleeces of our moving to Oxford depend on Michelle's admission to Emmanuel Christian School and finding a place to live.

ON THE LAST DAY OF THE SCHOOL YEAR, MICHELLE AND I board a red double-decker bus for Summertown in Oxford. Victorian residences with stone tracery at the windows line the entrance to this neighborhood where the spires of the Oxford colleges are visible above the rooftops. Emmanuel Christian School is housed in a 1970s single-story building that had been constructed as a school but had been idle for a few years. Before meeting the principal, Mr. Wilson, Michelle and I are taken to see Mrs. Stokes, the teacher who showed Michelle the computer during our last visit to Oxford. If admitted to the school, Michelle would be the fourth American girl in this class of fewer than twenty students. Has God brought America to Michelle, since she can't go to it?

Mr. Wilson is astonished to learn the circumstances of our journey, since I had not hinted about them during the telephone conversation. Now that we are face-to-face, I cover all the salient points: Michelle's sexual abuse, the criminal charges against me, our living on the run, and her father's diagnosis of AIDS. I bring no credentials as to the trustworthiness of these claims; all references begin with this journey. God alone is my witness.

Leaning forward in his chair to plant his forearms on the desk, Mr. Wilson extends compassion with the question "How can we help you, Mrs. Williams?"

"More than anything else, my daughter needs to attend a school without jeopardizing our safety. She needs to be registered as Michelle Williams, not using her passport name. I have money for school fees, although I don't know if the amount will be sufficient for a school like this one."

Mr. Wilson explains that school fees are assessed on a sliding scale, assuring me that admission, not necessarily money, is the obstacle.

"Mrs. Williams, your inquiry has been well timed for Michelle's admission. It was imperative that your petition be considered at the final board meeting of the school year. Would you be willing to tell them the story you have told me?"

Without hesitation, I agree to petition the board of directors in less than an hour. "Mr. Wilson, do you think they will admit Michelle, given the obstacles?"

"I don't know what the other board members will decide. The legal issue seems the most problematic. I pledge my full support on admitting Michelle, but all decisions must be agreed upon by the board of directors."

As our meeting ends, Mr. Wilson suggests, "Why don't you have some lunch, since the board will be deciding on other matters before hearing your petition? Michelle is welcome to eat with the children, and you are welcome to join the teachers in the staff room."

As we bring back sandwiches from a deli, Michelle is eager to eat with classmates. At the coffee area of the staff room, a blue and white mug catches my eye. The Wildcat mascot of the University of Kentucky (known there as U.K.) is on the mug with the slogan GO, U.K. None of the teachers remembers how it reached the U.K. from U.K. in America, but every sip of coffee brings a smile to my lips.

After lunch, the board members listen sympathetically to my story. Without deliberation, they agree to accept Michelle's application unofficially, contingent on the response of legal counsel. Catching up with Michelle during the closing assembly, she seems to have settled into the class. On the way to celebrate her conditional school acceptance under our tree at the Botanic Gardens, she pesters me to buy a school uniform at a shop on the High Street, but we buy frozen yogurt instead.

Everyone acknowledges that apartments in Oxford are scarce and tend to be expensive. The abundance of students drives up the rent, making competition intense for the inexpensive apartments. At a real estate agency near Summertown, few apartments within my budget are listed. Living options are as limited in Oxford as they had been in Perth.

When I call Janet about Michelle's conditional school acceptance and tell her my concerns about finding a place to live, she suggests asking at the church we had attended the autumn before with the Coupers. I'm skeptical about the likelihood of finding someone at the church on a Saturday morning, but she strongly urges me to give it a try. Since I don't have a better idea, Michelle and I walk in that direction.

Several blocks before reaching the church, Michelle stops to look at pictures of homes in the window of a real estate agency. Entering the agency on a whim minutes before closing time, I ask about the availability of furnished one-bedroom apartments, centrally located and near public transportation. The real estate agent suggests an apartment in Headington that will become available in September. Before she gives me the tenant's name and telephone number, I ask what options exist in lieu of signing a year's lease. Justifying this request more than necessary, I elaborate about researching a graduate thesis, which makes the length of our residency in Oxford uncertain. A way of escaping a year's lease exists: six months' rent up front and one month's deposit, a non-refundable fee, to be paid two weeks before occupancy.

On the way to a public phone, Michelle and I pass the home of the Coupers (now on their way to the Czech Republic) and the church, our original destination. When I call the tenant, he invites us to see the apartment, which is only a ten-minute walk away.

The second-floor perspective offers security and detachment from the busy flow of pedestrians and traffic on the London Road. Although the one bedroom is small (barely enough room to enter the bed from the sides), the spaciousness of the kitchen and the living room makes up for the cramped sleeping quarters. Fireplaces that had once been fitted with gas heaters now add only character to the rooms, where electric wall heaters supply the warmth. Michelle offers suggestions for rearranging the furniture, which means that she likes it. This cozy apartment would be a haven, a place for closing the door and shutting out the world.

If the real estate agency had been open, I would have secured this apartment immediately, despite Michelle's whining about being hungry. Paying the six months' rent in cash, and the nonrefundable fee, two weeks before occupancy without making a special trip to Oxford seems to be the only complication. Sending a check from Scotland in the name of Chris Williams would be impossible without proper identification.

Responding to Michelle's call for food, we order sandwiches at a nearby shop. Although I want to eat in the café's garden, I give way to Michelle's desire to picnic at the park the tenant mentioned. After eating, I push Michelle on a roundabout in the playground until I feel nauseated. With no one to push her, she loses interest and heads for the swings. Hanging back from nabbing the empty swing, she has something to tell me. Staring at two girls in the adjacent swings, Michelle whispers, "Those girls were at the school yesterday."

The other girls express self-conscious recognition of Michelle, but no one initiates contact. When I hear one of the girls call out to her father nearby, I make a move. Their father, Francis Prittie, confirms that Hannah and Rachel, as well as two older children, attend Emmanuel Christian School. When I mention our intention to move to Oxford, Francis invites us home to meet his wife, Sally, and talk about the school and Oxford.

While Michelle and the girls play in the backyard, I discover that Sally and Francis know the Coupers well, both through school and through attending the same church. This association paves the way for relating the circumstances of our moving to

Oxford. Sally and Francis encourage me with their compassion and willingness to help us.

Both confirm that the rent on this apartment in Headington is quite reasonable. According to the tenant, we hadn't been the first to view it. Since competition for apartments is so intense in the area, Francis suggests dropping off a letter of interest at the real estate agency. When I mention needing to come to Oxford two weeks prior to occupancy, Sally and Francis look at each other and smile. They have been praying for someone to stay at their home during their family vacation the last two weeks of August. If Michelle and I were to stay at their home and care for a young kitten during these two weeks, our mutual problems would be resolved. I accept the house-sitting offer contingent on securing the apartment.

Committing to the apartment before Michelle receives official school admission is a risk, but the sequence of events during the past three days encourages taking it. On the way back to the bed-and-breakfast, I slip a letter signed Chris Williams through the mail slot at the real estate agency.

When the agency reopens, Michelle and I are waiting at the door to stake our claim to the Headington apartment. If the agent requests passport identification, the deal will be off. Registering our legal name and address would be too risky. The agent accepts the nonrefundable fee, which holds the apartment until two weeks before occupancy. No identification is requested, but it helps to deal in cash. The leasing contract, in the name of Chris Williams, will be ready for signing then, when the six months' deposit will be due.

A few days in Oxford have yielded new friends, a place to live, a house-sitting offer to facilitate the timing of our move, and unofficial admission to Emmanuel Christian School. God has gone beyond confirming the wet and dry fleeces. Through Michelle's steps, God directed us to the window of a real estate agency, to a playground, and possibly to other Divine appointments whose purposes are not yet evident. The appointment by the swings would have been lost in the sands of time if my willfulness had prevailed—a poignant lesson for the future.

EARLY ONE MORNING IN MID-AUGUST THE THREE BLACK BAGS are once again lined up in Janet's hall, waiting for an all-day train ride to Oxford. Saying goodbye to Janet, I momentarily lose my nerve. Perhaps leaving the security of Janet's support to strike out toward unfamiliar surroundings is foolhardy, a decision we will regret. The Oxford apartment will be unbearably lonely after weeks of daily exposure to Janet's friendship.

At the Waverly Station in Edinburgh, I heave our bags, one by one, onto a luggage cart, heaping tote bags on top. One holds a round metal tray decorated with birds, a gift from Scotland for my mother. The cart lumbers along under its heavy burden until a jerk sends the tray skimming across the terrazzo floor like a stone on water, creating such a clamor that all eyes in the waiting room turn in our direction. Being the focus of attention in a travel center filled with Americans is as jarring for me as the noise had been for them.

When I ask the conductor about where to put our bags, he shakes his head, knowing, as I do, that they are too heavy for the overhead racks and too large for the floor space between the seats. The end-of-season luggage fills the racks at the ends of the train cars. After confirming that our destination involves no changes, he motions me to follow him toward the end of the train. Opening the mail car, he heaves our bags inside. Indiscreetly, I swear that no bombs have been concealed in these bags. When I express concern about the security of our luggage, the conductor assures me that they will be safe traveling with the mail and are too heavy to "walk away."

On the train, an English couple who have been on vacation in Scotland sit down next to us. By initiating conversation, I learn that they live in Headington, a few doors from our apartment.

Sitting next to future neighbors confirms the move to Oxford once again.

Knowing that the train remains at Oxford for only a few minutes before departing for Reading, Michelle and I are the first passengers on the platform. Our bags will end up in London unless I quickly locate a conductor to retrieve them from the mail car. At first, the conductor doesn't take me seriously. "Luggage isn't stowed in the mail car," he says, ready to brush me off. When I persist, he follows me to the back of the train and opens the mail car to reveal three black bags. Through the iron fencing, Sally, Hannah, and Rachel are standing by their station wagon, ready to receive us and our bulky load. The stress of saying goodbye to Janet, the exhaustion of heaving bags, and the melancholy of arriving at a city that is having its first downpour in weeks all combine to generate doubts about making Oxford our new home. The warm hospitality of the Pritties' home puts things right again.

NOW THAT I CONDUCT FINANCES IN TRAVELERS CHEQUES, I'M no longer accustomed to carrying large amounts of cash: pounds sterling this time. On the short bus ride from the bank to the real estate agency, I become uneasy for another reason. If passport identification is required when I sign the leasing contract, the apartment will have to be sacrificed.

Initially, the real estate agent counts a stack of pound notes, more than fifty of them. Minutes drag on precariously as she sorts through the paperwork. I glance at the wall clock to ease apprehension. All plans for living in Oxford are in the balance until the contract is signed. If the words "Can I see your passport, Mrs. Williams?" are voiced, all would be lost. Eventually, I hear the words I have been waiting for: "Mrs. Williams, please sign here." I leave the office with a contract, legally significant for Chris Williams, whoever he or she may be.

After an orientation on the workings of their house, the Pritties depart on vacation. Since I'm allergic to cats, Michelle takes charge of the kitten, a role that she happily assumes. Within a few days, living in close proximity to the kitten produces an allergic reaction, but road-map-like, itchy eyes are a small price to pay for a lovely place to stay during a time of need.

A portion of every day is spent exploring Oxford, usually ending up downtown to purchase items for our new home while resisting Michelle's pressure to purchase a school uniform before receiving official acceptance. Telephoning the secretary to the board of directors confirms that official acceptance won't occur until they meet again, just prior to the beginning of the school year.

Frequently, shopping trips conclude with ice cream under our birch tree in the Botanic Gardens, where we watch boaters maneuver through the water. Some struggle with entangling the pole in tree branches or the mud, making little progress through the water while expending a great amount of effort. Michelle and I giggle impatiently at their clumsiness. Later, I am humbled when my ineptness at handling the pole makes the children in my boat wonder if they will ever return to the boathouse.

AT THE BEGINNING OF SEPTEMBER, SALLY MOVES US AND OUR black bags into our new apartment. Both of us walk through it, praying for God's protection in every room. The horror of a police officer or a private investigator knocking on our door flashes across my mental screen. Sally's prayer for halting the mildew advance in the bathroom jerks me back to reality. Only one person knocks at our door on this first day in our new home: one of the board members, who delivers the official letter of Michelle's acceptance at Emmanuel Christian School.

Carrying one's house is self-limiting. Moving is transformed when possessions fit into three bags; everything is unpacked and arranged within a few hours. I wonder if I will remember the freedom and enjoyment of owning fewer possessions when we return to America and the opportunity to stockpile is restored.

It's not known how many cloaks hung on the hooks above where Jesus slept, or whether He packed a bag when visiting friends in a distant village, but He did instruct His disciples on how to pack for a preaching tour: "Do not acquire gold or silver or copper for your money belts; or a bag for your journey, or even two tunics or sandals or a staff; for the worker is worthy of his support" (Matt. 10:9–10).

ON THE FIRST DAY OF SCHOOL, MICHELLE AND I BOARD A double-decker bus at the stop outside our door for a thirty-minute ride that takes us within two blocks of the school. All the children in Michelle's class are younger, but a friendship forms on the first day with another American girl, Stephanee, who is also a newcomer to Oxford.

Michelle's school attendance is a treat for both of us. What a delicious feeling it is to walk along a street alone, popping into a shop without resistant discussion from my daughter. What enjoyment it is to seek a workout gym, a salon for haircuts, and a shop to buy coffee on my own! A search of secondhand shops turns up a small black-and-white TV for our Friday night celebrations, now moved to Saturday, a more celebratory night for BBC programming.

Once Michelle settles in at school, she begins taking dance lessons, which have become a canary-in-the-coal-mine indicator of this journey. If and when resources are no longer available for this privilege, the viability of the journey is at stake. I shall return to America before depriving Michelle of safe housing, good nutrition, schooling, and her treasured dance lessons. A question sits on the back shelf of my mind, one which I periodically remove and examine in the light of prayer. Is Michelle's life more secure in hiding with me than it would be living in America in the open?

Desiring an evening of entertainment other than television and pizza, I accompany the Coupers to a performance of Dvořák's *From the New World* symphony at the seventeenth-century Sheldonian Theater, where Oxford University graduations are held. As we sit in a hall inspired by a Roman amphitheater, the guest artist, Scottish percussionist Evelyn Glennie, tunes the kettle drums. Stretching to lean out over the drum, Ms. Glennie, who is deaf, presses her body on the surface to feel the vibrations. With fingertips resting on the drumhead, she listens through her fingernails for fine-tuning adjustments. Her second performance is as stellar as the preparatory one has been, bold percussion lighter than the clouds painted on the theater's ceiling. Hearing the familiar refrain of the *From the New World* symphony, the melancholy notes "Daa . . . dee . . . daa, daa . . . dee . . . daa," I recall lyrics that Dvořák lifted from slave songs in America: "Goin' home . . . goin' home . . . Yes, I'm goin' home." Throughout the evening, these words strike a harmonious triad chord of body, soul, and spirit. Michelle and I will return to America someday, but goin' home may be a long time comin'.

Now that false hopes and pipe dreams are draining from the pit of reality, expectations of spending birthdays and holidays in America don't provoke desperate phone calls home for an update on Jim's condition. Recent news from America has been more speculative than substantive. Little is known about Jim's life, his health, or how vigorously he is searching for us. I know that Gabriella in Italy and Janet in Scotland, both known to Jim, have not been contacted.

ONCE LIFE IN OXFORD SETTLES INTO A ROUTINE, THE SWIRLING waters of survival, which have kept the adrenaline pumping, diminish. Gone is the security of being on the move. The predictability of staying put threatens our safety, particularly in a city frequented by American tourists. Every day I look into their faces, hoping against recognition, but the faces who see me without my seeing them worry me the most.

The boggy pit of resignation is pockmarked with depressions that engulf unstructured time like quicksand. I express to Linda, a friend and teacher at Emmanuel, the frustration of living in a city rich with bibliographic resources but being unable to access them for researching my thesis. She introduces me to a friend, Andrew, an academic affiliated with Oxford University.

In a former Victorian residence that has been converted to university offices, I explain why it would be difficult for me to obtain a reader's card, even though I am (or have been) a bona fide graduate student in America. Andrew informs me that obtaining a card requires passport identification. Registration could be risky if someone at the university were to contact San Francisco State University for verification. Until now, I have been careful not to leave a paper trail of my true name, except on immigration and Moneygram forms.

After a night of pondering the possible consequences of this application, I compose a letter of request, including my passport number as well as outlining my thesis topic. Accompanied by Andrew's letter of recommendation, the application is submitted. Prepared to lay aside a rule I had pledged allegiance to at the beginning of the journey, I sense a greater need within me: fulfilling intellectual work. I feel that the neurons of my brain are lounging around, no longer snapping to attention. My contemporaries, all the other forty-four-year-olds in the world, are going forward with their lives as I slip farther behind in mine. A week later, I receive a reader's card with privileges to use one of the most outstanding libraries in the world. I read articles about fava beans and favism at a long table with a leather inset top in the reading room of the Radcliffe Camera. For the first time in years, the potential exists to make this journey count toward professional goals.

———

ALTHOUGH FRIENDS AND ACTIVITIES ABOUND IN OXFORD, loneliness stalks me, particularly on Sundays, when the daily routine is suspended. From the church pew, I stare at the injunctions inscribed at the top of the stained-glass windows: IN FAITH, OBEY. IN FAITH, ENDURE. IN FAITH, PRAY. I have obeyed; I am enduring; and I am praying that God, the One who has the power to change the course of the future, will resolve our situation. Our second Christmas season while on the run is approaching. My heart aches to relax at my parents' home with a cup of coffee, hear my name called every day, and smile at the future. Sitting reverently in the church service, inside I'm wrestling with God to reveal some sprigs of hope from the crevasses of a landscape void of future plans. Jacob, during the loneliest time of his life when he was separated from his family and fleeing from the wrath of his brother, Esau, wrestled with God in the flesh all through the night. At daybreak, Jacob's endurance paid off when the blessing was received, but his life would never be the same. He received a new name, Israel, and would limp to his grave, thanks to a dislocated hip joint (Gen. 32:24–29).

As I stand for the last hymn, I'm astonished that my hip joint supports me. Why had it been necessary for Jacob to strive with both God and man at the same time? I ask myself. I'm fed up with striving to understand God's timing and purpose. I want it to be over. Like the limited shelf life of manna in the wilderness, hope can't be stockpiled for the future. But, like Jacob, I don't depart from God's presence empty-hearted, but receive a momentary dispensation of hope from God's unlimited supply.

SEVERAL MONTHS INTO THE SCHOOL YEAR, MICHELLE'S teacher, Sally Stokes, and I plan an evening get-together, more for the purpose of becoming better acquainted than a parent-teacher conference. Earlier in the school year, Sally had reported that Michelle was adjusting well in the class and that her academic progress was steady and good.

"You really are an adventurer, aren't you?" Sally states, more as a matter of fact than a question.

"Not by nature, but I'm becoming one. I feel restless when I stay in one place too long."

"You've only just arrived in Oxford. Are you thinking of leaving already?"

"Leaving is always on my mind. If our safety were threatened, we would leave within minutes. Whatever happens, less than three months remain on our tourist visas for the United Kingdom."

"There must be a way to stay in the United Kingdom to allow Michelle to complete this year of schooling. If you need to know where you stand legally, I know a trustworthy lawyer who could advise you."

"I don't see how he could help me. Overstaying could mean deportation if I'm caught. Staying in the United Kingdom would necessitate leaving the country and risking reentry."

"Taking the ferry to France could solve the visa problem. Another six months in the U.K. would allow you time to catch your breath in Oxford."

"Sally, I'm not sure that I want to catch my breath. I'm more comfortable when we are on the move, but for Michelle's sake I have to stay put for as long as possible."

"Chris, you may find it difficult to adjust to normal living again, once all this is over."

Returning to life as it was in America becomes more challenging with every new country of residence. A restless spirit accompanies me everywhere.

THE BBC TELEVISION SERIES *CLASSIC ADVENTURES* BECOMES regular viewing. Since leaving San Francisco, I have called our travels an "adventure," although, more recently, Michelle refers to it as "our journey around the world." This TV show documents ordeals about solo sailors traversing oceans, climbers conquering mountains, and trekkers crossing deserts, but never the ordeal of a fugitive running with a child.

Common threads run through all the adventures: risk, uncertainty, endurance, and perseverance. All the television adventurers express feelings of isolation, loneliness, or wanting to be elsewhere, particularly toward the end of their journeys. When all comfort is gone, obsessions develop: the sailor dreams of a hot bath; the trekker in the desert thirsts for ice-cold water. Weariness dulls the threat of risks during the ordeal. The long-distance biker in America slumps onto the handlebars from sleep deprivation, threatening to swerve off the road. Reaching the goal is all that matters. Exhilaration, as well as the sweat of exhaustion, shines from the faces of these television adventurers who have been pushed beyond their natural limits. All leaned on the support of others to reach their goals.

If our adventure were depicted on *Classic Adventures*, it might be represented by a round-the-world sack race, with two unmatched legs running in one sack. Hearts and hands reach out to us from the sidelines, cheering us on, extending the glass of water when needed, or offering a supportive arm when my steps falter. There have been too many helps to consider them coincidental. An unseen advance team has been mobilizing support at each and every turn. An unseen Hand has been holding mine. Breaking through the barriers of my natural limits has allowed me to tap into God's stamina, receiving power that is perfected in weakness.

9

Crushed Grapes

Whether the Cup with sweet or bitter run,
The Wine of Life keeps oozing drop by drop . . .
—*The Rubáiyát of Omar Khayyám*

ON MY GRANDMOTHER'S BIRTHDAY, FOUR DAYS AFTER CHRIST-mas, Michelle and I board the ferry at Portsmouth for Le Havre in France. Leaving the United Kingdom (for a brief time) is imperative to remaining here—legally. Michelle and I stand in line with passengers who have presumably spent Christmas in the U.K. and are returning to the Continent for the New Year. For us, this crossing is the initial leg of a scouting mission to YWAM in Switzerland. The immigration officer looks at my passport, but he doesn't hand it back immediately as he has to the others in front of me.

With official sternness, he asks, "Do you realize that your tourist visa for the United Kingdom expired seven days ago?"

"Umm . . . yes. When I was planning this trip, I didn't think that a week would make that much difference." The look on his face communicates that I made the wrong response, even though it had been the truth.

"Not paying attention to dates stamped in your passport can

make a big difference. There are no grace periods for immigration visas."

"I'm sorry that we didn't leave on December 22, but I wanted to spend Christmas with friends in the U.K. before traveling to France," I respond, checking my inclination to explain more than is necessary or prudent.

A warm flush creeps up my neck as the delay causes the people behind me to shuffle impatiently. After reiterating several times the importance of honoring the passport visa dates, the officer returns our passports. With this encounter, the risk of deportation has doubled; immigration problems can occur when leaving a country, as well as entering.

A TOURIST BUS TOUR ISN'T MY FIRST CHOICE FOR SEEING Paris, but it's an expeditious way to spend the afternoon here with a seven-year-old. On this day, New Year's Eve, Michelle could outwalk me through the streets of Paris. Recovering from the flu, a bus tour is all that I can manage. Taking Michelle to the Eiffel Tower had been a journey objective before leaving America, in addition to seeing Gabriella in Italy and Janet in Scotland. The last day of 1991 holds fascinating juxtapositions of place: gazing up at the Eiffel Tower, dining at the marketplace where Joan of Arc was martyred, and returning to a bed-and-breakfast in Rouen where a king of France had stayed. It saddens me that Michelle won't remember all that she has been privileged to see.

Toward midnight, Michelle and I hear firecrackers and merrymaking from the street. Even the family who owns the bed-and-breakfast is having a party below us. The whole world is partying without us, but staying up to welcome the first minutes of the New Year seems pointless. This time last year in Italy I would never have imagined the two of us in France, listening to New Year celebrations from our beds in the dark.

The TGV from Paris to Lausanne speeds so rapidly that the

stones alongside the track are a blur. In July 1992, six months from now, Crossroads, a discipleship training school for students thirty-five and older, will be offered at the YWAM base in Switzerland. The name of the course is intriguing, since our lifestyle is perpetually at a crossroads, and the YWAM leaders encourage me to apply. Decisions regarding applications will be made later in the spring, but my acceptance seems likely. In Switzerland, immigration visas are for three months, but leaving the country even for a brief time extends the visa another three months. The course lasts six months and begins three days before our forthcoming U.K. immigration visas will expire.

Walking through the forest trails next to the base, Michelle and I view the chalet from a new perspective. The prospect of attending the YWAM-sponsored French-speaking school excites Michelle, who already knows some of the pupils, children of the YWAM staff. Learning to speak French is a carrot for her, plus living at the chalet. During past visits to the base, receiving kind attention from the young people attending the training schools has delighted her. For me, survival is the primary, though not the exclusive objective for living at a familiar place. Getting to know God better is a strong secondary consideration. Other Crossroads students may be more focused in their spiritual goals, but none will be singular in their decision. Trust is gradually being restored through God's protection and provision, which is reinforced daily. The accumulation of these blessings is wooing me back into the circle of His love. Spiritual ground, lost to the enemy through disappointment, is being reclaimed.

ON THE RETURN FERRY TO ENGLAND, THE U.K. IMMIGRATION officer thumbs through my passport, asking few questions as he checks the date stamps. When the customary questions come, his terse comments cause my palms to dampen. Any attempt on my part to lighten or divert his line of questioning is met with a piercing stare. Feeling exposed, I want to run for cover, but Michelle and I are an hour out of port on the English Channel. Other non-European Community passport holders are fidgeting in the line behind us. The officer announces that he will need to keep my passport, instructing me to return in one hour's time. In two years of traveling on the run, my passport has never left my possession, except momentarily across a counter to immigration officers and American Express agents. Stripped of it, the journey is arrested.

As Michelle and I move restlessly around the ferry, I pray for God's intervention. For all I know, the officer could be notifying officials in Portsmouth to arrange our detention, which would result in deportation. There's no doubt that he suspects me of something. If he checks my passport number against an international list of felons (which undoubtedly exists in some computer file), his suspicions will be validated.

Sixty minutes later, when I step up to the immigration window, the officer's questions target the fact that we haven't returned to the U.S.A. in two years. Although I stick to my story of researching a graduate thesis, he's not convinced.

"How does your daughter's father feel about your taking her away for such a long time?"

"Well, it's a long story." I want to proclaim that her father is dead, but I would be unable to bear the look on Michelle's confused face caused by such a lie. The officer would notice it as well.

Looking down at Michelle as if reluctant to speak in her presence, I continue, "It's not a problem for her father, but it's difficult to explain at the moment."

Studying a page of the passport, he seems to have another question on the tip of his tongue, but it stays there. The questions halt above the din of the ferry's engines. I'm immobilized without our passports and fear that the slightest twitch of my body will tip the scales in Jim's favor. Only my eyes follow his hand as it moves toward the stamp, hesitating in midair. Then I hear the blessed *plonk-plonk*, which frees us to live six more months in the United Kingdom. I check myself from offering exuberant gratitude, and walk away as if no crisis has been averted.

While Michelle watches a video in the children's room, I go to the cafeteria for a cup of coffee. The immigration officer approaches me, holding a coffee cup. Perhaps he has reconsidered, but the passports have been stamped. He offers to buy me a drink, but I decline the offer, being on guard against social interaction. Apprehensively, I ask if he is on a work break to ascertain whether he is approaching me on official business or speaking off the record.

As I expected, he's on a work break. With no forewarning, he asks, "Are you involved in a custody battle? Are you running from your daughter's father?"

As one lie begets another, I blurt out, "Oh no. I'm not running from anyone." Judging from his expression, I haven't convinced him this second time that my daughter and I are on a carefree world tour.

Desperate to change the subject and to stave off any interest he might have in getting to know me better, I mention how my faith in God has sustained me during my travels. Although he acknowledges that having faith in God is a good thing, he concedes, "It's too late for me." This is a topic I can run with and not away from. Our conversation takes no more menacing turns, at least not for me.

THE EXHILARATION OF WALKING OFF THE FERRY ONTO THE home soil of England fades quickly. In the aftermath of the adrenaline surge during the crisis on the ferry, fatigue turns my arms and legs to Silly Putty. At 10 P.M., the bed-and-breakfasts in Portsmouth are either without vacancies or not interested in taking guests at this late hour. One guest house says no but to call back if I'm stuck without a place to stay. When I do, persistence pays off. Outside the ferry terminal in the dark and misting rain,

I hire a cab to take us to the guest house. Michelle's exhaustion produces instantaneous sleep. I lay awake, wondering if my limbs will recover by the next morning to permit us to catch a train for Oxford.

At breakfast, Michelle announces to everyone that today is her eighth birthday and that she will be having a party later in January. The guest house owners present her a gift—a handkerchief embroidered with lilies of the valley.

A WEEK LATER IN OXFORD, DURING A TELEPHONE CONVERSATION with Janet, I mention our close call on the ferry. Janet, aware of our return to the United Kingdom, had been attending a wedding in York at the time.

"Chris, what time was your passport withheld?" she asks purposefully.

"Let's see . . . The ferry left Le Havre about 4:45 P.M., so it must have been about 6 P.M."

"At about that time, I was in the hotel room, getting ready for dinner. Chris, I became so worried about your well-being that I knelt by the bed, praying for your protection, sensing that you might be having difficulties reentering the United Kingdom."

The electrifying power of the Holy Spirit crackles on the telephone line, causing me to put my hand over my mouth in awe of how, through the prayer of a dear friend, God saved us from deportation.

THE ENCOUNTER ON THE FERRY HAS QUICKENED AN URGENCY to know where I stand with U.K. immigration. During an appointment with the lawyer Sally Stokes had recommended last autumn, I divulge the legalities of my situation, my defiance of a court order to remain in San Francisco, and the child abduction charges Jim initiated after our fleeing. He confirms that these criminal charges would block employment in the U.K., even if my skills were unique enough to justify my being awarded a job over a British citizen. He warns me to be out of the United Kingdom before July 4, and to stay away for at least three months, the longer the better. A third tourist visa would not be issued after a short stay in another country. If I decide to over-stay, the risk of deportation would increase and lock us into staying in the U.K. for the duration of the journey, just as leav-ing could be closing the door on ever returning to the U.K. Only one scenario provides legal justification for staying: mar-riage to a citizen of the U.K. Both of us agree that this solution could cause more problems than it solves.

The inner turmoil of facing difficult decisions takes a physical toll. Without treatment, the stomach pains have intensified since the encounter with immigration on the ferry. The acid-reducing medicine prescribed in Italy was consumed months ago. One afternoon while shopping, the severity of the pain suspends our errands. On the walk home, Michelle and I meet a friend, who is the mother of a schoolmate and whose husband is a physician. Later that evening, she phones with a recommendation for a doctor in my neighborhood, a friend of her husband's. If I'm unable to obtain an appointment the next day, using her hus-band's name as a reference, I'm to call her back.

Throughout the evening, Michelle watches me bending in pain, the milk and antacids giving little relief. Her memory flashes back to Italy, when I was doubled over with pain in the school parking lot and taken to the hospital. Her emotions erupt like a geyser as she rocks back and forth on her heels, sobbing, "Mommy, I don't want to be left alone. I want Jesus to take care of me if you go to the hospital. I want Him to stay with me." Over and over again, she expresses her fear of being alone and her frustration at not seeing Jesus in person. Both of us cling to the hope of a medical appointment the next day, but staying out of the hospital until then is critical to Michelle's peace of mind.

Registering for medical care is a risk, but the pain leaves me no choice. The next afternoon at the local clinic I sit alone with the clipboard and the form, deciding to register as Chris Williams, a transient nonresident. After I explain the circumstances of my life, this compassionate physician prescribes the medication I need and opens the door of his clinic for Chris Williams to return as needed.

ON THE SECOND ANNIVERSARY OF OUR DEPARTURE, NEWS from America reports that Jim is beginning to have health problems. Although my interest in Jim's health for the past two years has arisen more from malevolence than goodwill, sadness, not joy, overwhelms me. Without mentioning Michelle's abuse, I write Jim a letter expressing sadness at how life has turned out for both of us and for our daughter. Sending it to my parents via a contact, I doubt that the letter will go any farther. My writing such a letter to Jim will be difficult for them to understand. The pain of separation from their only child and grandchild has been almost more than they can bear; moreover, they haven't been insulated from Jim's hurtful actions and angry words, as I have been on this journey. Repeatedly, when Jim telephones, my parents have pleaded with him to let us return to America. Jim's defiance rings in their ears, as he has regularly said to them, "I want full custody of Ellen."

Returning to America could happen at any moment, or it could happen years from now. When blindfolded to the amount of time left as a fugitive, I grope for plans as if playing an existential blindman's bluff. The uncertainty keeps me dithering about whether to commit myself to a six-month YWAM school. The news about Jim's health puts me into a mental holding pattern on life. Although the application and references were submitted to YWAM months ago, the deposit is outstanding. I look to America for direction, but guidance unfolds on this side of the Atlantic.

THE GRAY SKIES OF WINTER ARE BRIGHTENED BY THE LOVING concern of a woman who sits with us at church. Madge, who is the same age as my mother, relates to us from a grandmother's and a mother's heart. Our friendship commences when Madge invites us to her home after church to taste cooking from her homeland, Jamaica. Sunday after Sunday, Madge speaks with the conviction of one whom God has brought through pain to the joy on the other side, "Mark my words, Chris, God will plead your cause," quoting verses from Psalm 35, a prayer of rescue from one's enemies.

"Chris, God is on the job. Tell Him your heart and leave it with Him. Mary became a fugitive to save her Son. You are doing the same thing for your lovely daughter. Mark my words, God is pleading your cause."

Madge is right. God is on the job, working in Michelle's life, as well as my own. Michelle's eyes are opened to the truth during an eight-hour stomach virus, whose symptoms make her the sickest she has been on this journey. Staying close by her side, I find my attentive care reaps more fruit than I could imagine.

When the symptoms are gone by evening, Michelle declares matter-of-factly, "Mommy, you have been taking care of me all around the world. You have to think of so many things. It's like Paul Daniels, but only a bigger magic trick."

I am overwhelmed at being compared to Paul Daniels, whose television tricks of illusion awe Michelle every Saturday evening. During these past two years, Michelle hasn't acknowledged any appreciation of the difficulties I've faced. Although I had cared for her during illnesses in San Francisco, her medical care had been orchestrated by her father. Successfully caring for her on my own has earned respect and gratitude, previously reserved exclusively for him.

A mellowing in our relationship occurs. Whenever I am tempted to respond to Michelle in anger, I remember my status as being on a par with Paul Daniels. Reduced defenses on both sides lead to my telling Michelle more of our situation: how I broke the law by going against her father's wishes and the judge's decision when I took her away and now, for this action, I risk being sentenced to prison when we return to America. Michelle needs to know how things stand, particularly if I'm arrested and she is taken from me without warning. Bestowing on her these confidences releases her compassion toward me, empowering her to make a difference in my life on this journey. Thereafter, perceiving that I need encouragement, Michelle pats my arm saying, "Mommy, it will be OK," just as she had said during the first tentative days in New Zealand.

DURING THE SPRING OF 1992, MICHELLE AND I ATTEND A church meeting to hear Jackie Pullinger, a British woman who established a drug addiction rehabilitation program in the Walled City of Hong Kong. As a young single woman, she had left Great Britain to serve God, not knowing where she was going. When God directed her to leave the ship in Hong Kong, she brought the hope of Christ's saving power to heroin addicts and prostitutes.

Focusing her talk on the Good Samaritan, she encourages every Christian to use their own donkey for helping others, rather than calling on and expecting the church donkey to do what needs to be done. For the first time since leaving San Francisco, I envision a Divine purpose behind this journey, a spiritual parallax viewing the fears, pain, and weariness from a new perspective. None of our experiences will be wasted, as Michelle and I equip a donkey for helping others who travel along this path. God's power is uniquely aimed to turn evil intent into good, and no story in the Old Testament communicates this truth more dramatically than the saga of Joseph, the son of Jacob, in Genesis 37.

Sold into slavery by his brothers, Joseph prospered in Egypt, attaining a position of authority in Pharaoh's household through God's favor. When Joseph ignored the sexual advances of his boss's wife, she used deception to send him to prison for doing the right thing. When the potential for release finally arrived, God failed to jog the memory of the cup bearer whose job had been restored by Joseph's interpretation of a dream. Joseph spent another two years in the dungeon.

Evil intent was again turned inside out when Joseph's freedom was restored and his position elevated to ruler. As the dispenser of grain during a famine, Joseph spoke to his desperate and hungry brothers: "And as for you, you meant evil against me, but God meant it for good in order to bring about this present result, to preserve many people alive" (Gen. 50:20). Although I don't want to go to prison, the bottom line of God's power is drawn at His ability to use even a prison sentence for good.

Soon after Jackie Pullinger's talk, a television documentary stirs up my passion about equipping a "donkey" for serving others in the future. The BBC production, *Why Women Kill*, interviews women in American prisons who are serving prison terms for murdering a man, usually a husband, to protect themselves and/or their children. In all cases, prolonged abuse has been a factor. Pacing before the television, my heart aches for these women, isolated from their families and cut off from nurturing their children. Someday I may know their pain. Child abduction, like murder, is a felony.

WITH LESS THAN TWO MONTHS REMAINING BEFORE CROSS-roads begins, the nonrefundable deposit is mailed to YWAM and I notify the real estate agency that we'll be leaving the apartment. When the dithering about the future ends, my migraine headaches ease. Michelle looks forward to reconnecting with a YWAM base where she has fond memories, and I anticipate the discipleship school as preparation, spiritual conditioning, for what is to come in America.

About this time, we receive a large box from my parents: gifts of clothes and jewelry, sections of my graduate thesis, stickers of horses for Michelle, bits and pieces from America. Per my instructions, the parcel had been sent to someone in Colorado, who had sent it on to Linda, our mutual friend in Oxford. Gifts we can see and touch reconnect us after telephone conversations have faded. Even the local newspaper my mother had used for packing is saved and read.

Ordinarily, a notice in the church bulletin about a counseling seminar in Oxford wouldn't catch my eye, but seeing that the speaker, Professor David Seamands, is an American theologian from a seminary located a few miles from my parents' home, I register.

On the first evening of the Christian counseling conference, home comes to me through the speaker's Kentucky accent. On learning from his wife that her father had been the minister of my grandmother's church, I feel as if family has arrived. I tell the Seamands the circumstances of our coming to Oxford, and they offer to contact my parents once Michelle and I have left Oxford. Later, without mentioning times and places, Professor and Mrs. Seamands have dinner with my parents in Kentucky, reassuring them that good things are taking place in our lives, a witness that gives my parents hope.

Through the conference, I get to know Helen, who is a member of our church and a counselor whose ministry prompts Christians to listen quietly for God to speak to their spirits. We meet for a morning prayer retreat in the pastoral setting of an Oxfordshire village. After praying together, we withdraw separately to listen to God and meditate on a passage from Ephesians:

> that the God of our Lord Jesus Christ, the Father of glory, may give to you a spirit of wisdom and of revelation in the knowledge of Him. I pray that the eyes of your heart may be enlightened, so that you may know what is the hope of His calling, what are the riches of the glory of His inheritance in the saints, and what is the surpassing greatness of His power toward us who believe. (Eph. 1:17–19a)

The word "inheritance" stands out from the passage, not from a monetary standpoint but from the inheritance of time spent with my family. Deprived of savoring the last years of their lives, never knowing when any of them could pass on into eternity without a goodbye, I grieve the loss of these riches and resist placing them in God's keeping.

As I sit alone with my Bible, the quietness is disrupted by restlessness from within, which challenges even keeping my body still. Daydreaming, a tension-reliever since childhood, has become a lost art. Not even physical exhaustion calms the internal revolutions of my spirit. Helen prays for the liberation of sparkle and vitality in my life, which are being held hostage by a restless spirit.

Helen wisely recognizes that fun revitalizes the body and soul, as prayer does the spirit. On several occasions, the elegant sitting rooms of Oxford's Randolph Hotel are our venue for "fun" and coffee. On another day, we enjoy tea and crumpets at a hotel in the Cotswolds after praying together in a fifteenth-century church; since moving to Oxford, my heart's desire has been to revisit these villages, which I had seen on my solo trip to England ten years before. As the Scripture had called for, the eyes of my heart are being enlightened; God hears the cries of my heart, and they matter to Him.

Several days before we leave Oxford for Switzerland, a friend stops by to bring a parting gift and a gift of Scripture as a prescription for the weariness engraved on my face: "Come unto Me, all who are weary and heavy-laden, and I will give you rest" (Matt. 11:28). Although I'm too preoccupied with carrying the load to accept rest, Jesus stands ready to be yoked into carrying my burdens, whenever I let go of them.

LEAVING THE U.K. FIVE DAYS BEFORE THE VISA EXPIRES RAISES no objections from immigration. On the flight to Zurich, I am insecure about being the only single parent in Crossroads, or on the YWAM base for that matter. Although Michelle and I have not lived communally, living in the chalet couldn't be more difficult than living in someone's home and worrying about disrupting their privacy. Will I have the energy to deepen my relationship with God, with Michelle, and with other Crossroaders, as well as attend to communal chores and care for our needs? This agenda bespeaks exhaustion. To Swiss immigration in Zurich, I present a letter acknowledging registration in YWAM's six-month course.

Michelle and I settle into our own room on the top floor of the chalet with an expansive view of the French Alps.

During the opening worship service, with the group of thirty students representing eleven countries, I share verses from Ezekiel 34:26–27, verses of hope and restoration farther along in the chapter which had been so important to me before leaving San Francisco. Although nothing (that I can tell) is trumpeting the advent of showers of blessings, the revelation of timing belongs to God.

During the mornings, speakers from around the world deliver a week of topical lectures. The afternoons are spent attending small group meetings, as well as performing assigned chores. One weekend a month every Crossroader signs up for kitchen duty on a rota basis to relieve the weekday kitchen staff, a policy I will come to cherish.

While I attend classes and meetings, Michelle spends time in childcare with children of other staff members. Once school begins in September, the French language becomes an end in itself to Michelle, not an obstacle to education. An English-speaking friend in her class translates instructions from Michelle's teacher, who speaks no English. Switzerland fits Michelle like a glove: the lyrical language, ice-skating as part of the school curriculum, the snow-covered mountains, the liveliness of the YWAM base, and a cuisine that leans on bread, chocolate, and cheese.

Spiritual expectations before coming to Crossroads had been for inner healing through the process of forgiving Jim, but God has different expectations for my spirit. One of the school speakers, who has experienced the death of a son, gives me words from the book *Don't Waste Your Sorrows* by Paul Billheimer.

One is not broken until all resentment and rebellion against God and man is removed. One who resents, takes offense, or retaliates against criticism and opposition or lack of appreciation is unbroken. All self-justification and self-defense betrays an unbroken spirit. All discontent and irritation with providential circumstances and situations reveals unbrokenness. Genuine brokenness usually requires years of crushing, heartache, and sorrow. Thus are self-will surrendered and deep degrees of yieldedness and submission developed, without which there is little agape love.

Many years ago in San Francisco, I had a vivid dream where a hand had been squeezing a cluster of grapes and the extract of their juice had flowed into a chalice. Although the dream had seemed significant at the time, its meaning had been puzzling. Now, sixteen years later, the gist of this dream is depicted on a wall at YWAM through a painting by a Norwegian pastor. I understand that the integrity of the grapes is enhanced through their yielding to the Divine purpose of becoming wine, and so it is when my yielded spirit is crushed by the hand of God to produce a precious flow. In the Scriptures, so many spiritual elements are described as being poured out like wine: the Holy Spirit, the blood of Christ, the faith and service of believers, and the love of God. Can the crushing blows in life work to one's advantage, becoming a splendid vintage when the extract is placed in the hands of the Divine Vintner?

I read about Job, who is the epitome of a broken spirit, though not initially. Brokenness occurred when Job closed his mouth and opened his ears to God's revelations. When Job admitted to "knowing too little and talking too much," he lost his desire to complain, and to negotiate his own terms with God. If a broken bone heals incorrectly, it must be reset, often becoming stronger than before the break. God doesn't break our spirit to reset it. The broken spirit remains broken, for this is its strength; pride (defined as sufficiency without God) tends to reset it.

As I run after happiness, clinging to bulky expectations, Christian joy is defined as suffering pain with a good attitude. Does a broken spirit turn the tables on the spiritual law which says that only bone-crushing sorrow produces inner strength? Certainly, nonbroken spirits respond to God's nudgings only when their backs are against the wall of despair, but what freedom it would be to learn as much from pleasure as from pain!

A spiritual breakthrough occurs when a Crossroads speaker prays individually for us during corporate worship, calling us to the front for prayer as the Holy Spirit directs through our hearts. When the speaker mentions the past attaching itself to our lives as a leech that can suck vitality from the present, I step forward for prayer. No perceptible physical change occurs initially, but slowly over the course of months the revving in my spirit that has blocked relaxation subsides.

The key to maintaining a broken spirit is tossing away my own agenda to assume one planned by the God who created time and who knows the present, past, and future. To make certain that I heed the point, one of the final speakers in Crossroads focuses on the forty years of wanderings by the Israelites in the wilderness, a journey that should have lasted weeks. The prideful spirits of the Israelites refused to embrace God's instructions, forgetting how enemies had been swallowed up by the deep, how water had gushed from the desert rock, and how manna had appeared each morning on the ground. Their stubborn choices kept them traveling in circles, or, as the speaker puts it, "taking another lap in the wilderness." Perhaps, in my situation, the consequences of disobedience would mean traveling around the world again in the opposite direction.

Supported by the school leadership, I elect to remain in Lausanne for Michelle's schooling when Crossroaders disperse on mission trips to Egypt, Africa, and Italy in October of 1992. As a kitchen staff member, I assist in preparing meals and balancing the books on food expenditures. I don't like cooking, and the kitchen becomes a bivouac for wilderness training. Although the food on the base is tasty, the availability of fresh vegetables often depends on donations of produce coming through the kitchen door. When baskets of leeks arrive, the European students are delighted, but after weeks of leeks, the gold-digging cousin of an onion has worked its way into every soup, quiche, and stew. When leeks still remain in the pantry, a kitchen worker from Switzerland produces a printed recipe for leek breakfast porridge, which is prepared but rejected by all.

THE COMPLETION OF THE CROSSROADS COURSE AND THE DE-parture of students opens space in the chalet for the next school, a discipleship training school for younger students. One young man, an American from California, becomes a hero in Michelle's female-satiated life. Wanting to spend as much time with Steve as possible, Michelle pleads to eat at his table or hang out with him during free time. Sometimes it's OK, but when it's not, Steve sets boundaries of time and place with firm kindness. For the first time since the experiences with her father, Michelle feels comfortable in a man's company again, receiving from Steve that which had been lost, a restoration of trust. His friendship doesn't disappoint us, as God gently restores my trust as well.

Browsing through an American news magazine in the reading room, I learn of a Swiss-based philanthropic organization, founded by a countess whose goal is to dispatch her fortune to help those who cannot speak up for themselves. She considers children "the voiceless of the world." Once Helen had said to me in Oxford, "Chris, you've earned the right to speak," and I had marked a verse in Proverbs where the mother of King Lemuel (considered to be Solomon) advises her son: "Speak up for those who cannot speak for themselves, for the rights of all who are destitute" (Prov. 31:8). Fear silences some abused children. Others, who speak about their abuse, may not be believed. In an adult-powered legal world, sometimes children are destitute of credibility, particularly if their voice threatens the security of a creditable adult.

The future asserts itself into the present, not only through receiving this vision of megaphoning the voice of abused children when the journey ends, but also through the ticking of passport time in Switzerland. Now that four months have elapsed on our visas, a silent alarm sounds, warning me to make arrangements for the next step. Attending another YWAM school would be too expensive, but perhaps volunteer opportunities exist on bases in other countries. I contact YWAM bases in Ireland and Jamaica, but nothing clicks. Applying to YWAM's hospital ship, I realize that the work economics of a single parent and child aren't compatible with the ship's needs. Our occupation of a family berth would provide only a part-time worker, since much of my work-day would be spent caring for Michelle. I understand these logistics, but time is running out in Switzerland and overstaying isn't an option.

Watching *Anne of Green Gables* videos suggests Nova Scotia as our next country of residence. Halifax is geographically removed from the mainstream of Canada but close enough for trips to the mainland for a rendezvous with my parents, or a visit with a friend from high school who lives in the Horn of the Moon in Vermont.

NOVA SCOTIA AS A POTENTIAL DESTINATION GETS A BOOST during a money pickup trip to Vienna. After a successful money transaction at the American Express office, Michelle and I stand in line for a tour of the Opera House. As we wait for the tour to begin, other tourists push past us in order to be at the front. Annoyed by their disregard for those of us standing in line, I proclaim a biblical truth to the world at large around me, "The last

shall be first and the first shall be last." A man's voice behind me
responds, "But that won't happen until the next age." Frank is a
medical doctor who is studying German in Vienna. When not in
Vienna or visiting his home country, Canada, he works in a missionary hospital in South Africa.

After the Opera House tour, the three of us walk to the Central
Café, where Lenin and Trotsky reputedly played chess. Patrons, in
no hurry to leave, read books and newspapers behind cups of
coffee dolloped with whipped cream. At a grand piano, a musician
plays "Satin Doll," my father's favorite jazz tune. After selecting
flaky, cream-filled pastries from the dessert tray, I talk to Frank
about moving to Canada, without explaining our circumstances.
He agrees that Halifax has the benefit of being less expensive than
an urban area, such as Toronto, and is small enough for us to rely
on public transportation.

Putting the cart before the horse, dinner follows dessert as the
three of us dine at a fifteenth-century tavern in the old city. The
low-timbered ceilings and small rooms compress the hop-
scented air, heated by platters of steaming wiener schnitzel and
the collective body heat of diners who are agreeably escaping
the autumn chill outside. Dinner is hurried by Michelle's tiredness from sight-seeing, walking, and adult conversation. As I
sing the praises of YWAM's MedAir ministry, which flies doctors
into crisis areas, Frank, who is interested in aviation, expresses
interest in visiting us at YWAM in Lausanne. Saying goodbye,
Frank and I swap addresses for exchanging information on
YWAM and Nova Scotia.

ALTHOUGH FRANK HAS WRITTEN ENCOURAGING LETTERS FROM
Vienna about living in Halifax, I have held back from purchasing
air tickets because such an action wouldn't be following my heart.
My heart says that I want to spend Christmas in Scotland with
Janet and to say goodbye to friends in Oxford before crossing the
Atlantic. I recoil at the scenario of arriving in a new country a few

days before our third Christmas away from home to spend the holidays at a bed-and-breakfast in a strange city.

In Lausanne, Michelle and I shop for Christmas gifts. Walking through streets cut from a medieval template, the intersections are fluid, never gridlike. Holiday shapes framed in white lights float above us. The landscape in Switzerland during the wintertime is perpetually in holiday attire: the lace curtains and the carved wooden ornaments against a background of evergreens and snow-covered peaks. I purchase a small white Swiss Army knife with the motif of a cat watching a spider for Michelle and Swiss-made watches for both of us, having them wrapped for opening wherever we are on Christmas morning.

The week before Christmas, when airline seats from Zurich to Heathrow Airport and on to Edinburgh are available, I take them . . . rejecting Nova Scotia for the United Kingdom. Calling Janet in Scotland, I ask her to pray for our admission into the United Kingdom at Heathrow on December 20. Calling Sally Stokes, Michelle's teacher in Oxford, I ask her to inquire whether Michelle could be readmitted to Emmanuel Christian School if immigration grants us six months in the U.K.

On the day of our Lausanne departure, YWAM staff members who plan to remain on the base during Christmas come together for a candlelight breakfast focusing on friendship. Thankfully, Steve left the base for a mission trip to Chile the week before; otherwise, removing Michelle from Switzerland and YWAM would be more painful. Frank arrived the previous day to spend time with us before we leave Switzerland. When the invitation was extended in a letter, I imagined YWAM to be his primary interest in coming to Lausanne, but on his arrival his comments hint that his coming is weighted more in my direction than YWAM's. His offer to accompany us and the three black bags on the train to Zurich is a Godsend.

On the train, I tell Frank about our lives as fugitives. Moved by a desire to protect us, he mentions marriage as a solution. Michelle's mouth falls open and isn't restored to full operation until we have said goodbye to him at the airport terminal gate. The depth of Frank's friendship warms my heart, knowing that I can call on him for any situation. Without Frank's assistance, I could never have gotten everything off the train in time at the airport stop, which would have sent us in a different direction, causing us to miss our flight to England.

At Heathrow, Michelle and I join the long line of Christmas travelers. Heeding legal advice, Michelle and I have been out of the U.K. for six months, but our passports tell the story that we haven't returned to our country of residence in almost three years. Deportation to the U.S.A. remains the greatest threat. When the official thumbs through my passport and asks the usual questions, I respond that I have just completed missionary training in Switzerland. Hopefully, he will relate the numerous stamps in my passport to being a missionary. Showing him air tickets from Heathrow to Edinburgh, I express my intention to spend Christmas in Scotland. Whether it is the air tickets out of England, the spirit of the season, or my missionary zeal that influences him, he stamps our passports and wishes me a Merry Christmas. Maneuvering through customs, my mind is whirring. Now that we have been granted six months in the United Kingdom, Christmas in Scotland will become a reality. Imagining the New Year, nothing seems to block returning to live in Oxford, where Michelle can attend school. The urgency to cross the Atlantic has vanished. The future appears so bright, so hopeful, that I kick up my heels, leaning into the bar of the luggage cart.

As we pass through the portal in the airport terminal, hundreds of hopeful eyes are riveted on the advancing luggage carts as they round the corner. Having witnessed many joyous reunions at airports, my expectation of seeing a familiar face rises for an instant, but dissolves into the crowd by the time we pass through the barriers. As my thoughts turn toward the Edinburgh flight, I feel a tap from behind on my shoulder. At first, I stiffen at the unlikely occurrence that immigration has reconsidered, and then a familiar voice stops me in my tracks.

10

Incognito

But is there any comfort to be found?
Man is in love and loves what vanishes,
What more is there to say?
    —W. B. YEATS, *NINETEEN HUNDRED AND NINETEEN*

ON THE CHANCE THAT MICHELLE AND I WOULD MAKE IT through U.K. immigration, Sally Stokes has driven from Oxford to Heathrow to meet us. Michelle is bowled over to see her teacher, and I'm speechless at Sally's unexpected welcome. Since the flight to Edinburgh is delayed by fog in Scotland, the three of us make plans in the airport restaurant. Sally has been preparing the way for our return to Oxford by talking with a board member at Emmanuel Christian School concerning Michelle's readmission, which seems likely. Where to live is a bigger obstacle, although Sally mentions an available apartment that she will pursue, now that the opportunity exists for us to spend six months in the U.K. At this glorious moment, anxiety about tomorrow can wait. The joy of the present puts the future where it belongs.

After years of reunionless arrivals in airports, Michelle and I experience two in the same evening. Janet is waiting outside the barrier in Edinburgh, wondering whether we will be on this flight or on another heading in the direction of Nova Scotia. On the ride to Perth, I smile at the future because my heart hasn't let me down. Michelle and I will be spending Christmas with Janet at our home away from home.

Early Christmas morning, as the three of us sit on Janet's living room floor, opening gifts, there is a knock at the front door. The hour is too early for friends to visit. My mind leaps to the memory of a man Janet had told me about, who had waited in a parked car on the street outside her house one day. Through the curtains, she had observed him taking pictures of her home, looking as if he could have been a private investigator. She had watched him until, perhaps having seen her at the window, the man moved down the hill to photograph the field of sheep next to her house. Later, she learned that he had been sent by the local government, which is considering developing the field. If this man standing next to Janet's Christmas tree is a detective, he's brazen to enter her home on Christmas morning disguised as Santa Claus. My fears are relieved seeing that Janet, despite feigning surprise, appears to know the man under the red suit. A nearly nine-year-old Michelle watches Santa pull gifts from a bag, perhaps rethinking former conclusions. Santa Claus leaves by the back door to deliver the remaining gifts to the residents at the care home next door.

A Christmas call to the U.S.A. gives no indication that our journey is ending. The lack of news about Jim confirms plans to push ahead with moving back to Oxford. Sally Stokes telephones, encouraging me to call the chairman of the board about Michelle's readmission to Emmanuel Christian School. The accommodation that she had mentioned is an option to pursue. Ray, a member of the church where Keith, Sally's husband, is pastor, owns an apartment in Oxford that is vacant. The beautifully furnished two-bedroom apartment is located close to Michelle's school, above a chiropractic clinic. Although the bedrooms and living room would be private, the bathrooms and kitchen are used by the clinic staff. After clinic hours and on weekends, the upstairs would be exclusively ours. The only hiccup is that the apartment has been promised to missionaries for six weeks during January and February. I call Ray to inquire about it, and he sets the rent as whatever I can pay, expecting no assistance in paying the utilities, since he has been briefed about our circumstances. When Sally and Keith offer us lodging in the manse during the six weeks we must vacate the apartment, I accept. The next evening Michelle's school readmission is confirmed by telephone. Now we must replace the gray uniform skirts that were given away in Switzerland. Once again, details for moving to Oxford have fallen into place within a few days. Life flows jubilantly toward the New Year, 1993.

CHRISTMAS IS A WARM-UP FOR HOGMANAY, NEW YEAR'S EVE in Scotland. In Kinloch Rannoch, Janet and I go first-footing during the first few hours of the New Year. In times past, a first-footer, the first person to cross the threshold, brought to the household a piece of coal or peat to warm the fire, a bottle of whiskey to warm the insides, and oatcakes. Janet and I cross the threshold with gifts of shortbread and black buns (a rich fruitcake wrapped in pastry), although neither of us are dark-haired, the preferred color of a first-footer for bringing good fortune in the New Year.

On New Year's Day evening, everyone is ready to fling off fatigue to dance the night away. In a small church hall on the edge of the moor at the top of Loch Rannoch, several musicians provide the rhythm for dancers who have little room to maneuver, which is fortuitous for an American who doesn't know the Highland steps. At midnight, sandwiches and tea are put out to sustain us until the wee hours of the morning. In this remote venue, I'm one of three Americans in attendance, but I don't seek out the American couple from California for conversation.

WHEN THE TRAIN FROM EDINBURGH TO OXFORD ARRIVES ONE
and a half hours late, Keith is waiting for us at the station. After a
late supper with Sally and Keith, we meet Ray, our landlord, at
the apartment, which, newly decorated and with a modern
kitchen, is the most attractive living situation yet. Ray supplies us
with sheets and towels, even preparing the beds for our collapse.
In a few hours, the new school semester begins.

During the opening assembly, students sing "Happy Birthday"
to Michelle, who is nine years old today. Most are surprised, as
well as puzzled, to see her, perhaps thinking back to the final
assembly only six months ago when goodbye cards and gifts had
been presented to us. Michelle settles easily into a new class with
old friends, thrilled to take her place next to Hannah, Rachel, and
Stephanee, who hasn't yet returned to Colorado.

Changes occur even when one is away from a place for a few
months, making Oxford familiar yet different. Friendships are
renewed in all corners of Oxford, but this time around Michelle
and I live on the opposite side of town, frequent different shops,
and attend a different church. Living in a city for the second time
on this journey is an alien experience. During our first stay in
Oxford, I had seen a chilling television drama entitled *12:01 P.M.*,
about a man caught in a time warp, a lunch hour in the park.
When he eventually realizes what is going on, only one hour
exists to convince others of his predicament. Starting his mission
at ground zero, 12:01 P.M., each time around, his frustration
transforms to resignation at being doomed to repeat over and
over again the same segment of time. In the past, the challenge of
settling into a new place has occupied my time and mind until it's
time to depart, but now in Oxford the sense of progression is
gone. The haunting idea surfaces that I might be doomed to
backtrack and retrace our steps on this journey, never advancing
to the ultimate destination.

———

WHEN THE ACID-REDUCING MEDICATIONS FROM SWITZERLAND run out, the stomach pains return. Visiting the same physician from our first stay in Oxford, a more serious health concern turns up. In Italy, I had detected a lump in my breast, which appears to be increasing in size. In America, during the past fifteen years, numerous surgical procedures had been necessary to determine the nature of breast lumps. All had turned out to be cysts, except one, a benign tumor, but if this one turns out to be malignant, receiving medical care could be difficult, if not impossible. The United Kingdom won't assume fiscal responsibility for the surgery, chemotherapy, or radiation therapy expenses required by a noncitizen, and I am beyond the pale of insurance, as well as the emotional support of family. Michelle could end up being alone with no parent to care for her.

I am referred to a surgeon, and a biopsy is scheduled in her clinic. Never before has so much been riding on a long thin needle. Hope for the future is restored when the aspiration confirms the mass to be a benign cyst.

WHEN THE MISSIONARIES ARRIVE IN OXFORD, MICHELLE AND I vacate the apartment to become short-term lodgers in the Victorian manse next to Keith's church. For the next six weeks, Michelle and I live with Sally and Keith and two of their three children still at home, as well as two cats who purr contentedly on Michelle's bed. Attending a church house group that meets at the manse is uncomplicated now, since Michelle's bedroom is upstairs. Church members of various ages and callings meet every other Wednesday evening in the living room for teaching, discussion, prayer, and fellowship.

I had met one of the members in the church parking lot when I had helped balance the end of an antique church pew as he loaded it on top of his station wagon. At that time, I had discovered that John, who is a designer in wood, and I have mutual interests: faith in God, architecture, the creative process, and singleness. Our conversation had sparked my interest in getting to know him better.

Soon after we move into the manse, a visitor appears at the breakfast table one Sunday morning. David, a medical doctor and family friend of the Stokeses, has returned to Oxford during the night from South Africa. On a whim, I ask him if he knows Frank. Incredibly, David had dinner with Frank several evenings ago. Weeks before, Frank had written to tell me that he would be changing hospitals to relieve a doctor who would be returning to the U.K., but I never expected to sit across a table from the same doctor in Oxford. Believing this occurrence is coincidental requires more faith than receiving it as assurance that no circumstances are too great for God to engineer.

DURING THE WEEK OF OUR THIRD ANNIVERSARY OF LIFE ON THE run, the fever and chills of influenza almost prevent me from walking to the telephone booth for a U.S.A. call, but not calling at the appointed time would have unleashed my mother's imagination toward the direst straits. From my parents, I learn that Jim had recently taken a three-month leave of absence from the hospital for health reasons, although he has since returned to full-time work. Jim's health is shifting back and forth, as are my emotions, never knowing what to expect when I call Kentucky.

On the way home, I meet John while shopping for juice and medication. I had hoped that our paths would cross outside the house group, but not on a day when I look wan and feverish. His gentleness warms my heart, and my health improves on the ride home in his car.

WHEN THE MISSIONARIES RETURN TO THEIR MISSION FIELD, Michelle and I move back into the apartment above the clinic. Although living at the manse has been fun, it's good to be on our own again. In addition to Sally's tasty meals, the manse was a hub for church activities, particularly the house group. Attending those evening meetings now requires arranging for someone to stay with Michelle. One of the perks of living away from the manse is riding home with John, who lives only a few blocks from our apartment.

Returning home from the Good Friday service at church, I hear a knock at the clinic door downstairs. Thinking it's a patient who doesn't realize that the clinic is closed, I open the door to see John, who has brought lunch for the three of us. At the house group meeting earlier in the week, I had mentioned that Michelle and I would be traveling with the church mission trip to France during Easter break. After lunching with John, I'm not as keen on traveling to France. Our purpose for taking the trip is twofold: to support the church's missionary who is serving there and to update our passports for another six months in the United Kingdom.

Riding on the expressway on the outskirts of Paris, I see the Eiffel Tower as a speck on the horizon. Our destination is Le Creusot, the city that supplied Marie Antoinette with crystal chandeliers. In France, my thoughts travel back to Oxford, despite the busy week. Passing through immigration on the ferry in Sally and Keith's car makes coming and going from the U.K. like crossing the Red Sea on dry ground. Remaining in Oxford is allowed until October 1993.

ON THE MAY BANK HOLIDAY LAST YEAR, MICHELLE AND I HAD spent the afternoon wrangling with each other and American Express in York; a year later, I heartily support the United Kingdom's declaration of a Monday holiday that allows us to sleep in. Stopping by the manse to talk with Sally Stokes, I learn that today is John's birthday. Sally offers to look after Michelle if I would like to invite John out for a pub dinner as a birthday treat. Alone with the telephone in the dining room, I eventually push the numbers. When John answers, he accepts the invitation.

During the Good Friday lunch, John had mentioned showing me a bluebell wood in the Oxfordshire countryside. The blossoms are at their peak on this fine spring day. Late-afternoon sunshine sprinkles the indigo carpet, a covering so complete that we must step gingerly to avoid smashing the flowers. The visual enchantment of these woods would be the envy of any Hollywood set.

As we enter the Star, a seventeenth-century pub in a nearby village, "Take Five" is playing—a mutual favorite that John has played on a double bass with a jazz group. For his own enjoyment, he also plays Appalachian music from Kentucky on a dulcimer he made himself. John's musical credentials are noteworthy.

A full moon lights the meadow path as we walk along the Thames River past the ruins of a medieval nunnery, now a crumbling hulk in the silver light. John's creative genius has spun an evening as lovely as any tapestry that may have graced the walls of the Godstow Nunnery. At the clinic reception desk the next day, John leaves a note of appreciation on notepaper with a photograph of a bluebell wood, a dead ringer for the one we had visited the afternoon before.

The birthday evening with John softens the news from America about the decline of my grandmother's health. My mother has spared me the progression of my grandmother's downhill memory slide, which has moved her into a nursing home. The mental jigsaw puzzle accompanying Alzheimer's disease would prevent her from hosting the big party she hoped and planned for when Michelle and I would return to America. I feel as though I have lost her. I want to grieve with someone who knows my grandmother, but that's impossible. Michelle's memory of her is fading, and expressing my sadness would only upset her.

During the weeks to follow, John and I enjoy one another's company on a shoestring budget that includes picnics, kite-flying with Michelle at Port Meadow, and sampling John's ace cooking talents. God heard the cry of my heart in January by uncorking fun and spontaneity in my life and by leaning toward Oxford to put His arm around me. For Michelle, it seems as if God has reached down and yanked me away.

For over three years, Michelle has had my constant and undivided attention, which she now regularly shares with John. The more time John and I spend together, the more obnoxious Michelle becomes. The situation is complicated by the fact that she likes John. The threat of being excluded from the fun mitigates her unpleasantness. Finally Michelle gives up, realizing that her disagreeable behavior isn't driving him away.

IN JULY, A U.S.A. TELEPHONE CALL PULLS THE PAVEMENT OUT from under my feet in the phone booth. Jim has telephoned my parents, following up a three-page letter in which he asserted his victimization and outlined his resentment and hatred toward me. My father's deafness delegates my mother as the primary telephone communicator.

With resignation in her voice, my mother says, "Janie, Jim's heart hasn't changed at all, except maybe becoming more bitter. Although his voice didn't sound as strong as it has in the past, he wanted me to know that his health is good."

"Mother, that doesn't surprise me. He knows how difficult it is for me to be cut off from all of you. He's implying that he will be around for a very long time, hoping I will give up and return home."

"Well, I wouldn't expect to return home anytime soon. Jim mentioned that he will be delivering a medical paper in Bethesda, and he plans to attend a medical seminar in Oxford, England."

Cutting off my mother's remarks, I repeat with as much detachment as possible, "Oxford, England?" My clenched throat prevents me from speaking. Instinctively, I look over my shoulder, half-fearing, half-expecting to see Jim walking toward me.

"Yes, he wanted me to know that he feels well enough for international travel, but I don't think that . . ." I no longer hear what my mother is saying as I lean against the side of the phone booth to steady myself. For a few minutes, I talk about Ellen's (not saying Michelle's) dance lessons to divert attention away from inadvertently exposing our hiding place. My mother knows me well, and vocal vibrations could tip her off. With the seconds disappearing from the phone card, finding out about the Oxford meeting will be tricky without making my mother suspicious.

Offhandedly, I ask, "Did he say when he would be traveling to Europe?," not wanting to call attention to Great Britain.

"No, he didn't mention any dates. It's possible that he isn't even going . . ." The phone card beeps ominously, leaving us only a few seconds to say goodbye. My mother's mild drawl had expanded her words, consuming precious time units on the phone card. Today I had needed the space between her syllables to gingerly retrieve information. On the walk home, I worry that I had appeared too eager for information about Oxford. Expecting to see Jim's face at every turn, I am tormented by the necessity of brushing my tracks and taking more precautions.

THE MANSE HOUSE GROUP IS BLESSED WITH TWO MEMBERS WHO work at Oxford University's medical center, the probable host for an international medical meeting. The medical library staff member will be on the lookout for infectious disease meetings in Oxford, but the other staff member, Anthony, is more likely to hear about future meetings. The research lab where he works is situated next to the department of infectious disease, Jim's medical speciality. Three weeks after being alerted, Anthony overhears talk in the lab about the British Parasitology Society meeting at Oxford in mid-September. That's the one, and it's only one month away.

With only two months remaining on our United Kingdom visas, the thought of meeting Jim on the street in Oxford sends me to a travel agent to make flight reservations for Nova Scotia. Michelle pleads that we wait until the last minute to leave Oxford, giving her maximum time to attend school, enjoy midnight feasts with her friends, and have riding lessons with Anne, Ray's fiancée. Canada may be too close for our safety—Jim knows that I would plan a rendezvous with my parents whenever possible—but the airline reservations to Halifax stand. No other destination is handy, but both my parents and I have grave misgivings about our fleeing toward North America.

While I am wondering what direction to take, Steve from Switzerland calls from the *Anastasis*, YWAM's hospital ship. We have lost contact with each other for a while, but Steve has tracked us to Oxford through YWAM Crossroaders I keep in contact with. Although the ship is a possible destination, nothing in my situation has changed since the first application. I'm still a single parent who would spend much of my time caring for Michelle. Earlier in the summer, John, Michelle, and I had toured the ship in London, where it docked before heading for West Africa. Unknown to Michelle and me, Steve had passed through London a week later to join the ship before its sailing. I don't reapply, feeling as if I'm trying to force open a closed door of opportunity.

AS MY FRIENDSHIP WITH JOHN DEEPENS, THE UNCERTAINTY OF how long this journey will last and what will happen to me when it's over introduces the awkwardness of an emotional straitjacket into the present. In less than two months, Michelle and I will be moving to a new country. According to legal opinion, it's likely that I will be sentenced to prison, even if I remain in hiding until Jim's death. The relationship with John, or anyone, isn't secure until the legal situation is resolved. But this is my head talking—my heart sings a different tune. All we can do is take our friendship one day at a time, an optimal increment of time for living life, whether one is a fugitive or not.

The night before the school year begins, I cry out to God for direction on our next destination. Only five weeks remain on our visas, the reservation deadline for the Nova Scotia airline tickets is three days away, and I have no peace about purchasing them. The only confirmation for moving to Halifax has been Ray mentioning a medical colleague there.

The next morning, as parents linger outside on the first day of school, one of the mothers I haven't seen since the last day of school a few months ago approaches me purposefully.

"Chris, I have been wanting to talk to you, but I didn't know if you would still be in Oxford. I have met another mother in your situation, except that she is English, fleeing from an American husband. When I told her your story, she said, 'Tell her the safe place to go is Ireland.' "

The exquisite timing of these words strikes my ears as if God Himself has spoken them. Confirmation will be necessary, but the revelation of Ireland as the next step lodges firmly in my mind, even altering the day's plans. After leaving Michelle at school, I catch a bus for London to pick up a Moneygram at American Express. As planned, I stop by the Canadian tourist office for brochures on Nova Scotia and then impulsively seek out the Republic of Ireland's embassy. Asking general questions about how long Americans can stay in Ireland and what happens if one wants to stay longer, I learn that foreigners must register at the aliens office in Dublin, since no passport control exists between the United Kingdom and Ireland. Returning to England and Scotland will be a cinch. The following day I cancel the Nova Scotia reservations.

John and I take comfort in the idea of being separated by the Irish Sea, rather than the Atlantic Ocean. John telephones his brother, a minister in Oxfordshire, who has a minister friend in Dublin. The next evening, during a long telephone conversation, I explain our situation to Niall in Dublin, who extends enthusiastic support for helping us move there.

A few days later, I receive the housing page from the *Irish Times*, where Niall has circled apartments on the same side of Dublin as the church. The listings mean nothing to me, as indecipherable as a code. Establishing the basics of life several times a year during the past four years has left no enthusiasm for moving to Ireland, or anywhere.

Life is in a reduction phase, and the threshold lowers daily. Prolonged stress of indeterminate duration is depleting both the body's and the soul's resources. A regimen of rationing these reserves cuts out nonessential exertion. Journal entries have become sporadic, letters to friends have dwindled, and cooking, which never had a secure position, has gone by the wayside. It seems too great an effort to photograph the people and places I'm leaving. At the beginning of the journey, I had hoped to photograph for posterity every place where Michelle and I stayed, but this practice was suspended several countries ago. If only I could stop running on the moving platform. I don't want to think about finding a place to live in Ireland. I almost wish that John hadn't come into my life. The emotional pull of leaving behind someone I care about hasn't been there before.

A WEEK BEFORE THE OXFORD INTERNATIONAL MEDICAL SEMI-nar, the news from America surprises me. Jim won't be attending the meeting in England because his father is in the hospital in Kentucky. Relief, which can't be shared with my parents, floods every corner of the phone booth. On the walk home, another concern surfaces. I have accompanied Jim to medical meetings in the U.S.A., as well as in Europe, and my face might be recognized by any of his friends who might attend this meeting, even after the passage of years. For all I know, some may be on the lookout for a mother who looks like me with a young girl of about the right age to be Ellen.

At the manse house group, I ask Anthony if he could obtain a list of the speakers at this meeting. Anthony doubts that someone in his department would receive a program for a parasitology meeting, but he will be on the lookout for one. Several days before the meeting begins, a late-evening knock at the clinic door gives me a start. Apprehensively, I descend the stairs, wondering how we could escape if one of Jim's friends is standing there. Opening the door, I see Anthony with a piece of paper for my inspection. Without him asking, the program of lectures for the parasitology meeting had appeared on his desk, and, sure enough, two of the presenters are Jim's friends, who would certainly recognize me without a disguise.

The circumstances of the medical meeting aren't mentioned to Michelle, only that I will be spending more time at home to research my thesis before we leave for Ireland. Devising a strategy, I initiate the following precautions for the days before and after the meeting date, in case any seminar participants are sightseeing in Oxford. Walking near the university and the tourist areas of Oxford is off-limits. Michelle and I will avoid all public appearances together, even at our neighborhood shopping area. On school mornings, John will pick up Michelle in his car. In the afternoons, she will walk home with the mother of some schoolmates who live nearby. Whenever I leave the apartment, I will disguise my appearance. The simple disguise of stuffing my hair in a hat and wearing glasses is shown to be effective when a teacher at Michelle's school doesn't recognize me until I remove the hat.

The week of the medical meeting comes and goes without incident, but the thought lurks that someone could have seen me on one of my few excursions in the neighborhood. Even if the identification of Michelle or myself would be inconclusive, someone could contact Jim with their suspicions. He might then hire a private investigator in Oxford to search for us. It's a mystery as to why Jim hasn't contacted Janet or Gabriella during the past three and a half years. Perhaps this Oxford meeting will direct his attention toward Europe and the two households Jim knows that I would visit at some point. Fortunately, weariness nips this convoluted worry in the bud.

A YEAR BEFORE LEAVING SAN FRANCISCO MICHELLE HAD PRO-
fessed her belief in Jesus as Lord and Savior, but she hadn't been
baptized. Witnessing the baptisms of school friends in Oxford
has motivated her to do the same. During the past year, Michelle's faith has matured through associations at school and
church. Her friend Stephanee has encouraged her to join the Girl
Crusaders' Union (GCU), an organization for girls aged eight to
eighteen to learn about the Christian faith and its application to
life.

On our last Sunday in Oxford, teachers and friends fill our
church to witness her baptism. Michelle reads the testimony she
has written, attributing God's protection as what has made the
difference in her life as a Christian. Early on in our journey, she
had selected favorite verses from Psalm 63: "For Thou hast been
my help, And in the shadow of Thy wings I sing for joy. My soul
clings to Thee; Thy right hand upholds me" (verses 7–8).

After the service, Miss Cooke, Michelle's GCU leader, lets me
know that she has written to Mrs. Allen, the GCU leader in
Dublin and her longtime friend, briefly explaining our circumstances. She encourages me to phone Mrs. Allen when we arrive
in Dublin, having paved the way for another supportive contact
in a new country.

Later in the day, John and I walk in the arboretum, a special
place for him, as his love of trees is the source of his art. I pick up
a Japanese maple leaf at the peak of its autumn color to press with
a stem of bluebells in my Bible. The pressure of circumstances is
too great to offer our relationship a future, which snaps as a
branch from its own weight. The temporal is uncertain; there are
no guarantees. Only one hope will not disappoint, and that's
reserved for the eternal.

11

Amazing Grace

May the road rise to meet you,
May the wind be always at your back,
May the sun shine warm upon your face,
the rains fall soft upon your fields,
and until we meet again
May God hold you in the palm of His hand.

—AN IRISH BLESSING

THE JOURNEY TO IRELAND BEGINS AT CREWE WHEN I STOP traveling away from Oxford and toward Dublin. Preoccupied with shifting the three black bags, I don't see an entry on the platform monitor for an earlier train to Holyhead, but Michelle does. Her observant eyes assure our timely passage on the ferry to Dun Laoghaire. Sometimes the smallest of details, the least of encouragements, makes the greatest of difference in a new endeavor. Michelle's astuteness in England opens for her the door of confidence in Ireland.

Before leaving Oxford, I had reserved a room at the same bed-and-breakfast where Michelle and I had stayed during our first trip to Ireland. Two years earlier, we had traveled this exact route for a Moneygram pickup at the American Express office in Dublin, although at that time the perspective had been different. The beauty of the Irish coast and our enjoyment of the spirited city of Dublin had transformed our mission into a brief vacation. Now we will be making County Dublin home.

The setting sun backlights the coastal hills as the ferry enters the port of Dun Laoghaire. Since there is no passport control, no stamp documents our exit from the United Kingdom. The customs office, located several buildings away, is the only official office open at this hour, but the three black bags prevent us from walking there. We hire a taxi to take us the few streets to the bed-and-breakfast, where Mrs. D'alton greets us with the same geniality she had extended during our first stay.

The next morning being Sunday, Niall has arranged for church members who live nearby in Dalkey to pick us up. Only Imant arrives, since his wife Barbara is at home with their sons, one of whom is sick. The church, which meets in a school, draws members from all corners of County Dublin. Their exuberance momentarily lifts the pressure of establishing a new life, holding out hope in their lilting assurances that "something will turn up." Encouraged by their welcome, Michelle and I sign up for a church retreat the next weekend at Greystones, a seaside village in Wicklow, south of County Dublin. Following the service, all members and visitors are invited to gather at the home of Niall and Sue, his wife, for refreshments. During the afternoon, John telephones Niall's home to confirm our safe arrival, which ferries my thoughts back across the Irish Sea and away from the task at hand. Discussing housing options, Niall calls a friend, Carol, who lives in Dun Laoghaire. Carol knows of an apartment in Killiney that may be available. She invites Michelle and me to her home on Tuesday morning, hoping to have the information about the apartment by then.

Only one day remains on the U.K. immigration visa. Unless our departure from the U.K. is documented on our passports, it will appear that we have overstayed. The lecture by the U.K. immigration officer at Portsmouth still rings in my ears. Taking

DART (Dublin Area Rapid Transit), the transportation lifeline of County Dublin, downtown, Michelle and I wait for several hours at the Aliens Office. Hoping to document our arrival on Irish soil, we obtain a tourist visa application. The amiable agent, who has no clue of our circumstances, gives me his name as a contact to expedite the processing of the registration form. I have no intention of submitting a form that puts our passport name, address, and telephone number on file with the Republic of Ireland.

Determined to have our passports stamped before the midnight deadline, Michelle and I return to the ferry port in the evening, threading our way through a maze of warehouses, having been told that the customs office is tucked away inside one. At first, the customs official refuses to stamp them, seeing no justification, since the Aliens Office handles registration. Persistence prevails. Hours before the U.K. visa expires, our passports are stamped: CUSTOMS AND EXCISE, 18 OCTOBER 1993, LANDING STATION, DUN LAOGHAIRE, as if it applied to fruitcakes from America.

At Carol's home the next morning, I learn that the apartment isn't available. When our conversation meanders to other topics, such as places to exercise, she invites me to an aerobics class the following day. Ready to pound frustration into a gym floor, I agree to meet her at the class, which is held at a church in the neighborhood. After three nights of staying in a bed-and-breakfast and three days of eating in restaurants, I'm no closer to finding a place to live, or a school, than when we arrived. I can't keep up this level of expenditures. Recently, my parents have mentioned that their cash reserve is running out. If the journey lasts much longer, selling their home will become necessary.

Resilience isn't as springy as it was in New Zealand, Oxford, and all the countries in between. Accumulative exhaustion is weighing me down. No longer does the absence of opportunities in a new place signal the end of the journey. News from America supports this notion. Jim and his wife are attending a medical meeting in New Orleans.

Feeling as if I should be pounding a different pavement, Michelle and I still attend the aerobics class, expecting to see Carol. A friend of hers reports that she is ill. After aerobics, I inquire in the church office about housing, also asking if anyone knows Mrs. Allen, the Girl Crusaders' Union leader in Dublin. Not only do they know Mrs. Allen, but she is a church member and lives nearby. Encouraged to contact her, first by Miss Cooke in Oxford and now by the church office staff, I wonder why I haven't done so earlier and telephone her from the church. She suggests meeting us right away; Miss Cooke's letter has paved the way for our introduction.

During lunch at McDonald's, Mrs. Allen makes a startling proposal. Since some bedrooms in her home aren't currently being used, she offers two of them to us until next spring. At that time, her husband will be returning from England, where he teaches at a university, and her daughters and their families will be arriving for the Easter holiday. Two bedrooms plus kitchen privileges are offered at whatever rent we can afford, an offer coming from Mrs. Allen's heart, not from financial considerations. Concerned about the money I'm spending at the bed-and-breakfast, Mrs. Allen suggests we see the rooms this very afternoon. The decision to take them is made before we leave McDonald's. It is confirmed by the spaciousness of Mrs. Allen's home, the beauty of her flower garden, and the comfortable upstairs bedrooms. The name of the area, Glenageary, means "glen of the sheep" in Gaelic, but the sheep have long gone.

ONE DOWN AND ONE TO GO IS HOW I VIEW OUR IMMEDIATE situation. Carol directs us to a teacher at a local school, who will consider enrolling Michelle in her class. Seeing our weariness, Mrs. D'alton drives us to the school appointment. Although the teacher is willing to have Michelle as a pupil, this action requires special authorization from the school board. Now seven weeks into the school year, most classes in County Dublin are filled to capacity. I let the request drop, and the school quandary is put on hold until after the church retreat.

On moving day, Mrs. D'alton drives us and the three black bags to Mrs. Allen's home in time for Michelle's first GCU meeting. As I pack for the weekend retreat, the chatter of about fifteen girls filters up the stairs. In a matter of hours, Michelle puts down roots in Ireland with girls her own age who have common interests.

After the GCU meeting, Michelle and I board DART, whose stop is only a few blocks away, to travel to the church retreat at Greystones. Heading south toward Bray, the train leaves the tunnel opening to a stunning view of Killiney Bay. The wide crescent of the sandy beach hugs the coast, which tourist brochures describe as resembling the Bay of Naples. With the graceful cone of Sugarloaf Mountain rising from behind the beach, the landscape needs no comparison to enhance its beauty.

Bray Head, an imposing hulk of land at the end of the crescent, blocks the southern advance of DART. We board a bus at Bray and wind through the coastal hills, stopping at the village of Greystones, where the windows of the retreat house, Carraig Eden, or Rock of Paradise, are glazed with sea spray.

The church envelops us as if we have always been within its fold. The childbearing age of the congregation provides an abundance of playmates for Michelle. We share a room with another single mother and her infant son, whose own story bonds us. The friendship start-up time with Imant and Barbara, his wife, is immediate, and we receive an invitation—the first of many—for dinner at their home in one week's time. In every country, as my inclination to cook has waned, God has placed us in the proximity of excellent cooks. Barbara and Imant's friendship shortens the journey, as does the friendship of their sons, Philip and Dylan, for Michelle.

The speaker for the retreat is a YWAM staff member serving in England, who also happens to be an American from California. The spiritual theme of the weekend shifts my focus from the tyranny of temporal urgency to the exigency of eternity. Thinking of the DART line, I picture the Glory Train bound for Eternity, making stops along the way, even unscheduled ones, opening its doors to anyone on the platforms willing to step inside. Whether the traveler boards at the first stop or at the eleventh hour makes no difference, but being on the train at the destination's end is imperative. So it is with God's kingdom.

Walking along the beach at Greystones, I reflect on how far I've come in trusting God for provision and protection. Having sung the hymn "Come, Thou Fount of Every Blessing" many times in the past, I had never known the meaning of the phrase in verse two, "Here I raise mine Ebenezer." Reading about the Israelites, I learn that the prophet Samuel set a stone in a place he called Ebenezer, meaning "the stones of help" in Hebrew. The stone memorial had signified: "Thus far the Lord has helped us" (1 Sam. 7:12). Looking back, the path of our journey is littered with Ebenezers.

In Oxford, Miss Cooke mentioned another GCU associate in Dublin, Miss Stella Mew, who is the principal at a girls' private school, as well as a friend of Mrs. Allen's. With only the cost of renting rooms, money would be available for private schooling. Through an introduction by Mrs. Allen, Michelle and I meet Miss Mew to discuss Michelle becoming a student at Rathdown School, which is located within walking distance of our new home. After I explain the situation and the risk of registering in public schools, Miss Mew opens the door of admission to Michelle. Miss Mew's support and Michelle's eagerness confirm Rathdown School as being the right choice. Sensitive to the expense of my purchasing a complete school uniform, Miss Mew loans us a gabardine school coat, which has been left at the school unclaimed. A few days later, Michelle dons a pleated blue-green plaid skirt with a dark green sweater, becoming a third-year student.

Rathdown School goes beyond fulfilling Michelle's expectations. French lessons, Gaelic lessons, drama workshops, and sports throughout the year—field hockey, track, basketball, swimming, and tennis—are all enjoyed in the company of friends. The girls in Michelle's class welcome her enthusiastically, initiating a new name of endearment, Shelly. When Michelle participates in school activities involving an audience, she is supported not only by my presence, but also by Mrs. D'alton, Mrs. Allen, and Mr. Allen (when he is in town). Having grandchildren the age of Michelle, they become a surrogate family.

Letters and phone calls from John add anticipation to life, but cutting off contact would remove the sadness I feel when I think about him. Uncertain about whether seeing John would make me feel better or worse, I miss him and eventually encourage him to visit us in Ireland.

Traveling by train and ferry, John spends a few nights at Mrs. D'alton's bed-and-breakfast. Our walks by the sea are invigorating, as well as being physically and emotionally exhausting. The push-pull of mixed-up feelings makes letting go of John's devotion inconceivable.

AT THE AMERICAN EXPRESS OFFICE IN GALWAY, THE AGENT INforms me that the computer is down, temporarily blocking the Moneygram transaction. Waiting for any reason in a place where my passport name is known makes me uneasy. When the computer links are restored, the agent asks for my Social Security number. This is the first instance in four years when passport identification and the Moneygram reference number haven't been sufficient verification. Since New Zealand, my Social Security number has been jumbled in my memory, and I always forget to verify it when talking to my parents. Sloughing off forgetfulness as casually as possible, I hope the agent doesn't catch on to how peculiar this memory lapse would be for an American. When the request for authorization is sent through without a Social Security number, American Express delays approval. Communicating with both Dublin and New York, the agent remarks that she has never experienced such a protracted delay. Warning lights flash in my mind. Although this delay may result from the internal workings at American Express, perhaps my name and passport number have been flagged. A wave of panic overcomes me. Realizing that my passport is behind the counter, out of reach, I want to run into the street, but I restrain the urge to flee. Under my breath, I sing the words to "Amazing Grace," praying for God's power to release the money. After more waiting and more telephone conversations, authorization is extricated as inexplicably as the bottleneck materialized. Nothing can be taken for granted—least of all, past success.

RECONNECTING WITH YWAM IN DUBLIN, MICHELLE SIGNS UP for the King's Kids Christmas Outreach, which combines two of her passions: singing and dancing. In Switzerland, being part of the King's Kids had been a dream, restrained at the time by her age and the language. Weeks of singing and choreography rehearsals in Dublin, as well as a weekend retreat, make the advent of Christmas spiritually festive for both of us. Piling into vans to sing on Grafton Street in the center of Dublin, in a hospital, or in shopping centers about Christ's message builds friendships among the participants. Friendships with YWAM staff members strengthen God's Spirit within me to endure the difficult months to come.

The Christmas phone call to my parents is impacted by the presence of a cleaning lady in Mary Ellen's apartment. My mother codes her language as if she is conversing with a relative across town. From our muddled conversation, I learn that Jim is spending Christmas in Kentucky, perhaps delivering a medical paper at a university after the holidays.

The presence of the cleaning lady was distracting but not as disruptive as the time when lightning had struck Mary Ellen's balcony at the same time my parents arrived to receive my call. My mother had resolutely continued the telephone conversation as firemen filed past her.

Mary Ellen's friendship has been a bulwark of strength for my parents. Following the early morning phone calls in her home, she invites them to stay for breakfast. Revealing to no one, except Mary Ellen and Marcella, a previous telephone contact, the occurrence of these phone calls, these breakfast visits are times when my parents can express their emotions about what's happening with Michelle and me.

THE JANUARY RAINS IN DUBLIN FALL HORIZONTALLY WITH some drops never reaching the ground. Umbrellas are useless against the wet winds. Treetops in Dublin are littered with plastic bags that have been put there by updrafts from the unrelenting wind. Sometimes Mrs. Allen gives us a ride to Rathdown if a downpour occurs as we leave for school. Although friends faithfully pick us up whenever possible, a lot of time is spent walking in the weather to school and shops. Ill health is like an underground stream in my life, always flowing and often surfacing with flulike symptoms and respiratory illnesses. During U.S.A. calls, my voice is often raspy from respiratory congestion. When I express concern about how much longer my body can endure the stress, my parents engage a lawyer in Kentucky to initiate negotiations with Jim's lawyer about our returning to America. Jim is staying at his parents' home, presumably due to ill health. Ears in Kentucky haven't heard whether he plans to return to California.

As physical stamina ebbs, I work to build up spiritual strength through prayer, a devalued spiritual asset. Marion, the mother of Dawn, a GCU friend of Michelle's, invites me to a women's home Bible study through her church. These women embrace the circumstances of my life through prayer. Imant and Barbara host a weekly church home group, a place where members express a variety of emotions, calling out both to God and man for strength. As we pray for one another's needs, God's power transfuses into the circumstances, sometimes like water breaking through a dam, other times with the force of an intravenous drip. Barbara and I become partners in prayer, bringing our petitions and praises around her kitchen table to each other and God. I yearn to tell her about my secret pleasure on hearing my name in the Irish expression "Janey Mac."

Fortunately, the passport alarms don't sound any more, now that we have decided to remain in Ireland for the duration of the journey, but moving looms in April when Mrs. Allen will need our rooms. Through Barbara, I contact a lady at her mother's church who rents an upstairs one-room apartment with a small kitchen, but my primary concern is living in a single room with a ten-year-old. The room is bright and pleasant, like our landlord, Miss Welsby. From the edge of one window is an angled view of Sandycove and the ferry pier. Although this apartment is closer to shopping, it's half a mile farther from Rathdown, adding two miles to the day's walking. Walking the extra distance, particularly in the mornings, seems overwhelming. When Fiona, the mother of a Rathdown classmate, offers to pick up Michelle in the mornings, I take the apartment. Once again, Mrs. D'alton moves us and the three black bags to our new home. Michelle heaps attention on two local cats that have adopted Miss Welsby.

BEFORE LEAVING CALIFORNIA, I HAD PRESENTED TO SUSAN, a friend in San Francisco, a shoebox full of legal papers, the power of attorney on my behalf, and bags of Peet's coffee beans from my freezer. During these past four years, Susan has been pursuing all angles in attempts to advance my freedom in California. Recently, she has put my mother in contact with a lawyer in San Francisco who is pleading my case at the district attorney's office. Working in concert, Susan and my mother are orchestrating the advancement of my cause on two fronts: San Francisco and Kentucky.

Contacting the lawyer in Kentucky from a public telephone booth, I confirm that I would like her to represent me. As a result of communications with Jim's lawyer, she receives a letter expressing Jim's desire to see Ellen and a proposal for our return to America. If Ellen and I return to America, Jim will drop the child abduction charges against me. In return, he would retain full custody of Ellen, which the judge in San Francisco had awarded him after our departure. My visiting rights with Ellen would be limited and supervised. Did Jim really think that I would grab at this proposal after four years of living on the run for Ellen's protection? His proposal is ludicrous, even laughable, if the situation weren't so sad. I instruct my lawyer to make a counterproposal: Ellen and I will return if full custody is restored to me, Jim being limited to supervised visiting with the supervisor being me. I know this proposal will be rejected, but any compromise would threaten Ellen's protection. Jim could be a threat to my life if we return to America, as well as hers; he has nothing to lose. Regardless of Jim's desperation, I would return to America if he were to agree to my proposal and set in motion the appropriate legal actions. As well as being sensitive to the fact that this could be his last opportunity to see his daughter, I'm more sensitive to my daughter's feelings. Her fall-out emotions over never seeing him again are impossible to gauge. Relying on indirect communications, a legal resolution of our situation seems hopeless.

THE DAY FOLLOWING THE MAY BANK HOLIDAY WEEKEND, as I'm saying goodnight to Michelle, there's a knock at the front door downstairs. Doubting that Miss Welsby would be expecting a visitor at this hour, I listen as she opens the door. The caller's voice is soft, deep, and familiar. Hastening down the stairs, I see John looking up at me from the hall.

Smiling self-consciously, he says, "I thought I would drop by to celebrate my birthday with you." After I have introduced John to Miss Welsby, she withdraws to her living room. Seconds later,

Michelle appears on the stairs, giving a shriek of delight when she sees him.

Traveling from Oxford by bicycle, bus, and ferry for sixteen hours, John has walked here after checking into Mrs. D'alton's. Upstairs in our small kitchen, he unloads from a small duffel bag a carton of whipping cream and a mixer, a chocolate cake baked the previous evening, candles and matches, and a bouquet of bluebells from the Oxfordshire woods of our first date one year ago.

The surprise of his arrival (after I had given up hope) leaves me with few words. Mostly I repeat, "I can't believe it," as the three of us eat birthday cake in our kitchen. Barbara chides me later for not calling her about staying with Michelle on short notice. At the time, I didn't think about it, being overcome with the serendipity of the moment.

John leaves the next morning on the return ferry. His visit has been so fleeting that its reality may seem questionable in a few weeks' time, when the blossoms wither. The bluebells have pierced my heart with romance. I have no doubt that I will see John when we visit Oxford in the summer.

Now when I approach the telephone booth to call America, whether speaking to my lawyer or my parents, the instability of the situation triggers anxiety. Is Jim's death imminent, or will his health rally as it has in the past? As expected, Jim rejects my proposal for our return, reiterating his claim that he will never give up custody of Ellen. Jim's desire to see his daughter isn't top priority in his life. Whose counsel has his ear, or is he too ill to receive any? Pride, foolish advice, or something else is cutting off what could be Jim's last opportunity to see his daughter.

During a call to America in mid-May, Jim's name isn't mentioned once. Several days earlier, Nannie, my ninety-four-year-old grandmother and my father's mother, has died. My parents will leave Mary Ellen's house to attend her funeral after receiving my call. As I cross the street to buy another phone card, my sobbing makes the employee at the newsstand uncomfortable. He doesn't know what to say to me. No one does. None of my friends have the answer to the question: Why couldn't God have preserved Nannie's life until we returned? I had been the apple of her eye, her only grandchild. She had always been there for me. Jim had been banking on the separation from my family, as well as inadequate funds, to drive me back to America.

Michelle's memories of her great-grandmother are more limited, but she remembers searching through Nannie's bag for the ever-present roll of Life Savers, as well as playing with her collection of salt and pepper shakers. That night, as I comfort Michelle before saying goodnight, I perform a ritual that Nannie had done when I was a small child and unable (or unwilling) to go to sleep. Rubbing her fingertips together, she (playing the part of the Sandman) had sprinkled imaginary sand into my wide-opened eyes. Then her fingertips would close the lids and apply magical mud while reciting "Now I lay me down to sleep. I pray the Lord my soul to keep. If I should die before I wake, I pray the Lord my soul to take."

I think back to the day Nannie died. Michelle and I had been sight-seeing with Helen and Tony from Oxford, who had been staying in Dublin. On the bright and sunny day, the four of us had walked along the sea coast, ending our visit with afternoon tea at the Shelbourne Hotel in Dublin. I have been ignorant of my grandmother's death for three days; now I want to retake them, inserting sadness and mourning.

Walking on daily rounds to school and shops, sometimes I sing, but songs flow less frequently now. With my grandmother's death staring me in the face, the wind doesn't seem at my back. One hymn's chorus, which worked its way into my spirit through repetition at a young age, does come forth spontaneously. Emphasizing a different word each time, I sing, "On Christ the solid rock I stand, all other ground is sinking sand . . . all other ground is sinking sand." I feel myself sinking in the pit, but know that my feet will strike the "solid rock" before I'm overcome.

ONCE AGAIN, GOD BRINGS AMERICA TO MICHELLE, THIS TIME through an introduction in the workout room of the hotel where I attend an aerobics class. Another woman and I approach an apparatus at the same time, deferring to one another. As I notice her English accent, she recognizes my American one, which prompts conversation on living in America. Joanna, her husband, and their daughter, Alexandra, are staying at the hotel while he directs a Walt Disney movie in Ireland.

Alexandra, who is the same age as Michelle, invites her to swim in the hotel pool, as well as visit the movie set at the studio in Bray. Their friendship extends into the classroom when Alexandra is enrolled in Rathdown for the remaining weeks of the school year. One morning, after dropping off the girls at school, Joanna and I drive toward the Wicklow Mountains to have lunch at Johnny Fox's, the highest pub in Ireland. Joanna, who is a screenplay writer, encourages me to write our story. Although I have been keeping a diary and making notes, attempts at putting pen to paper haven't materialized beyond a few pages. Concern about the outcome of the story blocks my enthusiasm for writing; a prison sentence would provide ample time to write the story, as well as the graduate thesis. Judging from the prison documentary I saw in Oxford, another positive benefit of serving time would be losing weight.

TWO WEEKS LATER, A U.S.A. PHONE CALL AGAIN UNEXPECTedly spotlights death. In a moment, all is changed. Jim has died at his parents' home in Kentucky from complications related to AIDS. Although my mother has been commenting on the decline of Jim's health during the past several months, his death comes as a surprise. Janet had said that it would come when I least expected it, as is true for so many things. My thoughts are like bumper cars bumping into and bouncing off one another. If both deaths were meant to be, why couldn't Jim's death have preceded Nannie's? Legal contacts had lifted my hopes that Jim's heart would change. Now all hope of having the charges dropped is gone. Relief is tempered by the finality of his death. Lodged in a recess of my heart had been the wish to talk with Jim face-to-face—reconciled. Spent of emotion, I can't talk with Michelle about another death right away. Will she strike out at me in anger, maligning me for keeping her away from her father? I ask myself.

After Michelle returns home from school the following day, I suggest a walk along the rocky shore. Michelle's enthusiasm jump-starts when I add stopping for ice cream along the way. Walking the short block to the sea, I begin with a deep sigh. "Sweetpea, I talked to Bebe and Granddaddy, who told me some sad news. Your dad died a few days ago in Kentucky." Michelle's prolonged silence makes me wonder whether she comprehended what I said.

Looking up at me with an expectant face, she asks, "Mommy, does this mean we can go home now?"

Caught off guard by her matter-of-factness, I stammer, "Uh . . . I . . . I don't know, probably not right away."

After more questions about where and how Jim died, she laments, "I know I should be sad, but I'm happy we're free."

As we walk, Michelle becomes more subdued. Reality is percolating through her consciousness that she will never again see her father whose memory has faded. At the water's edge, we hurl stones into the sea. Jim would have grieved in the same way— skimming stones across the water. When he had experienced the pressure of college exams, or later the pressure of clinical and research responsibilities, I had witnessed many a pebble fly from his hands. I can visualize the tilt of his body, leaning into his right shoulder before the release.

Later that evening, the reality of never seeing her father again hits Michelle as we say goodnight, a time of the day when we had prayed for him. Starting to cry, she moans, "I miss my daddy. Mommy, do you remember the night he brought me cough medicine?" I nod that I do, and she continues, "In the middle of the night he got out of bed and drove over to our house to bring me medicine. He took good care of me, Mommy."

Michelle had hit on Jim's gift. As a physician, he had been an excellent care-giver. What a loss for his patients! Sometimes, I had called him "the doctor's doctor."

Friends are at a loss to know how to comfort me. "Thank God" isn't what I feel; neither is "Oh, no, God." Regardless of the pain and disappointment, almost two thirds of my life was spent with Jim. Sadness persists.

At the best possible time, Michelle and I receive an invitation to spend a few days with friends at a hunting lodge in the Wicklow Mountains. This being our second visit, we know what beautiful surroundings await us. The way to Hollywood, Ireland, begins its climb through the mountains near Glendalough, the lovely lake and valley where St. Kevin founded a monastery in the sixth century. From the car I see the Round Tower, where monks fled for refuge from attacks. I want to flee from thoughts of death. Last autumn Mrs. Allen and I had threaded our way through the stone church ruins and Celtic crosses in the graveyard, which I now overlook. Legend says that hugging the base of one particular graveyard monument guarantees marriage within the year, if the fingertips touch.

Our hosts are Marion and her husband Frank, as well as Tom, Frank's brother, who lives year-round at the lodge. Michelle explores the byways in the green hills behind the lodge with their daughter, Dawn, who is a GCU friend. In the evenings, they play cards or board games, enlisting the participation of Dawn's older brother, Andrew. The adults sit in front of the fire with a hot drink and the hunting dogs at our feet—reading, talking, or playing cards.

During the weekend, the women from the Bible study group in Dublin come for an afternoon picnic with their families. Afterward, we hike up a gravel road toward the top of the mountain ridge, surrounded by glens of dark conifers and rocks pushing their way to the surface.

Marion's keen analytical mind is a brilliant sounding board for assessing future scenarios. If Michelle and I stayed in Ireland, my parents could visit us here, but that would leave my grandparents in Kentucky. Michelle wants to transport Rathdown School, the whole of Ireland, and a lot of other countries to America. Any return to America should occur after she attends a GCU camp in Yorkshire with her former Oxford GCU group. The camp is two months from now, giving time for things to settle in America.

Contacting my lawyer in Kentucky to assess the status of my legal situation after Jim's death, I find that he has left no dying wish that we return to America in freedom. His family express no interest in paving the way for our return—quite the opposite. Although my lawyer offers no assurance that I won't go to prison, no guarantee exists that I shall. Separation from Michelle grips me with terror more than the actuality of living in prison. Receiving legal help depends on avoiding arrest and extradition when passing through U.S.A. immigration and on making it back to Kentucky.

ONE NIGHT, ABOUT A MONTH AFTER THE DEATHS, I AWAKEN AT 2 A.M., not from a rapid heartbeat but from irrational terror. My head feels as if it is wrapped in a blood pressure cuff that is being pumped up. As my skin crawls with heightened sensitivity, I want to scream and run helter-skelter from the room. Turning on the light, I open my Bible, but it's impossible to read. Desperate to quell the war being waged inside me, I fear becoming a casualty on the battlefield. Using my earphones, I listen to a tape that Michelle had rescued from a wastebasket at YWAM Lausanne. The music soothes, but the singing of Scripture strengthens.

"Give ear to my words, O LORD, Consider my groaning. Heed the sound of my cry for help, my King and my God. For to Thee do I pray" (Ps. 5:1–2). Crying out to God to preserve sanity, I don't know how much longer I can keep the struggle silent without waking Michelle, who sleeps a few feet away. The next second a loud clap of thunder startles me, rocking the windows. God isn't speaking in the sound of a gentle wind tonight. The novelty of the thunderclap, one of the few I have heard in Ireland, cuts the panic like a sword. Remaining in bed, I wait, knowing that Peace is on its way.

The next morning, still shaken by residual fright, I'm worried about surviving intact. The winter has been too long, too wet, too gray, too draining. I crave to be out of the brisk cold wind, to sweat in the hot sun cooled by a gentle breeze, like the ones we had experienced in Greece. Before noon, I'm scanning vacation brochures at a travel agency in downtown Dublin. Gordon, who is a travel agent as well as a member of the church home group, advises a package tour to Greece, normally difficult to reserve this late in the season. Due to a cancellation that morning, a reservation opens for a two-week vacation in Corfu. Guilt flows over me as I make the deposit, but experiencing a vacation in two weeks' time is both expedient and prophylactic. It's a matter of paying now or later.

Corfu is hot and sunny, providing many opportunities to talk with Michelle about the future. After years of travel, this trip is our first vacation. Concerned that Michelle may learn information about her father's death from someone else, I explain about AIDS and that we have been tested for the virus several times, receiving good reports. When I talk about the possibility of going to prison, Michelle expresses her desire to live with Bebe and Granddaddy.

Two days after returning from Corfu, I sit across from Gordon once again, this time making airline reservations for Toronto. Years before in Italy, I had decided that it would be the portal for returning to America. On August 16, 1994, seats are available on a charter flight leaving Dublin for Shannon and Toronto. On faith, I reserve seats on a flight from Toronto to Cincinnati, where my parents plan to meet us, knowing that we may not make it that far. Later in the day, Gordon calls to report that the price of each air ticket has been reduced by £50, a reduction occurring only on the Tuesday flight of that week. Puzzled as to why this day has been singled out to reward the passengers, I believe it's confirmation that this is the day we are to travel home.

WITH ONLY TWO WEEKS REMAINING BEFORE OUR FLIGHT TO Toronto, Michelle and I travel to Oxford to say goodbye to friends and places. Ray graciously offers our former apartment as a place to stay, since the students who occupy it are away for the summer. Michelle departs with the Oxford GCU group to attend their camp in Yorkshire. In a week's time, I shall meet her on the platform in York to board a train for Perth.

While staying in Oxford, John and I see each other every day. The pain of enjoying his company is gone. My heart is somewhere over the Atlantic at this point and John makes no attempt to hold it back. Keeping in touch across the distance is a foregone conclusion.

The early morning rendezvous with Michelle requires that I arrive in York the evening before. Strolling through the streets as darkness falls, I pass a recessed shop entry where a man sits on the sidewalk with a black dog. Walking on by, I stop after a few paces, prompted to retrace my steps and initiate a conversation with him. He introduces himself as Mark Antony and his dog as Cleopatra, and it's apparent from his discussion on the powers of the occult that we serve different masters. Announcing that he is a warlock, he claims that the witchcraft powers were passed on to him by his grandfather at a young age. When he tells me that his Christian name is John Mark, I no longer see a man in his fifties who is holding his arm out to passing cars, presumably in a salute of malediction—I see a young child whose spirit has been raped by an adult whom he may have trusted. Perhaps the same was passed to his grandfather, generation to generation.

Addressing the spiritual gulf separating us, I say, "John Mark, we serve different masters. You're a slave to Satan, and I profess the Lordship of Christ. In the Bible, the Apostle Paul mentions being set free from the spirit of slavery and fear, which your master requires."

Smiling, he interjects, "You have said the right word," and pulls a piece of wood from his pack. On it, the word "slave" has been carved.

Hitting the mark of his spiritual condition sends vibrations through my own spirit. Adjuring him, I plead, "It's not too late, John Mark. You can decide to serve a different master. One who gives life and freedom, rather than death. Change your allegiance before it's too late."

Ignoring my admonition, he turns his attention back to the cars. As I turn to leave, he extends his hand toward me, looking me in the eye and knowing what's going on in my heart. I don't know what to do. At my hesitation, he thrusts his hand a bit closer. Perhaps my refusal to shake his hand would be interpreted as excluding him from the love of Christ. With the reluctance of plunging into a pool of cold water, I extend my hand. On the walk back to the bed-and-breakfast, I feel uneasy about this encounter, troubled by what has happened.

On the station platform the next morning, I notice a group of girls in a huddle at the other end. When Miss Cooke sees me, she signals to Michelle, who turns around. Seeing the white sling on her arm, I ask the obvious question. The previous evening she was using a chair to climb into the top bunk at bedtime. When the chair tottered, she lost her balance, and her arm struck the back rail of the chair. Miss Cooke explains that the camp nurse examined Michelle's arm, believing the wrist to be sprained. Opting not to go to the hospital on the last night of camp, the nurse still advises having it X-rayed.

Rather than seeking a medical opinion in York, we board the

train for Perth, where Janet could lend support if X rays become necessary. Although Michelle isn't in distress, the pain in her arm worsens on the journey to Perth. After dropping our luggage at Janet's, we walk to the hospital on the other side of the sheep field. Using Ellen's passport for registration purposes is no longer a problem. In a few days' time, I shall be surrendering to authorities in Kentucky if I'm permitted to enter America.

The radiologist reports that a bone in Michelle's arm is broken, requiring anesthesia to reset it. At midnight in the surgical prep room, Michelle pleads not to have a shot. As the intravenous line is inserted in her arm, the doctor focuses her attention on the cartoon characters painted on the ceiling. While counting the figures, her voice trails off.

Having worked as a secretary in an anesthesiology department, I remember a young law student who had been anesthetized for an emergency appendectomy. A freak drug reaction had caused cardiac arrest and death. Most likely, Michelle will be fine, but nothing can be taken for granted. We're so close to the end of our journey.

An operating room nurse who is going off-duty gives me a ride to Janet's home to retrieve what we will need for spending the night at the hospital. Although Janet is on duty at the residential care home next door, she runs me back to the hospital in her car before Michelle awakens. In the recovery room, I present Michelle with a bouquet of sweet peas that Janet had hurriedly picked from her garden in the dark for Squeak. A soft cast has been applied for travel in a pressurized plane, though not ideal protection for maneuvering in airports and crowded aircraft.

ON SUNDAY, OUR LAST DAY IN SCOTLAND, EWEN, JANET'S minister, who has also been my minister in Perth, has unknowingly planned a tremendous send-off service for Michelle and me. Months ago, the idea had come to Ewen to plan a family service at the end of the summer based on the theme of returning home after a vacation. During the "Going Home" service, participants offer music, poetry, and testimonies about homecomings, both temporal and eternal. As the congregation sings "Amazing Grace," none of the participants, not even Ewen, realizes the significant timing of the message until afterward. "Going Home" shifts the focus from arrest and imprisonment to reunion and homecoming.

ON THE FLIGHT TO TORONTO, I FEEL THE PUSH-PULL OF RE-turning to America, just as I had experienced it on leaving. Over the international waters of the Atlantic, the boundaries of national allegiance have lost their distinct edges, our survival having been aided by citizens of many countries. No one who shared the knowledge of our circumstances betrayed us. No one harmed us. In the course of traveling thousands of miles, I lost neither luggage nor cash. Only a bracelet, three earrings, and a zebra-striped sock (half of a Christmas gift from Michelle) failed to follow us. Remarkably, the sock found its way back to me two months later.

Perhaps I have been away from America too long. Everything will seem different, and acclimatization to the culture will take time. I have no health insurance, no driver's license, and only a few hundred dollars of cash. I'll be starting from rock bottom, since the judge had awarded Jim custody of Ellen and bestowed to him all my possessions and assets, my share of the house equity, and even my retirement benefits. Returning to America as a wanted woman is bittersweet. Although I have broken the law, I'm not a criminal. During the flight, Michelle writes a note to her dead father, expressing her wish that he had dropped the legal charges against me. In the postscript, Michelle writes: "God help us." She is terrified that I will go to prison.

Canadian immigration offers no resistance. At U.S.A. customs, I don't have ready answers, having concentrated on what I will say later at passport control. Once Michelle's X rays receive special handling in customs, I have no idea what to declare, realizing that I could be tripped up here just as easily. The journey has been so long that everything deserves to be declared. Few of the items packed in San Francisco have survived the journey. I panic when my mind goes blank. The customs officer, who has opened our black bags, exerts verbal pressure to respond as I struggle to remember their contents. Eventually, I declare the value of wool sweaters and scarves purchased in Ireland.

Walking down a corridor to U.S.A. passport control, I pray for wisdom. If the official inspects the passports carefully, he or she will notice that Michelle and I haven't returned to the U.S.A. in almost five years, which may be a red flag for immigration watchdogs. As I present our passports and airline tickets, his demeanor is friendly, not authoritative. Looking at Michelle as he thumbs through the pages of my passport, he asks, "How did you break your arm?" It is the only question he asks. Her broken arm proves to be an effective distraction. After consoling Michelle about the misfortune of it happening on a trip, he smiles and hands back our passports. In a matter of seconds, what I have been dreading for years is over. To celebrate the victory, I pull out the leftover coins, still wrapped in the roll Stephen had given us in San Francisco. It's been almost five years since U.S. currency has passed through my hands. Ceremoniously, I buy Michelle a hot dog.

On the flight to Cincinnati, our jubilation is difficult to contain in seats 11A and 11B. I tell our seatmate the reason for our excitement: the story is almost too incredible for him to believe, but his skepticism doesn't faze me. On the descent, I see the meanderings of the Ohio River and pray that the plane lands safely. We are so close now.

Our plethora of cabin luggage holds us back from being among the first passengers off the plane. My seatmate offers to carry something to help speed things along. My parents are waiting at the terminal gate on pins and needles, with no idea whether we are on this flight, having made it through U.S. immigration without being arrested. Every second of delay prolongs their agony.

Seeing my parents framed in the door of the gateway, Michelle runs into their arms. Her glee assures them that she has not forgotten them during the separation. Having had no photographs to catch them up on Michelle's development, they embrace her ten-and-a-half-year-old stature with astonishment. Blocking the way, the four of us clutch each other in wails of joy. My seatmate unobtrusively sets the black bag down. Other passengers eddy to either side of us, looking askance at the over-the-moon show of emotions.

Reaching the outskirts of the city, which is home to Jim's family as well as my parents, Michelle and I crouch in the back seat to avoid being recognized through the untinted windows of the van. If I am convicted, sentencing could be favorably influenced by surrendering, rather than being apprehended. Turning away from the direction of the city and toward the country roads where my parents live, we sit upright until headlights drive us down in the seat again. We pull into my parents' drive, and I taste what it must be like to be on the approach to heaven. The past is left behind. The future doesn't exist. Only the present matters. Arc, who has become an old dog with a whiter face, looks at me with the same adoration. He remembers me as I caress his velvet ears.

The answering machine handles any phone calls. I go through the house, noticing what furnishings have been moved or replaced. My parents are content to look at us and comment on how well they will sleep, knowing we're upstairs. For years, I have visualized looking out of the front window across the fields to a neighbor's barn. It's not the time to catch up on almost five years of living; it's the right time for savoring present delights.

As we walk into my lawyer's office without an appointment, she bursts into tears when she sees my mother, assuming me to be Janie. Her compassion encourages me. Plans are activated to arrange a court hearing for the next day. Returning home, I place calls to Scotland, Ireland, England, and San Francisco, requesting prayers for finding favor with the American legal system. In less than twenty-four hours, I could be waiting in a jail cell for extradition to California. I have visions of being handcuffed to a seat in a bus, although felons may be escorted by air.

On the following day, Michelle, my parents, and I meet at the lawyer's office, learning that the hearing couldn't be scheduled on such short notice. The alternative plan is to present my case to the sheriff. On the way to the county jail, I muse on how I have dressed for a court hearing, not a jail cell. In the parking lot, Michelle remains in the car with her grandparents while I am accompanied by my lawyer and another lawyer who is assisting her.

Walking to the entrance of the jail, the two lawyers explain to me what will happen on the inside. One brings up a point, which prompts the other to halt, saying, "Wait!" as my hand is poised to push open the front door. Thinking ahead, she continues, "It's probably best that you don't go in just yet, but wait in the car. I want to talk with the district attorney's office in San Francisco before you make an appearance." On the way back to the parking lot, the assisting lawyer explains that the sheriff would have been obligated to arrest me on the spot if I had crossed the threshold, given the felony charges against me. I had been one step away from certain arrest.

At the car, we confront the puzzled expressions on the faces of Michelle and my parents. Knowing little of what is going on inside, I surmise that persuasive reasoning is occurring on my behalf. What's the point of putting a mother in prison who needs to be free to nurture her fatherless daughter? As we wait in the car, the assisting lawyer listens patiently to our questions and concerns, encouraging us when possible. The flight instinct is still strong, but this time around, my motivation isn't as compelling. There's nowhere to run now, and I'm too tired anyway. It scares me to think how much time I might have to rest. Two hours later, my lawyer appears and opens the car door to make an announcement: "I have good news. The sheriff has been conferring with California, and the district attorney's office in San Francisco is dropping the charges."

Michelle lets out a whoop, and everyone follows suit. The threat of going to prison lets go its grip. The fear of living in hiding is gone, no longer stalking me. The slate has been wiped clean, as if no charges had ever been filed. At last, I'm free.

As one journey ends, a new one begins.

EPILOGUE: THE REVENGE
OF THE THREE BLACK BAGS

THE DOOR THAT I HAD EXPECTED TO OPEN THEN CLOSE BEHIND me with a solid thud hadn't done so. Freedom puts me at a loose end. Suddenly the future explodes with more choices than opportunities. I had assumed that I would be barred from making the decisions myself. During the first weeks of freedom, we spent our time inside my parents' home—hiding out until the felony charges clear the crime computer. If I were stopped by a police officer for any reason and checked, I would be arrested and questions would be asked.

Our self-imposed house arrest is where both Michelle and I want to be—reconnecting with our parents/grandparents and dog. The changes in their well-being during our absence is sad. My mother's blood pressure has skyrocketed and my father's energy has plummeted, but their spirits are buoyant. So are ours. Michelle wants to see all of America with them. Between bites of fried banana peppers from the garden, I introduce them to people and places around the world that couldn't be mentioned during our phone conversations.

Only Arc's health deteriorates quickly. Within six weeks, the loyal beagle into whose younger ear I had whispered so much heartache loses his strength to live. My father buries him on a peaceful fence row next to their dog. Arc's last act of devotion had been to hang on until our return.

When the charges clear, I initiate the legal process to reclaim what had been technically taken away from me: the custody of my daughter. In the twinkling of a tear-filled eye, the judge restores to me custody of Ellen (Michelle) and no one objects. I beam thankful messages toward the heavens: some destined for eternity and others received by satellites and relayed to friends in San Francisco, Ireland, England, Scotland, Italy, and Switzerland. Once the entourage of boxes (which follow us to every new country) arrive and the three black bags have been unpacked, I then permit the crisis mechanism in my nervous system to shut down completely after five years of nonstop operation. This letdown triggers exhaustion beyond any I experienced on the journey.

At my grandmother's nursing home, she gives me a faint smile of possible recognition; months later, she would call my name. On the piano in the activity room, I play her favorite hymns. Amazingly, she sings the verses from memory, at a time when her ability to carry on a conversation has gone. Down the hall, my grandfather (on the other family side) is rejuvenated from seeing us, the ones who had been lost but now are found. His already sharp mind is given a new edge by a merry heart. At the age of ninety-three, God grants me the privilege of praying with him—a prayer assuring him of eternal life. Until that life begins a year later, I listen and take notes as he tells stories from childhood and his younger days as a truck driver and a union organizer.

On my birthday, John calls to explain that the distance across the water is too far this time for him to bring a bouquet of bluebells. I am pleased that the idea had even been considered. His telephone calls are frequent, as well as painful. Our relationship is a memory without a future. On either side of the Atlantic, no mention is made of commitment. I suggest we limit our contact to letters, which, in time, dwindles to birthday cards and then only Christmas greetings.

Michelle decides to retain the name she selected for herself— to be used by everyone except family. Legally, she wants her name to be Ellen Mari Michelle. At school her hodge-podge accent is noticed by the other fourth graders in her class. Since

Michelle has learned in a variety of languages and teaching methods, she enters a grade behind others who are her age. Most of her classmates, rooted in American culture, are developing wings, but Michelle took flight from America before establishing roots. Everyone in her class has been to Florida except Michelle, who has seen the Parthenon but not Disney World. Now is the time to give her the continuity she has missed. Michelle takes tap, jazz, and ballet classes at the same school of dance. Summer after summer, she enjoys mowing the few acres of land where my parents live, a fifteen minute drive from our own place. Horse-riding lessons are sporadic, but she still dreams of owning her own horse. Echoing the words of her favorite Bible verse—"In the shadow of Thy wings, I sing for joy"—she sings whenever her vocal cords aren't occupied with eating, talking, or sleeping. As a teenager, she's happiest when the above pastimes include hanging out with friends.

Although the pace of life has slowed abruptly, the urgency to move on to the next country doesn't subside immediately. The rootless lifestyle hasn't prepared me for staying put. Rerooting in America is as challenging as the uprooting had been. Living in America is familiar, yet different for both of us, though Michelle gets in step to the rhythm of her new country easier than I do. As preparation for reentering the workforce, I complete the writing of my graduate thesis and receive a master's degree in geography from San Francisco State University. As a part-time faculty member at a university in Kentucky, I teach geography and dream of going around the world again in freedom.

FRIENDS FROM AROUND THE WORLD VISIT US IN KENTUCKY, beginning with Frank from Canada/South Africa, Sally and Keith from Oxford, Ray and Anne from Oxford, and Ann Marie from Dublin. I am pleased to show them who I am, and their presence pleasantly interjects our journey into life on this side of the world. Bonds of friendship are further cemented when Michelle and I return to England, Ireland, and Scotland for the purpose of promoting the British edition of *Fingernail Moon*.

Several of us incorporate an organization to promote the public's awareness of child abuse in Kentucky. The purpose of Abused Children Talk in Kentucky, Inc. (ACT in KY) is to encourage everyone to listen to children and to act on behalf of their protection. The political voice of children is faint and doesn't always carry through the halls of government. If the public megaphones a call for their welfare, then cannot mountains be moved to protect children from abuse? ACT in KY is in its infancy of development, crawling toward its goal, temporarily hampered by my preoccupation with writing this book, as well as being a single parent.

In the night skies every month, God shows me a reminder of His loving care and the unusual publishing path this book has taken. The process of writing exacerbates a problem brought on by moving the three heavy, black bags around the world. Sitting in a nonposture friendly position in front of a computer freezes my neck muscles. In time, the tension moves laterally across the muscles above my right rotator cuff, which had shouldered the heavy burden of the three black bags. Looking over my shoulder becomes impossible, which now isn't as critical as it had been as a fugitive. According to a neurologist, the heavy load may have injured a neck ligament that the tightened muscles never give a chance to heal.

The three black bags are now retired—collapsed in flattened heaps, collecting dust under my bed. They had rendered faithful service during bittersweet years of sojourning—never becoming lost or ripped or unzipped at the wrong time. As reminders of the baggage of pain I had once carried, they have been through too much with me to discard. In a similar manner, deflating emotional baggage can make the heart sad, even glad—realizing that a pain in the neck is only a pain in the neck.

Dear Reader,
      I hope that everyone who
reads this book can see how
abuse affects children. We need to
protect children and not put them
back into unsafe environments. I
am one of the fortunate ones,
because my mom listened to
me, even though the judge made
the wrong decision.
      When my mom and I were on
the run, we had to rely on God
to lead us and provide us with
friends, food, money, hope, and strength.
      I will never forget traveling
on our journey. Seeing different
countries was a chance most
6, 7, 8, 9, and 10 year olds don't
usually have. Sometimes, I
can't believe we are finally
back in America, safe and sound.

      yours sincerely,
      Glen Mari Michelle (age 14)